DATE DUE

FEB 2 1 '79			
MAY 1 6 1979			
SEP 1 1980			
MAY 2 2 1981			
SEP 1 1981			
30 505 JOSTEN'S			

Whitehead's Philosophy

Whitehead's Philosophy

Selected Essays, 1935-1970

Charles Hartshorne

University of Nebraska Press   Lincoln and London

Acknowledgments for permission to reprint copyrighted material appear on pages vii-viii, which constitute an extension of the copyright page.

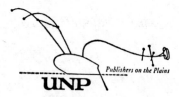

Publishers on the Plains

UNP

First Landmark Edition printing: 1978

Contents

Acknowledgments vii

Facsimile of Letter from Alfred North Whitehead to
   Charles Hartshorne ix

1. Introduction: Whitehead after Forty-Five Years 1
2. Whitehead's Metaphysics 9
3. On Some Criticisms of Whitehead's Philosophy 21
4. The Compound Individual 41
5. Whitehead's Idea of God 63
6. Is Whitehead's God the God of Religion? 99
7. Whitehead's Philosophy of Reality as Socially
   Structured Process 111
8. Whitehead's Theory of Prehension 125
9. Whitehead's Generalizing Power 129
10. Whitehead and Contemporary Philosophy 141
11. Whitehead's Novel Intuition 161
12. Whitehead and Ordinary Language 171
13. Whitehead and Berdyaev: Is There Tragedy in God? 183

Index of Persons 209

Index of Subjects 211

Acknowledgments

The author and the University of Nebraska Press acknowledge with thanks permission to reprint the following selections:

"Whitehead's Metaphysics," from *Whitehead and the Modern World: Science, Metaphysics, and Civilization, Three Essays on the Thought of Alfred North Whitehead*, by Victor Lowe, Charles Hartshorne, and A. H. Johnson, published by Beacon Press.

"On Some Criticisms of Whitehead's Philosophy," from *The Philosophical Review* 44 (July, 1935).

"The Compound Individual," from the book *Philosophical Essays for Alfred North Whitehead*, edited by Otis H. Lee, published by Longmans, Green & Company. All rights reserved. Reprinted by permission of David McKay Company, Inc.

"Whitehead's Idea of God," from *The Philosophy of Alfred North Whitehead*, The Library of Living Philosophers, Vol. III, edited by Paul Arthur Schilpp, © 1941 The Library of Living Philosophers, now published by The Open Court Publishing Company, LaSalle, Illinois.

"Is Whitehead's God the God of Religion?," from *Ethics* 53 (April, 1943), published by The University of Chicago Press, copyright © 1943 by The University of Chicago Press.

"Whitehead's Philosophy of Reality as Socially-Structured Process," from *Chicago Review* 8 (Spring-Summer, 1954).

"Whitehead's Generalizing Power," published originally under the title "Whitehead, the Anglo-American Philosopher-Scientist," from *Proceedings of the American Catholic Philosophical Association*, Vol. 35 (1961).

"Whitehead and Contemporary Philosophy," from *The Relevance of Whitehead: Philosophical Essays in Commemoration of the Centenary of the Birth of Alfred North Whitehead*, edited by Ivor Leclerc, published by George Allen & Unwin Ltd.; distributed in the United States by Humanities Press.

"Whitehead's Novel Intuition," in George L. Kline, Ed., *Alfred North Whitehead: Essays on His Philosophy*, © 1963. Reprinted by permission of Prentice-Hall, Inc., Englewood Cliffs, New Jersey.

"Whitehead and Ordinary Language," from *The Southern Journal of Philosophy* 8 (Winter, 1970).

"Whitehead and Berdyaev: Is There Tragedy in God?," from *The Journal of Religion* 37 (April, 1957), published by The University of Chicago Press, copyright © 1957 by The University of Chicago Press.

504 Radnor Hall
984 Memorial Drive
Cambridge - Mass, Jan 2ⁿᵈ - 1936

Dear Hartshorne

First, I want to tell you how touched
and pleased Evelyn and I have been by the
presentation of the volume of Philosophical Essays,
in anticipation of my 75ᵗʰ Birthday - It was a
wonderful experience.

Of course I have glanced through the contents, and
now I am slowly studying the individual essays,
before expressing myself to the contributors - I have
just finished a second careful perusal of your essay.

My general impression of the whole book, together with
my knowledge of the individual contributors, confirms
my longstanding belief that in the oncoming generation
America will be the centre of worth-while philosophy -

                    *   *   *

My belief is that the effective founders of this American
Renaissance are Charles Peirce, and William James - Of these
men, W.J. is the analogue to Plato, and C.P. to Aristotle,
though the time-order does not correspond, and the analogy
must not be pressed too far. Have you read Ralph Perry's

new book [2 vols] on James! It is a wonderful disclosure
of the living repercussions of late 14ᵗʰ century thought
on a sensitive genius.   *   *   *   But
I admit W.J. was weak on Rationalization. Also he
expressed himself by the dangerous method of over-statement.

How as to your recent work. Very naturally I have
been immensely interested in it.   Your article in the
Philosophical Review (July, 1935) gets to the heart
of what I have been endeavouring to say, in the most
masterly manner — Of course a short article omits whole
topics which require elaboration — But you do get hold of
the principles of approach, apart from which all my recent
writings since 1924 are a mere mass of confusion.
Of course, I fully realize that in the development of these
principles there is room for grave divergence and much
discussion.
Your essay in 'Philosophical Essays' on 'The Compound
Individual' is most important both in its
explanation of relationships to the Philosophical Tradition
and in its development of the new approach as it has
gradually emerged in the last 50 years —
Finally there is your book 'The Philosophy and
Psychology of Sensation' — It has entranced me by its
development of the result of a novelty of approach
to questions buried under the faulty presuppositions
of traditional thought —

I do hope that you have more work on hand.

There is one point as to which you — and everyone — misconstrue me — obviously my absent faculty of exposition are to blame. I mean my doctrine of eternal objects. It is a first endeavour to get beyond the absurd simple-mindedness of the ~~traditional~~ treatment of Universals.

As to the loci where I have treated the doctrine, of The Chapter on "Abstraction" in Science and The Modern World, and — Process and Reality, ~~scattered under the~~ evidenced the heading at the "Eternal Object", "Form", "Sensum", "Pattern".

The points to notice and (i) that Et. Obj.s are the carriers of potentiality into realization;

and (ii) that they thereby carry mentality into matter effect;

and (iii) that no eternal object in any finite realization can ~~apply~~ exhibit the full potentialities of its nature. It has an individual essence — whereby it is the same eternal object in diverse occasions, and it has a relational essence whereby it has an infinitude of modes of entry into realization — But realization introduces finitude [in Spinoza's sense], with its extrusion of the infinitude of incompatibles in the relational essence —

(iv) The relational essence of each "Etern. Obj." involves its (potential) ~~web~~ interconnections with all other eternal objects —

The traditional doctrine of the absolute isolation of universals is as great a (tacit) error, as the isolation of primary substances.

The realization of the compound individual involves a finite realization of a complete pattern of eternal objects –

The absolute abstraction of eternal objects from each other is an analogous error to their abstraction from some mode of realization, & to their abstraction of res verae from each other –

(V) The *simple*–minded way in which traditional philosophy – e.g. Hume, Bradley, etc – has treated Universals is the root of all evil –

This is the great merit of the Gestalt people –

I am afraid I have bored you – But this letter is a measure of my interest in your work.

Sincerely yrs

Alfred North Whitehead

Whitehead's Philosophy

Note

Comments added by the author when he reviewed the previously published essays prior to their collection in this volume are inclosed in brackets.

The essay texts have been edited for consistency in capitalization, punctuation, and spelling, and the footnotes for consistency in form of citation.

CHAPTER ONE

Introduction:
Whitehead after Forty-Five Years

Except for a hasty reading of *The Concept of Nature* and a still hastier perusal of early‑ passages in *Principia Mathematica*, I was, as a graduate student at Harvard, unacquainted with Whitehead and his philosophy. However, in 1925, as a young instructor, I began to hear him lecture, to grade student papers for him, and as his metaphysical writings began to appear, to read him intensively, while also, still more intensively, studying the writings of Charles Peirce. For the first time, after eight years as a college or university student, in this country and in Germany, I had the feeling of encountering philosophic genius in a congenial form and, in these two men, of encountering it twice over. For the first time, too, I found myself a warm partisan, under some temptation to substitute acceptance for critical evaluation. What I wrote about Peirce (most of it not published) in the late 1920s shows the strength of this temptation fully as much as what I wrote (mostly somewhat later)·about Whitehead. In the course of the nearly forty years since my (and Paul Weiss's) editing of Peirce, I have grown more objective, especially about Peirce.

To illustrate three of the many aspects in which Peirce and Whitehead were more "congenial" to my way of thinking than my undergraduate, graduate, and postdoctoral teachers, much as I learned from them, I select the following. I wrote a class essay (about 1922) entitled, "The Self Its Own Maker." Thus I was prepared for Peirce's generalization in his category of "spontaneity" or "Firstness," and for Whitehead's in his "Creativity" or "The self-created creature." I also wrote an essay defending the idea that it is a metaphysical blunder to base the justification of altruism upon self-interest, since the fundamental principle is love, self-love being but one expression out of many of this principle and in no sense its source or ground. Both Peirce and, especially, Whitehead have their versions of this doctrine, which I had previously found (less clearly stated) in Royce—and in Saint Paul's "we are members one of another." A third aspect of the partial "pre-established harmony" between me and my two chief inspirers was this: the only one of my Harvard teachers who was impressive as an interpreter of religion took personal immortality to be central, whereas for me this had long ceased to be, if it ever had been, a prominent aspect of the religious life. Here, too, Peirce and Whitehead were my kind of philosophers. For them also the "otherworldly" and undying factor is simply God himself, "the poet of the world" (Whitehead's phrase, but Peirce has the idea). Our permanence is in the way our earthly lives are woven (in part self-woven) into the poem, not in posthumous careers of our own.

On the three issues just mentioned, and many others, Whitehead seems to me clearly to have the more balanced and adequate doctrine. However, certain formulations of Whitehead (to be mentioned presently) which I have never been able to accept are not found in Peirce. Thus my development, from a brash young metaphysician (with already some local reputation for originality) who wrote a dissertation on "The Unity of Being in the Divine or Absolute Good" to—whatever I am today, came about in part through a sort of trialogue with two men of Leibniz-like scope and originality, almost entirely independent of one another, but with encouraging similarities and stimulating differences. If this was not good luck, what would be?

The essays span the years 1935-70. During this time my attitude toward Whitehead has undergone no drastic change. Throughout I took from him ideas I could assimilate, and ignored or touched on critically those I could not. I never cared for his "eternal objects," as a definite yet primordial multitude of "forms" of feeling or sensation, or for his analysis of the becoming of an actual entity (a concrete unit-happening) into "early" and "late" phases. I never could see in the "perishing" of actual entities anything more than a misleading metaphor which, taken literally, contradicts the dictum, entities "become but do not change." An entity becomes during (from an external point of view) a finite time and is succeeded by other actualities which objectify it along with their other predecessors, the objectifications being more or less abstract or deficient (qualified by "negative prehensions") except for the divine objectifications, in which, as I construe Whitehead, "there is no loss, no obstruction" or deficiency.

On one point there has been a change. For some years I disputed Whitehead's doctrine of the mutual independence of contemporary actualities. More recently I have defended Whitehead's view and regarded my early arguments to the contrary as mistaken. Two other changes, more of emphasis than of conviction, are the following. In several early essays I talk solely in terms of enduring individuals (Whitehead's "societies of occasions," especially those purely linear societies termed "personally ordered"), even calling them "substances," in spite of the fact that in the early twenties *The Concept of Nature* had convinced me that events are the concrete units of reality, not things, persons, or substances; also in spite of the fact that the doctrine of the discontinuity of becoming, the notion of objectively singular happenings, defended in the later works had never, once I encountered it, seemed to me mistaken. But I was slow to assimilate it fully to the extent of remembering it whenever it was relevant. I regard this as a real defect in chapters 4 and 5.

A similar slowness of assimilation is shown in the way I used to write as though it were only memory, in the usual sense, that connects experiences to the past, whereas I have never, so far as I recall, rejected the evidence, or Whitehead's assertions, concerning the equally retrospective reference of perception. This confusion was cleared up once I had formulated the distinction between "personal" and "impersonal memory," the latter being the same as perception. Memory in the generalized sense common to both forms is Whitehead's "prehension." I have little doubt that Whitehead would have liked this formulation, which is plainly implicit in his declaration that "causality is physical memory," since it is quite obvious that the standard personal meaning of memory (continued accessibility of one's own past experiences) will cover only one "strand" (in Whitehead's phrase) of causal connectedness.

The reader will see, I imagine, that my primary aim has always been to arrive at truth through Whitehead, or to make truth accessible to others through him, more than to ascertain or communicate the truth about Whitehead. In general I have tended to attribute to other philosophers as many acceptable ideas as possible. This may well have caused me, at times, to flatter the writers dealt with, making them even wiser than they were. Whitehead himself, somewhat notoriously, did this. My only defense is that this is at least better than the opposite procedure, making others more foolish than they really are. I have been particularly careful, for instance in the hundred book reviews I have written, to avoid the straw-man fallacy, attacking a man for holding opinions he in fact does not hold and could not reasonably be shown to have held. Nor do I recall being, as a reviewer, accused of this practice, which always confronts astute readers with the dilemma: Is the writer stupid, or is he too mean or lazy to allow the other fellow to stand or fall by what he actually thinks or writes?

It is already clear that my way of construing Whitehead is only one of indefinitely many ways, past and to come. If I have overpraised Whitehead, it seems safe to say that this excess of appreciation is at least balanced by the remarkable deficiency in the response Whitehead has received from the country in which he was born and educated and passed the first forty years of his adult career.

This reminds me that I have, in none of the essays, paid sufficient attention to Whitehead's relations to the British tradition in philosophy. Kant has often been extolled as the highly original German philosopher who did some justice to both Continental and British traditions. It is obvious that Whitehead can quite as readily be credited with being the highly original English or Anglo-American philosopher who assimilated essential aspects of Continental philosophy. In my opinion he understood Locke, Berkeley, Hume (also James), as well as Kant did Leibniz, and he had profound points of conscious agreement with all the great Continentals. Thus, for example, he was the first great system maker after Leibniz who made real use of the obvious point that man is far from the only kind of animal that has "experience," if this means perception, memory, learning, emotion, and purpose—or response to events as causes with expectable effects. What real use did the British, or Kant, or even Hegel, make of this truism? By generalizing fully the idea of varieties of subhuman experience Whitehead, here agreeing with Leibniz and Peirce, shows that the whole of nature can be interpreted in such terms. Agreeing with Berkeley and Leibniz, against Descartes and Locke, that mere extension, mere "primary qualities," cannot constitute the essence of anything concrete or actual, he also agrees with Leibniz and Kant that nature cannot be a mere set of ideas in human or superhuman minds; but at the same time, with the Hegelians, he sees that the idea of a *thing in itself*, both appearing to, and yet wholly hidden from, our awareness is an absurdity. Yet with Locke [and Leibniz] he can agree that the "constitution" of objects is indeed largely hidden from our direct and distinct perceptions. With Hume he is entirely convinced that mere dead bodies moving about cannot as such exhibit the causal connectedness of successive events; but with Kant (and how much more clearly) he sees that it is the temporal structure of experience as experience that constitutes the connectedness. With Hume, but unlike Kant, he sees that a merely infinite, absolute, immutable deity is an empty abstraction, and with Hegel (but how much more clearly) he knows that and how "the truth is the union of opposites," such as absolute and relative, infinite and finite, object and subject.

British philosophy has tended to be realistic—Berkeley's epistemology being an extreme, and Hume's skepticism a milder exception—especially taking this present century into account. Whitehead has discovered the very secret of realism, missed by nearly all previous philosophers: the temporal structure of experience-and-experienced, the paradigm of which is memory. Before Whitehead, did anyone unequivocally (Peirce and Bergson almost did it) perform the intellectual experiment of taking advantage of the known fact that distant events have already happened when we perceive them to convert the pseudoaxiom, "we cannot in memory intuit, enjoy as data, past events since these no longer exist" into the veritable axiom: Only events which have actually happened can be definite actualities, as such data for experience, since what is now happening is merely nascent actuality, not yet ready for objectification? In this sense memory furnishes the key to perception, not the other way. Here Whitehead is profoundly original, as he is in his concept of the objectively singular event or actual entity. (In both points, apparently without knowing it, he was anticipated by ancient Buddhism.) Through these ideas, the taint of subjectivism haunting modern philosophy (we are only aware of that very awareness itself) is definitely overcome. Every actual entity has other such entities given to it, and their otherness is guaranteed by their temporal priority. Yet the basic insight of all idealism and nearly all Asiatic philosophy that mere dead matter is but an abstraction and not a possible concrete reality is fully assimilated into Whitehead's system. Actual entities are experiences functioning as objects for subsequent experiences, which may or may not belong to the same personal stream of consciousness. Every kind of solipsism is as foreign to this view as every kind of mind-and-mere-matter dualism. Thus some of the worst diseases of modern thought are transcended. I add one more disease, the habit of skipping over the body in dealing with the question: How do we know (extrabodily) objects? Whitehead (like Merleau-Ponty later) never forgets, in his theory of perception, that experience is of bodily process, whatever other data there may be.

Probably it should not surprise us that so much insight should baffle many; perhaps particularly so in a tradition which has tended to make a merit of caution, unambitiousness, and amateurishness in philosophy. Whitehead was a highly technical and professional, as well as daring, philosopher in the decade 1925-35, in spite of having been chiefly a mathematician during most of his previous life. He came to philosophy much as Plato thought one should, but as "English Platonists" have generally not done, via intensive study of "geometry" as well as reflection upon the good and life generally. He had one thing Plato lacked, a developed formal logic as instrument in analyzing ideas. But, unlike some modern logicians, he knew or shrewdly guessed how far this logic was from fully exhibiting the structure of basic ideas; and this, I suspect, was one reason why, in his mature system, he seems to be making almost no use of that logic. Yet it is having a pervasive influence all the while. For one thing, it is probably a chief source of his insight, so rare in philosophy, into the dual necessity of admitting both intrinsic relational predicates (internal relations) and nonintrinsic relational predicates. Green, Bradley, Bosanquet, Joachim, Howison, and Royce lacked one side of this insight; Moore, Russell, at least the early Wittgenstein, R. B. Perry, Spaulding, even to some extent James, lacked the other. Peirce and Whitehead are nearly alone in seeing both. . . .

[Perhaps the most serious conflict between Whiteheadians and their philosophical contemporaries arises from the trend toward extreme behaviorism, a trend encouraged by the writings of Wittgenstein and Ryle as these are sometimes, possibly wrongly, interpreted. I remark: this issue is as old as Greek atomism; it has always left and, in spite of Feyerabend and others, still leaves unexplained almost everything, secondary and tertiary qualities, the unity of experience, whether at a moment or through time, our basic categories of causal influence and order, our freedom, what you will. As Peirce said, materialism leaves the world about as unintelligible as it finds it. Physical things, merely as such, are nothing but changing and moving shapes, the so-called primary properties. And these, in Whitehead's analysis, are simply very abstract, purely relational aspects of mind (subjectivity, feeling) on various levels. Materialism differs from Whiteheadianism by no positive assertions but solely by its omissions and denials. Nor have we been told how it could be known that such things as molecules lack even the most rudimentary forms of feeling.

Contemporary materialism appeals to the necessity that words have public significance. But there seems no real difficulty in understanding, on Whitehead's theory, how we can learn the meaning of words like pain, sorrow, joy, memory, perception, in spite of a certain limited privacy of these aspects of experience. "I am aware of having just felt or perceived a certain something in a certain way" is markedly different from "I am aware of your having just felt or perceived it in a certain way." Even more obviously, "I am aware of having just dreamt a certain dream" differs from

"I am aware of your having just dreamt a certain dream." These scarcely deniable differences are all that Whitehead needs. He has no need, on his premises, of asserting any absolute inaccessibility or incomparability of the experiences of subjects. The denial that momentary human experiences are real and unitary events seems to me purely dogmatic. Nor does it follow from the admitted truth, the reason for which Whitehead carefully explains, that the experiences are impossible without certain physiological occurrences. I wonder if current linguistic theory furnishes a reason, or only an excuse, for the materialistic preference?]

It is curious to reflect that, just as it was not Kant, but the more extremely Germanic Hegel, and later Heidegger, who really dominated German thought, so it has not, so far, been Whitehead but the more extremely British thinkers Russell, Moore, Ryle, Wisdom, Austin, and their followers, with the unclassifiable Wittgenstein (who in his later phase is, in an eccentric manner, ultra-British too) who dominate in Britain. In the more chaotic and in a significant sense freer arena in North America, no one quite dominates; and every idea, if intelligently advocated, has a chance. Whitehead preferred it that way, as do I.

CHAPTER TWO

Whitehead's Metaphysics

What has Whitehead contributed to the subjects of metaphysics and cosmology? By "metaphysics" I mean the study of the necessary, eternal, completely universal aspects of reality; by "cosmology," the attempt, combining metaphysics and scientific knowledge, to discern the large, comparatively universal features of nature as now constituted. Cosmology is science running more risks than usual, or indulging in greater vagueness, in order to achieve a more complete and rounded picture; but the risks and the vagueness may be less if some clarity has been achieved as to what makes metaphysical sense, as opposed to the confusion that results when we attempt to escape the inescapable or necessary—the metaphysical—traits of being and process.

Whitehead was a metaphysician as well as a cosmologist, and in my opinion supremely great in both roles. Indeed, I see no one since Leibniz to compare with him, and no one at all to compare with him in the adequacy of his conclusions. This of course does not mean that I believe there are no defects in his thinking or writing. (Once, when asked why he did not write more clearly, he replied, "Because I do not think more clearly.") Accurate definition of the merits of a philosophy seems indeed logically impossible without indication of how they are limited or bounded by errors—such as human beings can scarcely avoid. Nevertheless, for good or evil, this essay is written almost solely in praise, rather than criticism, of Whitehead. On this occasion, I am trying to outline some reasons that can be given for the above-suggested high estimate of his importance:

1. Whitehead is a rationalist who formulates and even practices a rational method! Rationalism is the search for views that are of necessity true because, owing to their absolute generality, they have no rational alternative. But the only way to be sure of this is, in every case, to explore the possibility of formulating an alternative. The "rationalists" of the past failed to do so. Leibniz assumes as rationally necessary the view that what a true elementary proposition describes must be an enduring individual, such as a human self; but there is the obvious alternative that what is described is an event, such as a human experience. Leibniz also assumes that the basic properties of a subject are nonrelative ones, those not containing other subjects as constituents, as A's relation-to-B contains B; but there is obviously the alternative that every subject must have relative properties, and so possess other subjects as constituents. Again, Descartes assumes that mind is to be defined as inextended, leaving the necessity for a not-mind to explain extension; but, as Leibniz partly perceived and James, Peirce, and Whitehead have shown, it is conceivable that the web of relations between minds, or rather experiences, is extension. Again, the older rationalists assume that God must be conceived as at once supremely actual and supremely nonrelative, "absolute," or independent of becoming; whereas it is conceivable that the supreme actuality is precisely the supreme example of becoming and relativity.

On all these issues and many others, Whitehead is much more aware than his predecessors of the alternatives that may (with greater or less coherence and consistency) be held. If he asserts that events and experiences are the ultimate subjects of predication, it is not because it has never occurred to him to regard "things" and "persons" in this light; but because he believes he sees that two thousand years of persistent effort to achieve rational coherence by this method have failed and were bound to fail. These are just some of the ways in which Whitehead is more of a rationalist than his predecessors.

2. In spite, or because, of his genuine rationalism, Whitehead is also an empiricist who actually describes experience—and not some pseudorationalist myth about experience. Locke and Hume and Mill, for example, treat experience as though it were something assembled primarily (but not too successfully) for the mere purpose of cognitive mirroring of the world around the human body, rather than an enjoying, striving, sympathetic (yet partly antipathetic), responsive (yet partly self-creative) activity, whose primary intuitive data are its own past states, its intentions for the future, and the processes within its "body." Again, earlier empiricists treat memory and anticipation as secondary, as at most mere ways in which we

know that existence is successive, instead of as constitutive features of our only [distinctly] intuited examples of that very successiveness itself. They speak also of experience as a duality of subject and object, of experiencing and what is experienced, but never quite identify the two terms of this duality, since their "ideas" or "impressions" or "mental states" are equivocal in this regard. Or again, Hume contrasts self-interest and sympathy, but does not observe—what is certainly the case—that self-interest is a sort of sympathy whose objects are past and future experiences of the same human person. Nor did the "empiricists" (or Kant either) realize that, as Croce says, all direct intuition is expression of feeling or that the basic principles of immediate awareness are aesthetic. Whitehead matches and surpasses the introspective subtlety of Bergson, Croce, and William James, and embodies the living process of experience in his philosophical description.

3. As a result of this descriptive accuracy, Whitehead is enabled to be perhaps the first realist who escapes from the egocentric predicament and shows how he does it. R. B. Perry did not quite explain his own escape from the dilemma: either a thing is unknown to me or known to me; in the latter case, its being-known-to-me is apparently one of its properties, and hence, if I wish to know what the thing would be were it not known to me, I find myself trying to know without knowing.

Whitehead solves the problem by pointing out that real relatedness is given only as prehension—feeling or awareness of—and that the prehended does not prehend its prehender and hence is not really related to it. Thus in memory we prehend and are really related to past experience; but this does not relate the past experience to the present memory, for we certainly do not remember the past as having anticipated or prehended or in any way referred to this present memory of itself. Nor does present experience refer to any particular future memory of itself. Memory is thus the givenness of a relatedness that runs one way only, that has no actual converse. Accordingly, whereas Perry and C. I. Lewis say that the relation of being known by a certain subject is at any rate not important to a particular concrete object, Whitehead can say that it is . . . simply nothing to the object. If this is realism, Whitehead is an absolute realist.

4. In spite, or even because, of this radical realism, Whitehead's theory is a thoroughgoing "idealism," if this means the doctrine that subjectivity is the principle of all being. Prehension being the actuality of relatedness, it is on the one hand established that to know a thing is to find, not to create, it—for we prehend actualities that do not prehend us—but on the

other hand, since the actuality we know must have some relatedness to its world, it must prehend that world. Every singular actuality (for Whitehead, as for Leibniz, perceived extended things are collectives) must be related to—in other words prehend—a world of antecedent actualities. In this regard, the actuality is a subject whose object is a world of antecedent subjects. But also, every actuality adds itself to the evergrowing totality of the real, which through it acquires a new member. In this regard, the actuality is a subject about to become object for subsequent subjects. An experience expects to become past for some new present, and this feeling of being about to become past (i.e., prehended by subjects not in the world of the initial subject) is constitutive of all experience. Every actual occasion thus is, and feels itself to be, a potential for objectification in future occasions. But this potentiality, like all potentiality, need not be actualized in just this way, or in just that way, by this subject rather than by that, so long as it is actualized somehow.

Or we may put Whitehead's discovery here as follows: That an object is a potential for objectification "blurs" the distinction between universal and particular.[1] For potentiality is universality. Any entity, O, involves the possibility, "some subject or other, any subject, prehending O"; but any-subject-prehending-O is a universal, of which this-subject-prehending-O is a particular instance. Now, although no universal can imply how it is to be particularized in a given instance (for then it would be particular and not universal), nevertheless, as Aristotle maintained, the universal can have being only as it is concretized somehow. Accordingly, that the object must be object for some subject rather than none (though it need not be so for this subject rather than that) illustrates the Aristotelian principle. (There can be fictitious or unembodied universals, but they are complex and derivative from embodied universals. "Prehension of O" is not complex in the relevant fashion—just as "about to become past" adds nothing to "present.") I can indeed know what the thing known would be though I myself did not know or feel it; but I cannot possibly know what it would be were it now unknown and unfelt; any more than I can know what an existent Platonic form would be were there nothing concrete to embody it. All being is prehended as indifferent to the particular prehension, but nothing is or could be prehended as indifferent to being prehended at all, for this would mean indifferent to being contained in any world at all, term of any real relatedness, past for any present. It is true also that there must be a divine present to endow an actuality with adequate objectivity, whereby with all its being it is immortally past—but this divine subjectivity (as here required) is not any particular subject.

This point will become clearer when the next three paragraphs have been read.

5. Whitehead is, in the Western world at least, the first great philosophical theist who, as a philosopher, really believes in the God of religion. (This statement may seem startling; it assumes that Socinus and Tertullian were not great philosophers; perhaps it is unjust to Fechner and the later Schelling.) The God of religion is a supreme person capable of relations to other persons, or at any rate—for the word "person" is not the point—one who knows, loves, and wills with regard to others who know, love, and will. A person is given not as a particular actuality, but as a principle of sequence of actualities. The principle is the personality or character of the individual, the actualities are the states, experiences, or acts expressing that character.

No great philosopher before Whitehead put this manifest fact of experience in clear technical terms. Personality is the "defining character- istic" of a "society of occasions" in linear temporal ("personal") order, these occasions being the successive experiences actualizing the individual in question. The defining characteristic is less concrete or particular than its expressions; it has a certain abstractness or neutrality with respect to alternative possible experiences and acts. Philip drunk or Philip sober is still Philip, but obviously not the same determinate or particular actuality. The extreme contrast to the universal or general is not the individual but the particular. The individual is intermediate, semiabstract, partially unparticular or indeterminate. If it were otherwise, a man's character at birth plus his environment would entail all his future actions, and he would be in the iron grip of determinations effected before he could do anything about them. Also, we would not know who John Jones was unless we could predict all his future experiences. The very function of proper names would be nullified. The traditional view of God as identical in his actuality with his character or "essence" entirely deprives him of freedom, personality, or individuality, and makes him either a meaningless universal embodied in nothing concrete, or a meaningless particular expressing no character, purpose, or individuality.

Whitehead, by distinguishing between the primordial essence or personality, and the consequent state or actuality (he probably should not have called it "nature") of deity is almost the first to deal seriously with the individuality of God. The primordial essence is absolute, independent, abstract, and (like everything abstract) neutral with respect to particular determinations. The essence is "infinite" and nonactual. All personal character, indeed, is abstract, neutral, free from wholly determinate limits, and is a principle or potency of actualization, rather than any actual entity; but divine personality is unique and transcendent in quality by being absolutely (instead of only relatively) abstract, infinitely (instead of only finitely) free or indeterminate, with respect to particularization. But, whereas earlier metaphysicians generally stopped here, leaving deity a mere unlimited essence, totally devoid of definite actuality, a power totally divorced from expression or achievement, Whitehead adds the other side of the divine portrait. The "consequent" actuality of deity is the sequence of determinate, contingent experiences expressing both the essence of deity and the de facto content of the world God experiences at a given moment. Whereas the divine essence is "absolute," impassive, the consequent actuality is "relative" and passive, with a supreme sensitivity or responsiveness that is, without equivocation, love itself in unadulterated purity.

This is the first clearheadedly honest intellectualization (for Schelling's and Fechner's analyses are less clear) of what religion has always intuitively meant by "God."

6. Whitehead, more than any other, has really "answered Hume." By his account of memory and physical purpose, generalized in his "reformed subjectivism," by his explanation of order in terms of aesthetic drives, focused in God, Whitehead gives causality a uniquely adequate grounding. He furnishes the "impressions" of causal connectedness that Hume calls for, and at the same time, by showing the subtlety of these impressions and the complexity of the problem of causality and induction, which is only solved (as Hume indeed suspected—see his Dialogues) when all main factors, including God, are reckoned with, Whitehead justifies Hume's refusal to be satisfied with solutions then available.

7. Whitehead is the first to embody modern relational logic in a fairly complete metaphysical system. (Peirce came nearest to anticipating this achievement.) Logic has discovered itself to be the study of relational structures as involved in meanings. Metaphysics ought to be the study of relational structures as embodied in reality as such, or taken generically. Instead of focusing on the meager, arbitrarily limited question of how particular actualities are related to universal properties, how an S is P, we need to focus on the general case of how actualities, as such, are related to actualities of the past, and to potentialities for future actualization; or how a subject is self-referent to other subjects, in both their particular and their universal aspects. This is what the theory of prehensions effects. By the ontological principle (perhaps sometimes forgotten in Whitehead's

exposition), relationship to other actualities includes all relationships and is the general case. This is what the Aristotelian doctrine of the universal-only-in-the-particular comes to, when we face the necessity that things must have relative properties.

The Philosophy of Organism here retains the old truth that properties must actually qualify something actual, some subject, but adds the new truth that we must recognize relational properties—those by which some portion of the system of particular things enters into the nature of each thing, and thus there is "immanence" of one thing in another. Yet Whitehead [discounting his tendency to overstress this side of his doctrine] avoids the modern error of Absolute Idealism which would impose no limitations upon this immanence and make all things constituents of each thing. At this point, Whitehead follows the sound lead of G. E. Moore and William James in defending the thesis of "external" relatedness,[2] but without forgetting—as Moore at least did forget—that every real relation must be "somewhere," in some actuality, internal to some term, though by no necessity to all terms. Thus, undeterred either by the specious simplicity of the ancient subject-predicate logic, or by the current logical fiction that "every relation has a converse," Whitehead seeks and finds the ways in which a thing may be self-referent to another thing, without the second thing having any reference to the first, so that aRb is an actual relatedness, while bRa is not. In this way, he arrives at the objective analogue of the relational structure of meanings, in a theory of partly self-creative, partly caused or derivative atomic creatures, self-referent to the world they are about to enrich.

This is the first theory of time worthy of the name. [Perhaps this is unfair to Peirce and Bergson.] For it is the first that ascribes to time an intelligible logical structure, while allowing for a principle of flux or passage that transcends all fixed or already determinate structures, since it is an inexhaustible source of new relationships, extrinsic to reality as already actual.

8. Whitehead is among the first [after Boutroux, Peirce, and Bergson] to see the philosophical generality inherent in the principle of evolution, the principle that the characters of things, as expressed in their ways of acting, are products of change, and to see that this enables us to dispense with the mythical notion of laws as eternally fixed, yet quantitatively definite, aspects of behavior. It is enough for us if nature changes sufficiently slowly in her more basic ways—those whose duration defines a "cosmic epoch"—for all our needs of prediction and mental reconstruction of the past. Whitehead also avoids the arbitrariness of Peirce's view that

the world gets more and more orderly. One order may change to another, but "more" or "less" orderly is an unwarranted, if not absurd, addition.

9. Most philosophers seem to regard the discovery of cells in biology as merely a tale told to them when they were young. For they speak of the body as though it were essentially one entity, one mass of stuff, or machine, or "material" aspect of one human individual. In fact, the body is a vast "society of cells," none of which is a human being, and any of which could (with minor modifications) conceivably exist and live in a suitable medium outside of any human organism.

Whitehead seems to be among the first to see that all this renders imperative a generalization of the idea of "environment," if that means, "the set of individuals with which a given individual interacts." The body is nothing but the most necessary, inseparable, intimate portion of our social environment, or field-of-relationships with other living beings, each living its own life. Whitehead draws the consequence that the primary nonhuman (and nondivine) datum of human experience must be cellular activity, objectified without distinctness as to individual cells, and instinctively taken as an index of conditions outside the bodily system, an index whose general reliability is due to evolutionary adaptation.

The view appears to fit every known fact. And at one stroke it explains both how we know subhuman reality, and how we are causally influenced by such reality. For the subject could not be uninfluenced by what it directly, even though indistinctly, intuits. This is a part of Whitehead's "answer to Hume."

10. Who before Whitehead presented a clear, fully articulated reason for temporal atomicity, a special quantitative illustration of which is given by quantum mechanics? Or for the wave structure pervasive in nature, which for Whitehead illustrates (though it would not, unless in extremely generalized form, be deducible from) the aesthetic laws of contrast and repetition to which all appetition is subject?[3]

11. Whitehead seems to be the only philosopher to note the universality of societies in the cosmos, at all levels; also, and best of all, he is the first to see that what is called an individual in common life (and much philosophy) can only be understood as a form of sequence of particular actualities socially inheriting a common quality from antecedent members; and that personality itself is a special temporally linear case of such social—that is, sympathetic—inheritance. Thus the account of personal self-identity which modern psychology substitutes for the pseudosimplic-

ity of the "soul" is integrated into a comprehensive generalization that is superlative in its sweep—apparently too much so for pedestrian minds. The ethical problem of self-interest and altruism can, really for the first time, now be analyzed without radical ambiguity as to what "self" is in question. Self-interest, so far as looking to the future, is seen as a case of sympathetic projection, not radically different from some other cases of such projection.

12. Whitehead is among the first to see that empiricism means the necessity of generalizing comparative psychology and sociology downward to include physiology, biology, chemistry, and physics as studies of the more elementary types of sentient individuals and societies. Biology has already begun to follow this lead. Agar shows how embryology, for example, is best conceived as the study of the responsive behavior of cells under the stimulus of a highly specialized environment (in the womb).[4]

Some readers will of course feel that the foregoing estimate of Whitehead depends for most of its plausibility upon the assumption that the universe really is the sort of social process of "feelings of feelings" that Whitehead thinks it is. I venture three remarks here.

Whitehead certainly has not chosen this view because of inattention to its alternatives. He obviously knows why the idea of mere matter, or "vacuous actuality," for example, has appealed to so many. Quite a portion of his life must have been passed in meditation upon this question, meditation focused upon the main facts of modern science and the main trends of modern philosophy.

Also, the sole way to refute Whitehead's declaration—that we shall never succeed in elaborating an explanatory metaphysics until we have stopped trying to include in such a system the alleged concept of vacuous actuality—the sole way to refute this negative prediction is to produce a metaphysics which accepts vacuous actuality and which yet rivals Whitehead's in coherence and width of applicability to experience.

Third, to the complaint (which Morris Cohen and others have expressed) that modern science, far from having eliminated the concept of matter, has rather arrived at a more subtle and adequate one, and thus has confirmed "materialism" instead of refuting it, the answer is that so far as matter means vacuous actuality, no such concept functions in science at all. In other terms, if "matter" means something alternative to experience (to subjectivity in the broadest sense), then precisely this alternative status, this definitely asserted possibility of no-experience, no-feeling, no-sociality, this alleged neutrality or possible vacuousness of matter, by which it was formerly contrasted to mind, is the very set of aspects, or pseudonotions, that advances in scientific subtlety and adequacy have been eliminating, until, as Whitehead says, not one such aspect remains. Physics does, to be sure, need the notion of physical reality, reality with spatiotemporal characters, and this notion Whitehead accepts along with science and common sense. But since, according to his observations and analysis, experiences as such have spatiotemporal characters, and since no unmistakable samples of concrete actuality other than experiences are directly given or positively imaginable as actualities (with quality as well as relational structure, causal connectedness, intrinsic becoming, etc.), it is, he holds, meaningless to say that besides experiences there are also the merely physical realities. Experiences are physical realities, and our only way of positively generalizing the notion of "real" or "physical actuality," beyond the specific traits of human experiences as sample realities, is to generalize the notion of experience itself so as to enable it to include a vast and indeed infinite range of possible types of nonhuman experience, not forgetting divine experience. If this cannot be done, then we are incurably ignorant of what can be meant by "real" or "process" in general, as we must certainly be of any positive characters distinguishing the parts of nature to which we deny the characters of experience.

A difficult concept in Whitehead is that of the Creativity, or the ultimate ground, or substantial activity. Is this a sort of God beyond God? I have some doubt whether all his utterances on this topic can be reconciled. But we are told that the creativity is not an actual or concrete entity. My suggestion is that we regard creativity or the principle of process as an "analogical concept" functioning in Whitehead's system somewhat as "being" functions in Aristotelian theology. There are diverse kinds of being, according to Thomas Aquinas, with a major division between the necessary being of God and the contingent being of all else. So, for Whitehead, it is impossible simply to identify creative action with divine action, because every actual entity, as partly "self-created," has its own action. (This, of course, is one aspect of the explanation of how evil results from action.) Moreover, the divine action is unique because, just as the divine being in Thomism was held to exist necessarily and eternally, so in Whiteheadianism the divine process, since it is, in its primordial aspect, the ground of all possibility (the eternal objects), is likewise necessary, in the sense that it is not a possibility that there should be no such process, and this distinguishes it from ordinary kinds of process. Thus creativity-as-such is no more a God beyond God in this system than being-as-such is in

Thomism. The difference is mainly in the shift from mere being to process—as the ultimate analogical universal or form of forms.

My own conviction is that if there is anything in the passages dealing with this topic not capable of the foregoing interpretation, it probably ought to be discarded, and would have been discarded by Whitehead himself, had his attention been brought to bear a little more fully upon the question. My only alternative or supplementary suggestion is that one or two of the remarks about creativity might possibly be applied to God instead, on condition that they do not contradict the basic primordial-consequent structure attributed to deity.

In conclusion, one may say that the basic principles of our knowledge and experience—physical, biological, sociological, aesthetic, religious—are in this philosophy given an intellectual integration such as only a thousand or ten thousand years of further reflection and inquiry seem likely to exhaust or adequately evaluate, but whose wide relevance and in many respects at least comparative accuracy some of us think can already be discerned.

Reprinted from *Whitehead and the Modern World: Science, Metaphysics, and Civilization, Three Essays on the Thought of Alfred North Whitehead*, by Victor Lowe, Charles Hartshorne, and A. H. Johnson (Boston: Beacon Press, 1950), pp. 25-41.

CHAPTER THREE

On Some Criticisms of
Whitehead's Philosophy

Concerning Professor A. N. Whitehead's most comprehensive work, *Process and Reality*, a reviewer has said: "Whether it is the product of thinking that is essentially unclear but capable of brief flashes of penetrating insight; or whether it is too profound in its thought to be judged by this generation, I do not know. Reluctantly I am inclined to accept the first alternative."[1] It may as well be said at once that, if the choice must be made, I for one would feel compelled to adopt the second alternative. But the possible attitudes toward Whitehead's philosophy are not exhausted by the particular disjunction proposed. That this philosophy is clearly thought out in all its aspects I do not believe; nor I think, does its author. And certainly I for one would not lay claim to its full understanding. But that many critics of Whitehead's writings have in important respects misinterpreted his intentions I am no less convinced. My purpose in the remarks which follow is to indicate a number of these misconceptions, as they seem to me to be, and to suggest some of my own reasons for thinking that in most of its main outlines Whitehead's system is clear-cut and consistent, as well as original and well grounded. I shall also indicate what seem to me the least defensible aspects of the system.

How far the misunderstandings which I allege are due to deficiencies in Whitehead's literary exposition it is very difficult for me to judge, since my first acquaintance with most [some] of his ideas was by means of the spoken rather than the written word. How far, again, understanding of his work will have to be reserved for future generations depends (I am enlarging upon a suggestion which Stebbing herself makes) very much

21

upon the extent to which the present generation is really interested in systematic philosophy as such. To follow a fundamental reconstruction of philosophical ideas requires an effort which will not be made by anyone who believes that only piecemeal work upon neatly isolated problems is worthwhile.[2] I must add that this belief itself seems to me no more reasonable than would be the notion that the most valuable scientists are those multitudes of workers whose problems are highly restricted, rather than the Newtons and Einsteins who revise nearly the whole system of their science. Isolation of problems is possible as a matter of emphasis, but as such it occurs in the most systematic philosophy, the expositions of which must perforce pass from one topic to another. Outside of a system we never know fully what any philosophical category means, since only other categories can explain it—as, for instance, "necessity" is partially explained as the "impossibility" of the "opposite" [contradictory] —and since a system is nothing but the thorough carrying out of such explanation. Of course, categories possess some meaning independently of this process, since they all refer to experience and to traditionally ingrained habits of thinking about experience. But to rely upon such traditional and unclarified meanings in general in order to clarify certain problems in particular is appropriate only in an age when no fundamental advance, no radical revision of conceptions, is required or possible. Who can think of the present age in this fashion? Only after we have a general program of thought, such as Whitehead offers, which faces the new intellectual situation *in toto*, can we settle down again to a concentration upon lesser tasks. In this way and in no other has advance been made in the past, whether in philosophy or in physics.

The first possibility of misunderstanding Whitehead's philosophy which I wish to consider concerns the famous rejection of the "bifurcation of nature." It is of course clear that this rejection is a protest against the conception of a world consisting exclusively of primary qualities, bare spatiotemporal patterns, such as Newtonian physics appeared to posit. It has not, I fear, been equally clear to all of Whitehead's readers just how the required reinstatement of the secondary (and tertiary) qualities is to be effected.[3] The difficulty is due partly to the fact that the actual situation, as Whitehead sees it, is not simple. The answer proposed is complex; and the complexity has been taken for ambiguity.

In what sense are the secondary qualities objective, really *there* in nature? The most obvious sense is of course that we, or our experiences, as including the qualities, are real parts of nature. This has seldom been denied, and can hardly be all that Whitehead wishes to assert. In fact the division of nature into two parts, in but one of which occur the secondary qualities, *is* the bifurcation. The denial of the latter means that *all* parts of nature possess qualities of this type. A second, more subtle, answer is that any part of nature possesses qualities when and insofar as it is related to perceiving organisms. The table which to me appears as red really does so appear to me; and this fact is as much a truth about the table as it is a truth about me. When things are in certain relations, they really are in those relations. Is this doctrine, which is called Objective Relativism,[4] an adequate solution of the bifurcation question? Perhaps it is such a solution upon one condition, that objective relativism be combined with panpsychism. For suppose this condition not to be granted. Then whatever things do not happen to be present to sentient organisms, to be felt, will be without actual secondary qualities; and thus nature will consist after all of two parts, in but one of which qualities occur. Such division of nature can occur either on spatial or on temporal lines. It may be that some things in the present world around us are not felt by an organism. If so, there is bifurcation. It may be that all sentience has emerged from a world in which no such thing originally existed. If so, a very drastic bifurcation in time must be admitted. And the point is that the objections to bifurcation as such apply quite as well to these special forms of it as to any others. If a world, indeed any individual reality, without quality beyond bare spatiotemporal form is in the strictest sense inconceivable—and it is—then it is of no consequence whether the hypothesis of such a world, or of such a reality, places it in the distant past or somewhere off in space. Berkeley's objections to Locke's philosophy have no relation to such matters of locus. Indeed, from the standpoint of these objections, it seems a fair question whether Locke was not precisely an objective relativist; that is to say, so much of one as is logically possible to a thinker who does not accept panpsychism.

An objection to the foregoing might be that things which are not felt, and so possess no actual qualities, may nevertheless be regarded as in potential relation to sentience, and so potentially clothed with quality. Here is a new bifurcation, one of still subtler guise. The division now involves not merely space-time but also the dimension of actual-possible. What is gained? As before, I cannot discover. For, apart from the fact that the distinction is dealt with by Locke and Berkeley, insofar as the quality of a thing is merely potential, its actuality is so likewise; it is a possible individual at most. Furthermore, there is no intellectual value in the ascription of a possibility to something unless the actualized aspects of the thing's nature throw light upon, are intelligibly related to, this potentiality.

When have the opponents of panpsychism offered us anything even purporting to render intelligible the relation between stimulus (in its final stage as nervous process) and color or smell? On the contrary such relations are regarded by them as perfect examples of ultimate facts which we have merely to accept without further analysis. The purpose of "speculative philosophy" is to avoid such barriers to inquiry.

From the standpoint of panpsychism, objective relativism assumes a very different and a more intelligible meaning. To say that to be felt by us is an aspect of the book as truly as of ourselves is of doubtful value unless we can really see how this fact helps us better to understand the book in its *remaining* aspects, especially those which are studied by the physicist. For it is to be observed that this requirement *can* be fulfilled on the converse side of the relation. We do understand *ourselves* better in terms of such things as perceiving a red book. But what do we learn about the book? It seems clear that we learn either too much or too little to justify the nonpsychistic form of objective relativism. Too much, if the contribution of "being-felt" to the book is to change it from a qualityless pattern, a mere abstraction incapable of independent existence, into a concrete individual determinate with respect to quality. Too little, if the book already has some nonsentient quality—in which case we gain no understanding of how the contributed quality fuses with the other to form a new total quality. I frankly confess that I fear all that we really are being offered here is the tautology: a thing which is perceived is a thing which is perceived. The panpsychist substitutes for this tautology a significant assertion, which is that, not the book, but the individual molecules or atoms, or whatever real parts it may be composed of, are not simply felt by us but also themselves feel. It follows that what we are feeling in the book may be in part—a very minute part, to be sure—the feelings of its molecules. These latter feelings, in their turn, are also feelings of feelings, including as an unimportant but real part our feelings of the redness of the book. Primarily felt by us in the redness are the feelings of the molecules of our own bodies. Primarily felt by the particles of the book are the feelings of the particles around them, and only as an almost infinitesimally faint echo, our own feelings. As to the qualities of feelings, these will be specific to the kind of organism having the feeling. The primary quality of our feeling, that which is clear and in the focus of attention, will have only a distant analogy with the primary quality of the feelings constituting the external object. Still some analogy will obtain; for all feeling has its specificity in terms of certain ultimate dimensions, such as intensity, positivity-negativity (pleasantness-unpleasantness), passivity-activity. The word feeling indeed is simply a reference to these dimensions, the final measures of all qualitative differentiation. Those who reject this word and these dimensions do not address themselves to the task of providing an alternative analysis of the dimensions of quality; but offer us at best the mere word "quality," if they do not strip parts of the world bare of all claim to the category. As for the assertion that the ultimacy of a category implies that it cannot be explained (in terms of other categories), this is the precise equivalent of the denial that philosophy is possible. For the application of categories to particular things is the business of the special sciences, leaving the explanation of the categories themselves as the sole task of philosophy. Moreover, modern mathematics and logic have found that the distinction between primitive and defined ideas is subject to a relativity with which Descartes and Leibniz (and their contemporary followers) seem not to have reckoned in their assumption of simple indefinables as the intellectual foundations of knowledge. The whole conception that explanation in a circle is necessarily, as applied to categorial notions, fallacious is a relic of the older logico-mathematical ideas which it is time to discard.[5]

The suggestion has been made that in reducing all things to modes of feeling (or rather, of feeling of feeling) Whitehead has committed his own "fallacy of misplaced concreteness."[6] For, just as the materialists stripped the psychological predicates from nature, calling the truncated remainder reality, so Whitehead has stripped off the physical properties and dignified the remaining class of properties—"feelings"—in a similarly arbitrary fashion.[7] The answer is that by feeling, Whitehead does not mean any particular set of properties which experience exhibits, but *dimensional characteristics found in all* such properties, those traits of structure which physics exploits being in no way excluded. It is somewhat amusing to see a physicist and mathematician like Whitehead accused of forgetting the structural character of the universe! No such forgetting has in fact occurred. Here we must note that it is not feeling *simpliciter* but feeling *of* feeling, that is, in the widest possible sense, *social* feeling, that is in question. Now this social feeling just as such has a structure. The contrast between self and other is never wholly absent from it. This contrast has four dimensions, and these dimensions are those of space-time. Space and time (and therefore motion) are simply the modalities of the "of" relation in "feeling of feeling." All this is worked out by Whitehead in considerable detail. If there is any important concept of physics that is left out of account, it should be worth mentioning which one it is.

One may verbally believe that the universe contains other kinds of entities than social feelings; but it is an entire misunderstanding of the fallacy of misplaced concreteness to suppose that it applies to the presumed contents of the universe in any other way than via a prior inspection of experience. The old-fashioned materialist abstracted from the *experienced* secondary and tertiary qualities; Whitehead omits no experienced qualities whatever. If he does, these qualities should be pointed out.

It may indeed seem to many that the experienced qualities of color, sound, or smell are not properly describable as feelings. This, however, is a question of observational fact. A distinction between sense-data and affective tone is certainly traditional in psychology and philosophy, and Whitehead's denial of this distinction may appear dogmatic. In one sense, indeed, the denial is not only dogmatic but certainly false; for affective tone is generally—though by no means universally—taken as unidimensional; and sense-qualities display at least three dimensions. It follows that the traditional idea of feeling-tone cannot be used as an adequate description of sense-data. On the other hand, the attempt to divide experience into those portions which do and those which do not display feeling-tone has not yet led to consistent results. There are good reasons for doubting whether it ever will. Moreover, the unidimensional view of feeling is equally open to question.[8] The fact is that psychology has recently come, to its great surprise, upon numerous facts which it has yet to reconcile with the view of a departmental division of data into sensory and emotional. Indeed not all psychologists believe that there is any need to attempt such a division. The moral for philosophy is that the question is not one to be settled by offhand personal impressions, or dogmas based thereon. Rather it can only be settled by improvements in the technique of observation, such as are now actually being made. There is one fact on the basis of which I venture to predict the outcome of these advances. This fact is that it is the open secret of aesthetic experience that sense-datum and feeling-tone are absolutely one in the phenomenon of expression. If psychological theories of sensation had been originally devised for the purpose of explaining this phenomenon, the dichotomy of sense and feeling would not have been set up. Historically, the concept of sensation as nonfeeling experience was devised for very different purposes; and the result has been that every real advance in aesthetics has been in spite of this concept. The attempt to preserve the latter has resulted in numerous artificial hypotheses, such as that of *Einfühlung,* by which the unity of expression was to be attained on the assumption of a dichotomy of sense and feeling. Criticism of these ingenious evasions is driving aestheticians ever nearer to the uncompromising admission that the truth of the aesthetic experience and the falsity of the assumed dichotomy are one. [This was too optimistic. The dichotomy is still widely assumed, e.g., by some writers in the *Journal of Aesthetics.*]

[Murphy complains that when "feeling" is given the extended meaning it has for Whitehead it becomes as abstract as the concepts of physics. However, as I have pointed out elsewhere, there are two sorts of abstractness. One consists in neglecting specific or individual forms of a general property, the other in neglecting general properties. Physics is abstract chiefly in the latter, metaphysics, if sound, only in the former sense. Physics neglects all forms of nonstructural or genuinely qualitative properties in favor of structural ones. It neglects all forms of value and purpose except only the purpose and value of seeking and finding the truth. I deny that Whitehead neglects any general property whatever. The aim of metaphysics is not to find concepts that are concrete in the sense of being specific, but to find the concepts that express what it is to be concrete. Concreteness itself and as such is the abstraction that is sought. Murphy has some understanding of this, but questions either the worthwhileness of the project or, it is not always clear to me which, the way in which Whitehead carries it out. He fears that we may become imprisoned in a definite concept of concreteness and so become blinded to aspects of experience that do not fit. He recognizes that Whitehead does not claim certainty and secure finality for his theory of concreteness, but he seems to hold that this openness to further experience might be better provided for by giving up the metaphysical quest. But perhaps what we really need is simply that there should always be both metaphysicians and intelligent critics of metaphysicians, always both Whiteheads and Murphys! A theory of concreteness is a tool for that "criticism of abstractions" which, according to Whitehead, is philosophy. But certainly the abstractions used in the theory cannot be exempted from criticism. All theory is tested in some sense or fashion in experience, finally in practical experience. Whitehead and Murphy are in partial agreement on this central point. And, unlike some critics of Whitehead, Murphy read and taught Whitehead with care and throughout his career. I am glad now that my wife persuaded me not to publish a highly polemical article I wrote long ago to combat Murphy's early attacks on Whitehead. We both had something to learn, and meanwhile Whitehead's reputation could manage fairly well with or without us.]

Suppose, for the sake of following Whitehead's argument, that one were to grant the category of feeling as adequately descriptive of the immediate data of experience. Could one not still object to the extension of this category to all reality? Against such a panpsychism it may be objected that it is really nothing but an argument by analogy, "a striking metaphor."[9] The answer is that the doctrine is certainly an inference by analogy, but that it is two other things besides, and that its claim to validity rests upon the interplay of no less than three types of evidence. Of the three, it is not analogy that is the most fundamental.

First and above all is what might be called "the argument from categories." If feeling is the most general character of the immediately given, then we can form no more general category by which to describe existence in general than this very character. It is not a difficulty of finding some method of proof for a nonaffective reality, but the prior difficulty of finding any meaning for our words—for such a word as quality, for instance—except via an illustration in experience, perceptual or imaginative. Whatever the criterion for truth may be, that for *meaning*, we are nearly all agreed today, is experience. All this is only another way of saying that the basic argument for panpsychism is that any alternative commits the fallacy of misplaced concreteness.

The second argument, which is really a specialization of the first, is that not simply feeling but, to repeat, feeling of feeling, is *immediately given*. In psychology this point is beginning to be recognized in the concept, based upon very careful experimental inquiry, of "objective" feelings. These are feelings which at least seem to stand over against us as characters of objects. The supposition that this effect is mediate, a sort of involuntary and false inference, is scarcely borne out experimentally, but remains speculation. Now, in Whitehead's terms, this result, which has somewhat puzzled the psychologists, depends upon the fact that immediacy is essentially social or sympathetic. The life of feeling which is ours is not ours alone, but is also other life in which we share. Primarily it is the life of the body, of its living members, the cells (ultimately the constituent electrons also). By virtue of such givenness of other-feeling in our feeling, we have not only a general clue, via the categories, to the sentient character of physical reality, but particular evidence of the particular feelings which constitute at least one small portion of the physical world. Thus the intensity of a bright light may be descriptive not only of our sensory feeling but also of the feeling of certain cells. And so on through the other dimensions of feeling. Such direct evidences of nonhuman feelings, however, are because of faintness incapable of distinct observation with respect to all objects except the bodily parts. And even with respect to these there is much vagueness, due to the fact that our feelings prehend those of the body not with individual distinctness, but en masse, according to principles beautifully stated by Spinoza long ago. [Here I perhaps flatter Spinoza.]

But we can have recourse finally to a third principle, that of analogy. Structurally and behavioristically, i.e., as known through our sensory feelings plus inferences therefrom, physical objects in general exhibit analogies to that object which is the human body. These analogies may be obvious, or may require science for their discovery. In the first case we have animal bodies in the commonsense scope of this classification. In the second, we have apparently dead things, but things which science demonstrates to involve so much more than their everyday appearances that the question of the animate or inanimate character of their constituent parts cannot for a moment be regarded as within the competence of mere common sense. The fact is that science has forced us enormously to extend the notion of life and has destroyed for the present all possibility of drawing a definite line between living and dead individuals. What seems a mass of mere matter may be a colony of bacteria; and between bacteria and the molecules there are the viruses, so that it is the remarkable fact that all individuals whatsoever that are capable of being seen, even with the most powerful microscope, together with some even smaller, fall into the class of animate individuals.

The reader will of course understand that I do not regard a chair as an individual, but as a swarm or mass of individuals. Its unity, in other words, is superficial, as even prescientific speculation was able to infer, and as modern science shows. The effective units in nature which are not obviously living are submicroscopic, and our knowledge of their structure and individual behavior is still highly incomplete. It is these little-known individuals only to which the term inanimate can still be applied, and then only on the basis of our ignorance. Whatever is known fits the hylozoistic hypothesis well enough, certainly far better than anyone could have anticipated who supposed that Newtonian science, with its rigid determinism, eternal atoms, etc., was justified in these life-denying absolutes.

The argument by analogy, however, encounters another difficulty besides that of our ignorance of the lowest individual systems. Granting that bacteria are alive, it does not follow that they are sentient. Hylozoism is not panpsychism. The beginnings of the nervous system [seem to] afford a good basis for distinguishing the psychic from the merely animate. But . . . the point of the nervous system is coordination of behavior, and this occurs to some degree with it or without it. It is therefore always a question whether an [invertebrate] "organism" is to be viewed as an individual or as a colony. Whitehead's description of a tree as "a democracy" may also apply to multicellular animals that are not endowed with a nervous system. Thus sentient individuality may be found at a lower level than that of the nerve-possessing animal, for the single cells of nerveless metazoa have a functional unity which the animal as a whole lacks and which is analogous to the coordination brought about by a system of nerves. And were this not so the question of molecules, atoms, electrons, etc., would still have to be considered on its merits. Panpsychism merely says that *if* things act individually they feel individually. In any event we are debarred from resting content with an absolute distinction between sentient and insentient by the arguments from categories and from the immediate givenness of other-feeling. Moreover, the latter gives us a means of corroborating the results of analogy at one strategic point in the scale of living creatures, the bodily cell. It is a matter for empirical inquiry whether or not the behavior and structure of the cells most concerned in a particular human feeling suggest by analogy that these cells possess somewhat similar feelings.

This last statement calls for explanation; but I am content here to remark that I see no way of knowing that the satisfactory execution of the program of inquiry indicated could be accomplished in any particular period of time. Perhaps it will take a thousand years. Indeed, there is perhaps no reason why it should ever be completed in such a way as to leave no room for improvement. Meanwhile, panpsychism has this advantage over every rival hypothesis, that it promises a higher degree of eventual integration of knowledge, particularly as between physics and psychology, than any other. For it suggests that a generalized comparative psychology will one day include all science, whereas other doctrines— whether they be called idealistic or realistic—differ only in the explicitness with which they admit that physical and psychical processes are irreducible to any common principles capable of explaining in detail their interrelationships. [I suspect this is true even of today's "identity theories."]

It is well known that, according to Whitehead's doctrine, every event prehends its ancestors; but doubt has frequently been expressed whether this applies strictly to the totality of its ancestors, and also whether the same principle applies to an event's contemporaries. Concerning the ancestors there need I think be no dispute: Whitehead has expressed himself emphatically and repeatedly upon this point. Every actual entity prehends the entirety of its own actual universe and this actual universe consists of all entities in its causal past. There has been question of his asserting this only because of one or more of the following sources of confusion. (1) "Negligible relevance" and "negative relevance" have been taken as zero relevance; but if Whitehead had meant this he would, I take it, have said it. (2) He certainly does deny that everything implies everything else, if the first "everything" includes abstract entities or eternal objects; for these are indeterminate with respect to their particular instances, and therefore do not in any way contain them. (3) He also denies that future events in their fully individual characters are ever prehended while they are still future. They are not parts of the actual world except as somewhat indefinite outlines, the indefiniteness expressing the degree of contingency permitted by the only relatively exact laws or habits of nature. (4) Recently Whitehead has made it clear that he even denies that contemporaries are internal to each other.[10] He actually defines contemporaneity, following physics, as the absence of influence, so that no contemporary event is ever internal to another. [I have come to agree with this.] The matter is complicated by the physics of relativity. In spite of the difficulties, I venture to suggest, against Whitehead's own opinion, that the unqualified inclusiveness of prehension (always excepting universals in relation to particulars, and earlier in relation to later events in time) is required by his system as a whole. For it is the only means which the system seems to provide by which the world can be constituted as such, as a real whole. Nor is there any need for a limitation of the principle in order to safeguard the individuality of things; for the *principium individuationis* of the system is not only compatible with that of the solidarity of the world, but seems actually to require it. This is the principle of Leibniz: every monad reflects the totality of monads, but each monad does this with its own perspective, its own distribution of emphasis. External relations between coexistent monads, so far from increasing their individuality, would diminish or destroy it; for it is precisely the nonindividual or universal factors of the world, such as the eternal objects, which are thus independent of their contexts. Also, external relations between individuals would imply [?] Bradley's vicious regress of relations between things and their relations. [Mutually internal relations imply a truly vicious regress.] The . . . denial of internality among coexistent events involves the further difficulty that all events prehend God, who in his contemporary or consequent nature prehends all actual things.

An obscure, if not definitely erroneous, feature of Whitehead's view is his notion of eternal objects. That these are legitimately distinguished from ordinary universals or essences is I believe a point well taken, but one which is by no means consistently carried out. In spite of much dogmatism to the contrary—in which Whitehead himself has sometimes indulged—there is no reason why characters may not have a certain degree of universality without possessing the absolute degree of it which is eternity. Independence of temporal context may be relative as well as absolute. To use the current term, "essences" may perfectly well emerge in the universe, not merely in the world of actuality but in the total universe of actuality and possibility. It is true that, before an essence emerges, there must be a possibility of which its appearance is the actualization; but the question is whether such a possibility need be as *definite* as the quality which actualizes it. The objection to supposing this is that the process of actualization is thereby reduced to a mere shuffling (Whitehead's "selection" is all too suggestive of this view) of primordial qualitative factors. In short, creation in the proper sense is denied, and with it the nature of time as recent philosophy has revealed that nature.[11] The distinction between possible and actual is that between the relatively indefinite and the relatively definite, the determinable and the determinate; or it is a distinction of which no intelligible account has ever been given. It follows from all this that the strictly nonemergent factors of the universe must be simply its most general determinables, that is to say, the categories in the strictest sense of the word.[12] Now are Whitehead's eternal objects [all] categories? And if not, as seems to be the case, why not? That Whitehead has anywhere adequately treated this question I have not as yet been able to find. In *Science and the Modern World* we learn that "a color is eternal." But how this statement is to be justified is not explained. In terms of Whitehead's descriptive method one may suspect that no justification is possible.

To argue that it must be eternally true that red is red and not blue, and that hence red itself must be eternal, is merely to beg the question. Of course it can never have been *false* that red is red, but if red is an emergent in the universe, then before this emergence it was neither true nor false that red was red—or anything else. For truth and falsity alike require ideas, and it is just the question whether an idea of red is or is not an eternal ingredient of the universe. The proposition *red is red* can never have had any but a positive truth-value; but if there was once a time when there was no such proposition, then at that time "it" could have had *no* truth-value, or any other property whatever, for there was no such it. Nor is there any criticism of Whitehead's work which has been more uniformly made even by sympathetic interpreters than this one of the unsatisfactoriness of the eternal objects.[13] It would be unjust, however, not to add that in many another recent philosophy the problem of mediating between essence and existence is left immeasurably farther from any apparent solution, as witness Santayana's debonair division of the universe into "realms" for whose mode of integration into one cosmos he disclaims intellectual responsibility.

The bearing of this problem upon the question of world-solidarity is as follows. Lovejoy has argued with considerable cogency that since it cannot be the eternal objects, nor the events as constituted by them, which internally involve other actual events, therefore the solidarity of the world, with its corollary, the denial of simple location, can only mean that the bare space-time locus of each event involves reference to the loci of other events.[14] Qualitatively, events remain outside each other. I confess to a virtual certainty that this is not Whitehead's meaning. But I am far from certain that he has succeeded in providing us with a clear statement of what he does mean. Nevertheless, there are plenty of hints at least pointing to the conclusion that the qualitative nature of events is not simply the aggregate of eternal objects ingredient in them, but a more definite determination of these determinables producing a unique single individual-essence; and that it is this unique quality which does prehend the unique quality of at least every antecedent event.[15] But such an interpretation seems to imply a very clear division of essences into eternal and emergent, and this requirement is perhaps not wholly met by Whitehead's exposition.[16] There is need also for a very sharp statement of the fallacy of supposing that qualities as embodied in different things can be the same qualities in any other sense than that the same determinable (i.e., somewhat vague) quality can achieve determinations which are qualitatively different, however slightly, in these different things. This is the truth of Stout's contention that the qualities of things are as particular and unique as the things. When we think that two objects have or can have the same hue of color, we are thinking in terms of approximation; the idea that the two hues are ever exactly the same is either a sheer assumption or it presupposes as its verification an absoluteness of qualitative comparison which itself is a sheer assumption, controverted by much significant evidence. Thus Stout's idea is less mysterious than he himself regards it as being.[17] It is the only view of universals that is not purely dogmatic and unverifiable. The same essence can be in different things; but only if by essence we mean an entity which in itself, and not merely as we see it, is vague.

Upon the idea of vagueness depends, in still other ways, the world-solidarity. There are two possible accounts of the fact that we do not distinctly intuit all reality. We may say that there are parts . . . of the real which we just do, and parts which we just do not, intuit. The difficulty is that the individuality of real things includes all their parts (we have no other way of distinguishing universal from particular) as a unity, a *Gestalt.* If we intuit any individual reality at all, we must intuit it as a whole. . . . But it is simply not a fact that we distinctly intuit any single reality in this exhaustive fashion. Therefore, we must choose between saying that nothing individual is intuited as such, that reality is a sheer inference from the intuition of more or less general characters, or possibilities, and admitting that indistinctness is not due to the (assumed) fact that some parts of the real are quite outside our intuition. In other words, indistinctness is qualitative and not quantitative merely. But then there are all intensities of this quality, and it inexorably follows that there can be no [empirical] evidence whatever *against* the solidarity of the subject with its entire world. One has only to suppose the indistinctness sufficiently great to account for any empirical inability to detect, say, the inhabitants of China in our immediate intuitions.[18] Furthermore, it is inconsequent to admit that we prehend at least our immediate neighbors, and these prehend theirs, and so on, and to deny that each prehends all the others. William James used to say that each thing was solid with its immediate surroundings but not with its ultimate surroundings, and some still adhere to this doctrine. But I fear the transitivity of the relation of implication or inclusion renders the suggestion nothing more nor less than the invitation to a holiday from logic. The real intention of James was surely to prevent such a chain of transitive necessity from leading *into the future*, or from the past into the present. But this aim is sufficiently accomplished by denying that even the immediate future follows necessarily from or is contained in the present, except in the sense in which alone the future, while still not present, is in being, namely in a somewhat general or nebulous form.[19] The proposition, *all individual being prehends all other individual being*, is thus not contradicted by holding the future in its details external to the present. For as external these details are a mere general class; they are not examples of individual being.

The solidarity of the world includes at least the past. The only alternative is to suppose that the past is subject to the same indefiniteness as the future. If there are determinate truths about the details of the past—and it is paradox to deny it—then the past is not simply dropped from the universe, in the passage to the present, but preserved. It is no good to say that its definiteness is preserved but not its reality. For the definite *is* the real as distinguished from the possible. There is nothing in reality over and above potentiality except definiteness. The conclusion is obviously the necessity for a cosmic memory by which nothing is forgotten.[20] If this is more startling than the contemporary aspect of solidarity, the reason lies in the stronger suggestion of infinity in the content prehended.

Each of us is vaguely what omniscience would be distinctly. Now it is arguable that the vaguely inclusive form of prehension implies the existence of the distinct or omniscient form. For insofar as vagueness is the last word, there seems no answer to the question, "What would be the difference between a feeling which vaguely remembers something, say as I vaguely remember my physical birth, and a feeling which did not remember it but is otherwise just like mine?" The feeling itself provides no answer insofar as it is vague. In some sense the fact that I vaguely remember just that unique event in all its particularity and no other must be a perfectly definite fact. The available solution was given long ago—that unclear ideas are only possible as aspects of the clear intuitions of God (cf. Spinoza). This is also Whitehead's answer. But there is a difference which is enormously to his advantage. In Spinoza there is really no place for unclearness in the world, since in the ground of things is no hint of such a property. (This is equally true of Scholastic theology.) But for Whitehead human unclearness is simply [is analogous to] the unclearness (unclearness, not confusion or error) with which even God surveys the future, but in an exaggerated form or as applied to objects which, unlike the future, are in themselves definite.

We have arrived at the final question, the question of the role of the Divine in Whitehead's metaphysics. It has been suggested by more than one critic that the use of the term God is not justified by the place which this entity actually occupies in the system. There is irony in this. For nearly two thousand years theology has invested its intellectual fortunes in the concept of the timeless absolute; and for some three hundred years, beginning especially with Spinoza, much of the best thought of modern metaphysicians has tended more and more irresistibly toward the conclusion that this timeless absolute is not the God of religion. In Bosanquet the demonstration is particularly persuasive. Now Whitehead's endeavor has been to eliminate the nonreligious aspect from theology. The result, that he is accused of using the religious term with impropriety, is, I say, somewhat amusing. For consider. Putting God, the eternal, in time gives back the ancient conception of a "living God," one who can pursue purposes, i.e., *as yet unrealized* values; whereas to the timeless all ends are realized eternally and hence are only in a Pickwickian sense ends at all.

Yet, in the doctrine of the Primordial Nature of God, justice is done to the motives which led medieval theology to exalt the nonemergent or eternal character of the Absolute. Nor is it only in connection with time that Whitehead's God is peculiarly deserving of the name. Most theologians have admitted in their cosmology some element of sheer dead matter, and thus have divided their world into a living and spiritual part, which reflects the living spirit at the foundation of things, and a lifeless, wholly nonspiritual part, which does not, except in some evasive Pickwickian sense, reflect this source. Leibniz was the first to see that this would not do, but there are vestiges of materialism in his system, as there are in Berkeley's. In Whitehead the inconsistency is cleared up; all things are for him spiritual in their degree, and hence are not dead matter, nor windowless monads, nor lifeless, Berkeleyan ideas, but, in the lowest terms, sentience, intuitions of value, socially interlocked with other such intuitions. What is this but to say that all things literally embody what may fairly be called love? Is this or is this not the religious idea of the immanence of God? To me it seems the most consistent and candid interpretation of that idea ever set forth. God is that clear and distinct grasp of love by which, as Dante says, all things are bound together. The "things" are more or less imperfect expressions of the same principle of social feeling. In the older theology it is intellect and not love which reigns; hence the neutral conception of matter, and many other features whose religious meaning is not apparent.

But we must consider the question whether the system really requires the factor of deity, so conceived, except in the objectionable fashion of a cure-all for mismanaged problems. The ultimate answer must rest upon the results of taking seriously the view of metaphysics as "a descriptive science." In the end, God must not remain a mere inference, but must be interpretable as a descriptive term for the ultimate horizons, the infinite dimensions of experience, and for their interrelations. But are there such infinite horizons *within* experience? The [A] clue to the answer lies in the observation that the thought of infinity is involved in every branch of human knowledge, from mathematics to ethics, aesthetics, and astronomy. If the descriptive view of ultimate categories is sound, then, theology or no theology, we are obliged to search experience for an immanent infinity. One can also argue dialectically that it is impossible without contradiction to deny that we possess meanings that refer to infinite dimensions of being.

If the problem of theology has seemed hopeless, this may well be due to two circumstances: the descriptive view of metaphysics has only recently won something like general acceptance, and the infinite has generally been defined negatively. This negative mode of definition forms a natural but treacherous short cut to transcending the limitation of the finite. Neither the correct formula for relations between finite and infinite, nor the descriptive attitude by which alone—we are nearly all agreed— metaphysics can become a science, has been customary in theology. The formula in question is that the finite necessarily possesses, to a partial degree, whatever properties are found in completeness in the infinite, and conversely. Thus the ultimate being is not lacking in spatial or temporal extension, but is, as Spinoza said, spatial extension in its completeness (which, according to the new astronomy, may even be finite in quantity), and also as he should have said, a factor enduring throughout all time. Again, the so-called deadness of the basic material in the world cannot be absolute if God is aliveness in superlative degree. The concept of the imperfect must be treated as a partial contraction of that of the perfect, and this cannot be if either term is regarded as the sheer negation of the other; e.g., if God is timeless, or if matter is lifeless. The transition from a merely qualitative to a quantitative or graduated, and from a dialectical to a descriptive, doctrine of the primordial being is the most sublime achievement of which the scientific method holds promise. In Whitehead we are at least a long stage nearer to its consummation than in Spinoza, who was perhaps its first major prophet. For instance, Whitehead avoids the trap of supposing that the complete being must contain the actualization of all possibilities, and thus be incapable of growth. The nonrealization of a part of the possibilities is not a matter of finitude or of incompleteness, but of consistency, since possibilities involve incompatible alternatives, and it is hardly an implication of the supreme that it should be self-contradictory—unless, indeed, the concept of perfection is altogether impossible and meaningless, and theology nothing but an attempt against reason, a conclusion which would at any rate not have appealed to Spinoza or the Catholic theologians who with him have denied to God the capacity for growth. [This paragraph seems to me now somewhat confused in its use of "descriptive," "infinite," "perfect," "complete."]

Compared to the great systems of the past, Whitehead's doctrine presents such distinguishing characteristics as the following: (1) It combines a recognition of the organic unity of the world—a thought which has inspired every modern thinker who has been able to find his way through the morass of epistemological controversy into a positive statement about the nature of the world—with a no less vigorous assertion of the reality of contingency, individuality, and time. Whitehead's is the first *uni*verse that is not a "block universe." So far as the theory of relations is concerned, he is to a remarkable extent the reconciliation of Bosanquet and William James. (2) In its epistemology the long struggle which modern thought has waged against the subjectivism injected into it by Descartes, and carried to extreme consequences in Hegel and Comte, is finally successful; the full positive meaning of realism is vindicated, but at the same time, the positive content of idealism, or the doctrine that the object which we experience, while not just our own mental state, is yet akin to it in nature, is given no less ungrudging acceptance, and the two views shown in no wise to conflict. (3) The ancient conflict between atomistic and continuous views of space and time (as shown for instance in the paradoxes of Zeno) is resolved in such a way as to exhibit the correctness of one view in application to actual, and of the other in application to potential, occurrences. (4) The one-sided intellectualism of modern philosophy, indeed of much ancient philosophy as well, is effectively corrected by the exhibition of the evaluational content of thought, and of every phase of consciousness; but at the same time the rights and glories of that particular mode of evaluation which is intellectual procedure are much more positively admitted and asserted than in most other attempts to counteract the intellectualist fallacy. (5) The problem of the changing and the permanent, the generated and the primordial or eternal, is given a distinctive (though perhaps not wholly adequate and consistent) treatment. The differentiation between the primordial nature and the endless series of consequent natures [or states] of God seems to me easily the most illuminating thing that anyone has contributed to the theological problem for a hundred years. For want of this distinction, medieval theology failed, turned indeed, in the hands of the first exponent of its premises who was not restrained by the determination to conform to some orthodoxy—I refer of course to Spinoza—into a doctrine in which theism and atheism were irretrievably confounded and confused. From henceforth theologians will not be permitted unchallenged to pass from the concept of an underived or eternal being (a being which at all times and necessarily is), a positive and analytically necessary conception, to the really very different, merely negative, and groundless one of a timeless being, a being not in time at all. (6) Whitehead is the first metaphysician to do justice to the necessity of compound individuals, individuals consisting of parts which are individuals. His "cell-theory" of reality is relatively new in philosophy, and of great significance for natural science. This sixth point is an aspect of point (1) above.

There is one final question. Is Whitehead's philosophy pragmatically relevant? Can it aid humanity in its struggle against the incompetence, greed, and inertia which now threaten its very existence in civilized form? I believe there are two sides to the question. In few, perhaps in no other philosophic writings of our time, however pragmatic in intent, can be found saner or more penetrating comments upon social problems than are scattered through Whitehead's last five or six books. For a philosophy of social action a wonderful background is here. But something more is required at the present time. During the next few decades intelligence will race with catastrophe. It will avert catastrophe not merely by improving upon its stock of general ideas but also by bringing more fully to bear those which it already has. Action is inevitably one-sided, emphatic in temper. It is necessary to set *certain* truths in strong light, even at the risk of obscuring others. Today, what must be driven home, better fanatically than ineffectively, is the basic contradiction of a society democratic in political form and theory, and largely feudal or despotic in its economic, which at present means its determining, conditions. Now Whitehead is aware of and points to the basic factors that are here involved. But there is too little emphasis upon just those factors which need to be made central. The single and, even in the eyes of one who is not a Marxian, excessively unappreciative reference to Karl Marx in *Adventures of Ideas*, the relatively complete lack of emphasis upon the need for a vastly greater degree of economic equality than now obtains, and upon certain other matters whose importance was first adequately set forth by none other than Marx, these are some of the details of what I have in mind.[21]

All this may be much less a criticism of Whitehead than a confession of faith. And certainly we of the younger generation can ill afford to scorn his majestic vision just because a more narrowly focused philosophy is a destiny from which we ourselves cannot rightfully escape. Nor can the obscurities of his thought, due in part to a perhaps excessive use of technical terms, greatly diminish our admiration for Whitehead so long as no one else among the living—and, if we except the astonishing Charles Peirce, none among the recently dead—even approaches him in comprehensiveness and subtlety. If upon the wreckage of Newtonian materialism a new world view is to arise, then Whitehead's system is the most important single indication of what that world view is to be.

Reprinted from *The Philosophical Review* 44 (July 1935): 323-44.

CHAPTER FOUR

The Compound Individual

Atoms, cells, and the idea of substance.—Nearly twenty-four centuries ago appeared perhaps the greatest scientific invention of the Greek mind, the atomic theory. Over a hundred years ago the existence of atoms began to emerge as demonstrated fact. Before this demonstration was completed, empirical evidence had also shown that the atomic principle held sway just where its applicability had been least suspected, in biology. The discovery of cells meant that organic life is atomized, that organisms contain simpler organisms as invisible parts. Today, with all these events long passed into history, their significance seems still largely overlooked, both by scientists and by philosophers. As to the latter, it is almost incredible, but I shall try to show that it is a fact, that not until the twentieth century were philosophical categories developed capable of convenient and fruitful application to an atomic reality, and that anything like a general discussion or even awareness of these categories awaits the future.

Whatever an atom or a cell may be, it is clearly an individual. Of course we are sometimes told that an atom is merely a "construct," an abstraction, or a convenient way of summarizing certain experimental phenomena. But it is to be objected that, if the atom is a construct or abstraction, it is one of the special kind which posits individuality in the reality which it interprets, and not of the kind which merely refers to a universal, as does the concept "square." Besides, the cell, at least, cannot easily be regarded, even for a moment, as anything less than a concretely existent individual entity. On the whole the construct theory of atomism is a beautiful example of the widespread attempt of philosophers to adapt the atomic facts to categories which were developed on the assumption that there were no such facts. It is an evasion of the challenging discovery that the variety of individuals in nature is immensely greater than common sense could have guessed and that all individuals apparent to the senses are compounded of numerous much smaller individuals.

If an atom is an individual, then the philosophic problem of atomism is that of the nature of the individual as such; that is, of whatever is not a universal or mere quality, but is a particular [singular] subject or "substance" or existent to which such abstract properties may be ascribed. The word substance is rather unfashionable at present, but if, as there is fair historical warrant for doing, we regard it as simply the technical term for individuality as a philosophical category, then the problem of substance is inescapable. Indeed, the dislike of the word is in part simply an aspect of the modern evasion of the problem of individuality, although it is also a legitimate revulsion from certain outworn attempts to deal with this problem.

Five theories of substance.—History shows that five main views have been held concerning the general properties of the individual. Four of these agree in taking literally and absolutely the etymological meaning of "in-dividual"—that is, indivisible, without real parts, simple. The remaining view arose through the discovery that, like so many other doctrines, this one of noncompositeness (to be referred to in this essay as "simplicism," or absolute individualism, or absolute substantialism) occasions difficulties until it is restricted, relativized in some fashion, that is, made a matter of degree rather than of all or nothing.

The notion that the individual has no real parts means that it has no parts which are individuals. Substances can then never contain substances as elements. Substances do not compound to form more complex substances in which the simpler ones retain their substantiality (however this concept is to be defined). Perhaps this veto upon substantial composition has never been rigidly adhered to. But that would of course by no means imply that the objections I have to offer against the noncompositional view are historically irrelevant. For what is needed is a definitive and tenable doctrine concerning composition, not vagueness or inconsistency in adhering to an impossible one.

Monism.—Historically the oldest of the four principal forms of simplicism (as a sharply formulated doctrine) appears to be the conception of the entire universe as a single indivisible entity. The first clear-cut metaphysics was the monism of Parmenides. Moreover, monism dominated

Indian thought from a very early stage of its development until now. It is also interesting to note that after many centuries of experiment with pluralistic forms of absolute substantialism Europe has seen the potent revival of monism in Spinoza, Bradley, and others. One might seek to explain these facts by suggesting that, in a sense, monism is the most philosophical of simplicist doctrines. For if individuals have no parts then either the universe is the only individual (since others could only be parts of it) or it is not an individual at all. But the latter alternative is little better than a refusal to consider the problem of the cosmic totality; and is not that problem precisely the characteristic and central one for philosophy? On the other hand, monism is highly paradoxical, a fearful defiance both of common sense and of science, and indeed, in itself, a self-contradictory or meaningless conception. So long, therefore, as absolutism rules over theories of substance, one of two things must occur; science and common sense will be discouraged, as in India, or philosophy will be hindered from concentrating upon its chief problems, as in Europe; and in any case the chief philosophical problems will not be solved. In Europe the relation of God to the world was never really faced, because the universe, the whole formed by God *and* the world, was scarcely admitted as a topic for discussion; while in India the world was almost given up as a bad job, as essentially negative or illusory. In Bradley and others the West has also sometimes followed the Oriental example.

It results from the foregoing considerations that the scientific discovery of the truth of atomism was not, in mere logic, required to show to philosophers the inadequacy of the simplicist view of individuality. For this view cannot deal with the universe, and its incapacity to do so is evident quite apart from the existence of atoms. But even philosophical geniuses are not guided always by strict logic, and it was not until scientific atomism was well intrenched that the hope of finding a tenable version of simplicism began to fade, and the search for a compositional view of substance to begin in earnest. Not that discoveries in natural science were the only cause of the change; for perhaps even more important were developments in pure mathematics, and in aspects of logic related to those developments (particularly the supersession of the "subject-predicate logic" by the logic of relatives).

Atomism.—The second oldest version of simplicism is materialistic atomism. For the Greek inventors of this theory, imperceptible particles were the only real positive existences—"in reality, atoms and the void"—all else, such as human consciousnesses, being mere appearances, mere accidental collocations, or simply gross superficial views, of the basic reals.

The void or space (termed "not being") was of course a puzzle, as was consciousness, or appearance, not to mention the totality formed by the atoms and the void and appearances together.

Aristotelian commonsensism.—Sharply opposed was the Aristotelian view, which found individual reality in the macroscopic objects apparent to human perception and denied it to the alleged microscopic constituents. This might be called commonsensism in the theory of substance, for of course common sense expects real things to be of sensible magnitude. Savages believe that there is more in nature than meets the eye of ordinary inspection; but that the real constitutents of nature are largely hidden simply because they are so minute is apparently a speculation occurring only in high cultures and to a few great minds, not to men generally and as such, i.e., as endowed with common sense. Commonsensical in Aristotelianism is also, at least according to a common view of the matter, its dualism, its division of substances into those which do and those which do not possess a soul. But this is not strictly a commonsense view, since primitive peoples seem scarcely to hold it. Also the final causes which Aristotle ascribes to all individuals are difficult to interpret except as traces or germs of soul inherent in even inanimate things. (How else could God influence the world "as the beloved the lover"?) Still there is a real connection between commonsensism, or macroscopic pluralism, and dualism. For if the senses are to be trusted to reveal the individual units of nature, it is not easy to defend the view that all such units are (in principle, or allowing for differences of degree) of one nature. A stone is just not—it seems—an individual in the sense in which a man is so, and if we admit that it is nonetheless an individual, then the division of individuals into two basically different types is scarcely avoidable. Primitive animism, which vaguely ascribed souls even to stones, breaks down at this point, leaving final causes as puzzling attenuated ghosts of the spirits that preceded them.

It might not appear that Aristotelianism is correctly classifiable as a form of absolute substantialism. Is it not held that the distinction between form and matter is relative, so that what is in itself form may be matter with respect to a higher form, and is not the Aristotelian conception of substance so dependent upon those of form and matter that any relativism applying to these must apply also to substance? Would not Aristotle agree that a brick is a substance relative to clay, and a house relative to the brick, so that the brick is a part of a substance and yet in some degree itself a substance? It is to be observed, however, that any such implications of Aristotelianism are too slightly developed and dubious to constitute a very important factor in the situation when viewed in the large perspective suitable to our purposes here. If simplicism is really untenable, then of course no great philosopher ever fully adopted it; for a philosophical view capable of complete undeviating adoption is not untenable. [Even if Aristotle might have agreed that a brick is a substance in a substance, this would not have amounted to relativism in the sense to be set forth presently.] The test case of the attitude of the Aristotelians is seen in the doctrine of the human soul. This is defined not simply as "form of the body" but as *the* form, the sole substantial essence, of it. This means that whatever parts, cells, atoms, the body may prove to contain will have no forms of their own and hence no individuality. It is interesting to imagine Aristotle looking through a microscope and beholding the obvious individual forms, dynamic and directive, as well as statically descriptive, of the cells. Would he have remained an Aristotelian? Or would he not have had to confess that his guess had been a bad one? Only Thomas Aquinas, with his theological compulsions, must perhaps have continued to deny cellular individuality in the face of observations to the contrary. Yet either Aristotle or Aquinas would have been quite justified in denying substantiality to cells on their assumption that such substantiality must be absolute if it is to be real at all. Undoubtedly cells are to some extent limited and overshadowed in their independence of action, or in their final causes, by the body as a whole. But there is equally good reason for saying that the soul, as the form of the whole body, is limited by the individual cells. In this way the concept of true reciprocal relativism is reached. But this is to anticipate.

Berkeleyan subjectivism.—The fourth and last great theory of substance as absolute is subjectivism, or the view that the only individuals are human minds or, at least, minds not vastly different from the human, with perhaps the exception of a single vastly superior or divine mind. The Berkeleyan principle that physical things are only ideas resulted from the application of absolute individualism to experience. Things as experienced are parts of the experiencing individual, and this, according to absolutism, excludes their being individuals themselves. Kant only repeats the reasoning, while at the same time grimly insisting that there must be a, to us, wholly inconceivable remedy for the subjectivist difficulty to which it leads. Things must, he holds, be something in themselves, or apart from us; but it is far from clear how, on Kantian principles, we can affirm this. Hegel also gives no effective solution of the Berkeleyan problem. Many recent realists try to evade it by denying the one sound premise from which Berkeley had argued, the assertion that things as immediately given are parts of the momentary subject to which they are given. To deny this premise leads only to the result that the subject is void of content, a whole without real parts, and that there ·can be nothing which is in any intelligible sense immediately given, at any rate nothing individual. (Cf. American Critical Realism.)

It is noteworthy that subjectivism is a form of commonsensism. Berkeley proudly proclaimed as much, and—except perhaps for the pride— with justice. For basic to his view was the conception of the *minimum sensibile* as the smallest thing that can exist (or rather, subsist as an idea in a mind). The microscopic realm was thus excluded by fiat. Moreover, in rejecting the dualism sometimes regarded as a commonsense doctrine, Berkeley was ridding the common man of an embarrassing encumbrance, since the evidence upon which this dualism rests is invalid if one accepts modern science, with its demonstration that sticks and stones and other dead things are too inadequately revealed to sense perception for the semblance of deadness with which the latter invests them to constitute significant testimony. And the common man in modern times is not ready to defy science. Thus Berkeleyanism is the last stand of common sense in that region in which science shows, if it shows anything, that common sense is superficial and inaccurate—in very truth a system of "constructs" which are more convenient than literally descriptive of reality. Those who today defend Aristotelianism by calling it "the commonsense philosophy" are simply inviting us to begin the foredoomed process all over again. Every new Aristotle can only usher in a new Berkeley; and both will be in opposition to science.

In order to avoid Berkeley's error we must first note that his "ideas" were not individuals. This yellow which I now see is not perceptibly different from others which I have seen or may see again. It is *this* yellow for me because it is the one I *now* see. That is, its individuality [as known] involves the subjective context. Insofar it is indeed my idea. But since, unless some genuine individuality besides my own is given, the epistemological difficulty, the egocentric predicament, is inescapable, the right conclusion can only be that "external" objects as known through sense data are not the point of our most immediate [and clearest] contact with reality. That point is within, not without, the body. Green snakes may, in a case of delirium, be "given" visually when no such snakes are at hand, but never when certain activities in the nervous system are not at hand. The mode of awareness which makes this primacy of the body in givenness almost unmistakably apparent is, as Whitehead well points out, the sense of emotional disturbance. In this sense we are aware of compulsions to undergo certain feelings, and the immediate source of these compulsions we more or less clearly realize to be in our viscera. It is these latter, and not extrabodily objects, which are then given to us. And the visceral upheavals are really there, unlike the madman's snakes. Surely the least that can be required of the given is that it should exist. If vision of extrabodily objects is normally, and within limits, trustworthy, it is not because visual objects are givens, but because those states of the nervous system which genuinely are given and guaranteed by visual phenomena are normally produced only when the external objects really are at hand, and this again is due to the biological adaptation of organism and environment, not to the direct relation of givenness to its given. When, for instance, we see that an object is between two others this betweenness as immediately intuited is a relation between elements in the optical nerve system. The body more or less accurately *duplicates* the [spatial] pattern of the external object, first in the image on the retina, then in patterns of excitation to and in the brain. This final duplicate pattern is the one we intuit. For the view that the body also closely reproduces something qualitative, like color, in the object we have at present no evidence. Nor is it easy to see what biological purpose would be served, since from [extrabodily] qualities no biological utilities seem to follow. On the other hand, since the color is certainly given, and since pattern [as such purely relational] can in any case not exist without qualities (without terms, no relations) there is no escaping the conclusion that what is given as arranged in patterns must also be given as having quality, and as having the quality which alone is given, that is, the color. If, also, what is given is individual, then one or more individuals, not the subject, must be given as colored; say, as yellow. Admittedly there is no very distinct individuality about the yellow patch as given. But science tells us that nerves have a degree of individuality, and the upshot of the whole matter is, accordingly, that in sense perception the immediate datum is the quality inhering in certain cells, whose separateness from each other is blurred by the nonabsolute or imperfect character of the givenness. [Cf. Whitehead's "transmutation."] For here, too, relativity applies. To intuit any individual whatever with absolute distinctness would be to reach divinity in this respect and, necessarily, all others.

Thus the epistemological problem is one of our relations to individuals, first of all to those individuals with which our direct relations are incomparably the most vivid, the organisms composing the organism we call our body. But Berkeley and most modern philosophers have neglected the individual as such, besides having been strangely obsessed with the extrabodily object as the typical terminus of the mind-matter relation, the body being regarded as [at most] the mere cause or instrument of this relation.

To say with Peirce that modern philosophy has been mainly nominalistic is not inconsistent with our assertion that it has neglected the individual. For universal and individual are ideas that are clear only in relation to each other, and where either conception is neglected the other will suffer also.

This situation is well illustrated by the brilliant doctrine of American New Realism. This doctrine grants that an entity can be a part of experience and yet real in other contexts as well. But the entities thus "neutral" to experience are not unambiguously individuals, and the wholes which they form will not be clearly distinguished from complex universals. Even if the entire complex of space and time be brought in, still, by virtue of the "externality" of the relations, alternative space-time systems are equally possible, and only the ineffable word "reality" distinguishes the actual from the possible systems. . . .New Realism has nothing very illuminating to say concerning the ancient problem of universals, and how they differ from and yet qualify individuals. Altogether, a considerable part of recent realist effort to escape from the epistemological tangle into which Berkeley fell has been blocked by the repetition of the mistakes responsible for that fall (neglect of atomism and of the necessity that individuals be given, lack of an adequate theory of the universal). Nevertheless, in destroying the proud and self-confident pseudoidealism which was based upon the same errors, New Realism and Critical Realism have certainly deserved our gratitude. But the former, at least, abolishes all recognizable individuals, even the human person, which Berkeley makes almost the only true individual.

The Leibnizian compromise.—The four forms of absolutism in the theory of substance are now before us. They are: cosmic monism, microscopic pluralism, and two forms of macroscopic pluralism—dualism and subjectivism (neutral pluralism being, as just noted, hardly a theory of substance, or of the individual, at all). None of the four gives a real answer to the inevitable question: How do many things form one universe? Three of the four are contrary to the most obvious findings of science. And the one which alone can accept these findings, microscopic pluralism, is utterly unphilosophical, as Aristotle showed long ago, and for even better reasons than he gave. Above all, like New Realism it contradicts the obvious unity and individuality of experience, the epistemological basis for all conceptions of unity. And finally, each of the four views has real merits as compared to the others, yet is incompatible with them. Clearly the only hope lies in a new principle by virtue of which these merits can be united in one consistent doctrine, together with the merit lacking to them all of explaining the greatest of existences, the universe itself.

It seems apparent that if atomism is in any sense true, and if [some] macroscopic individuals are also real—as they assuredly are, for we are such individuals—then it cannot be true that individuality is so far absolute as to be exclusive of genuinely individual parts. I say that this seems apparent; yet one great mind expended much of its powers in trying to escape the conclusion, while accepting the premises from which it follows so manifestly. This mind was Leibniz. None ever insisted more than he upon the simplicity of the individual, its lack of real parts, its exclusion of all other individuals. Yet he insisted equally that both microscopic and macroscopic individuality is genuine. He is at once atomist and common-sensist. How is this done? By supplementing the real simplicity of the monad with its ideal or virtual compositeness, connecting the two with the pre-established harmony. No monad actually embraces another; but all monads contain representations of the entire collection of monads. Thus the human soul ideally contains the colony of monads constituting its body and, to a weaker degree, those monads constituting its environment. Conversely the bodily units have representations, though of a lower order, of the human soul. Thus on the ideal or virtual side, substantial unity is basically relative, and substances certainly are compounded of each other; while, on the real side, substantial separatedness is absolute. It is a grandiose proposal, but an evasion. For the cosmic unity implied in the pre-established harmony is more than virtual, else there is a regress of harmonizers. The monads do have windows toward God, they do really contain God, since without him they would be absolutely nothing, creations not yet created. Virtual relativism thus paves the way for true relativism. Leibniz, indeed, came very near to stating the precise logical basis of relativism. The older subject-predicate logic regarded a predicate as that which posits a subject in which it inheres, while a subject posits nothing but itself—"is never a predicate." Leibniz accepted this. But, he asked, what is the relation of inherence of predicate to subject? His answer was, the subject is *identical* with the integrated whole of its predicates. In current terms the subject is a *Gestalt* and the predicates are partial, abstracted aspects of that *Gestalt*. This was a great advance over the old dualism of form and matter. But two problems arise. The first concerns predicates which are relational in character. Each such predicate posits not one but two or more subjects. Yet this predicate which applies to two or more subjects is itself not two things but one. What becomes of the separateness of subjects thus united? Or, how can one say that such a subject posits only itself? Clearly it posits at least one other subject as term of its relations. The relativity of substance is the legitimate conclusion from this consideration. And Leibniz, on the ideal side of his ambiguous doctrine, fully recognizes this. Each monad internally represents its relations to all others. We have only to remove the ambiguity, and substantial relativism is reached. It is noteworthy that the resulting compound individual contains as its parts not only those inferior substances, such as cells or atoms, which ordinary science regards as such but also those perhaps equal or superior entities which constitute its neighbors, its environment. These too, though spatially outside, are in some fashion or degree also integral parts of its being. Paradoxically we might say that only some parts of an entity are internal. All this is, after all, only another aspect of the truth which Parmenides and Spinoza set forth, that the cosmos is also an individual, in whose unity all distinctions between lesser individuals must be—not abolished, as these thinkers seem to say—but limited, relativized.

The other problem concerns the temporal relations of predicates to each other and to their subjects. Leibniz held that the *Gestalt* which *is* the subject must at all times have the same total content. For, if it were to lose or gain in content, it would no longer be the same substance, but a different one. Identity through time means that past predicates are preserved and future predicates virtually realized already. The older doctrine had distinguished between essential predicates—those defining the identity of the substance—and accidental predicates. The latter constitute changes of the subject, but without preventing its endurance as the selfsame subject of these changes. Leibniz, on the other hand, explains endurance too well. He virtually denies change altogether. He falls into the vice of absolutism in demanding that identity be so complete that nothing new can enter the substance. And this absolutism is little more than another aspect of his other absolutist doctrine that actually each substance is simple and outside of every other. For if nothing can enter the substance which is not already a part of its identity, then to explain its adventures no other substance need or can be considered. So Leibniz declares that monads have no windows but yet act in an orderly manner with respect to each other because all are inwardly determined [or selected] by the initial plan of God. In this way the mutual externality and the absolute determination of the future by the past and present support one another and together prevent Leibniz from discovering the compound individual.

It follows from the foregoing that the distinction between essential and accidental predicates [of substances or individuals] cannot be set aside, as Leibniz proposed, and as every determinist in effect proposes. But on the other hand, Leibniz was brilliantly right in his doctrine of the past. Once a subject has acquired a predicate, it can never absolutely lose it. That which makes the subject the same subject today as yesterday is not, as Aristotelianism taught, merely the enduring common essence, but also the *past accidents*. Reasons for this doctrine are many. First, the past is the realm of facts, and what has been will always have been. In other words, facts about the past are immortal. But what are facts if not propositions whose referents exist? (To say "have existed" begs the question here.) Thus, the immortality of facts means the immortality of events to which the facts refer. The present is a *Gestalt*, part of whose content is the past. Another reason for this view is that memory is a fact; and memory either dissolves into Hume's paradox of present impressions corresponding to previous impressions even though the very word "previous" is, in terms of impressions, meaningless, or else memory *is* the past as part of the content of the present (subject, like all direct awareness, to erroneous elaboration and inference, to illusions). Here are two reasons, either of which seems to me rather convincing, for Leibniz's great doctrine of the past. The present is a compound individual, of which previous presents are individual parts. And this compounding is, for Leibniz, literal, not virtual merely.

However, in extending his doctrine to the future Leibniz fell into a new version of an error involved in the very doctrine of time he was rejecting. This error is the neglect of the asymmetry of time. For the old view, *neither* past nor future details were embraced in the *Gestalt* of the present substance. (Where this was combined with determinism, the result was an implicit self-contradiction.) This was a symmetrically negative or exclusive view of time. Leibniz adopts a symmetrically positive or inclusive view, as was natural for many reasons. Natural, but unfortunate. For while it is at least highly awkward to deny "once a fact always a fact," it is much more plausible that until an event has occurred its exact character may be undetermined, i.e., not a fact except that, as a matter of fact, it is indefinite. And after all, the future differs somehow from the past. Why not in this way? If the reader will look back at the reasons given for the immortality of the past, he will see that none of them can easily be used to support the pre-existence of the future. Indeed, they are incompatible with it. Corresponding to memory is anticipation; but it differs from memory precisely in the way required by the theory of asymmetry. Memory concerns details (cf. hypnotic recall of long-forgotten particular occurrences, circumstantially reproduced), anticipation concerns generalities, the more distant the more general. And certainly if the arguments did apply symmetrically to past and future we could not speak of the immortality of the past but only of the eternity of all things in a world void of distinction between "past" and "future." If the past is part of what still exists, it must yet be distinguishable from that new whole of existence which is the present event. Indeterminism provides for this distinction by making the new a further determination of an indeterminate feature of the old.

But is the present, then, uncompounded with reference to its future? Does the doctrine of relativity fail at this point? No, for in whatever sense there *is* a future it is embraced in the present. This sense is given empirically in the generalizing character of anticipation already mentioned. The future contains no particulars, but only the law that certain more or less broad or narrow generalities will be *somehow* further particularized. This law is part of the present, and is the future as such, i.e., as a fact in the present.

There is one feature of Leibniz's doctrine which almost completely anticipates a thoroughgoing relativism. This is his spiritualism or panpsychism. In formal aspect, it is his "law of continuity." All individuals are one in principle, but some are immensely diverse in degree. It becomes only a verbal question whether we say the least monad is a very low-grade "mind" or "soul," or something different from this only by representing peculiarly low values of the same variables by which minds or souls are compared with one another. Leibniz is the founder of true idealism—not Berkeley or Hegel with their hostility to microscopic and submicroscopic individuals. And the basis of idealism is not epistemological solipsism (the subject aware only of its own states) but the compound individual and the law of continuity, both being aspects of general relativity. The subject is directly aware only of what in this awareness *becomes* part of itself, but from this we must infer just the opposite of the Berkeleyan conclusion that the object is *merely* such a part. Rather we must hold that objects are of such a character that in becoming parts of our individuality they do not cease to be individuals themselves. This can never be if the character of objects is to be dead matter. Thus the basis of idealism is not the egocentric predicament, interpreted first solipsistically and then, inconsistently, in terms of the absolute mind; but rather the social, the altruistic, nature of immediacy by virtue of which the subject participates in the life of the object, makes this life a part of its own without destroying its characteristic reality. Naturally it could not do so if the object were lifeless. In other words, the natures of the subject and its object, while not entirely the same, must differ in degree only, as the law of continuity posits. Using a term of Peirce, this idealism or panpsychism based upon continuity or relativity may be termed "synechistic" idealism.

The demand of realism that knowledge should not alter or be internal to its object can be readily met by an idealism that respects the asymmetry of time. For if the object is given by memory, then the givenness is indeed extrinsic to the given, since it is related to it as realized detail of its future, which as such, or as in the past, lacked details.

If the directly given object is a contemporary of the subject—which Whitehead, perhaps wrongly, denies to be possible—then indeed the awareness must be intrinsic to the object, but this internality is mutual and makes the object no more dependent upon the subject than vice versa. Moreover, although knowing would in this case alter the known from its state previous to the knowledge, the alteration might be slight, and in any case the object would be known as it was at the moment of knowing, and further use of this knowledge in memory would be subject to the asymmetry of time which guarantees the past against alteration. [But then A knows B as knowing A as knowing B, etc., etc.] . . . .

Leibniz did not invent any one of what we have regarded as the five great theories of substance, because this tolerant politically minded spirit combined several quite incompatible theories, concealing the conflict even from himself under one of the most ingenious intellectual camouflages ever constructed (the pre-established harmony). But Leibniz certainly came closer to compound or relativistic individualism than any man between Plato and Peirce. About all that is needed is to translate representation into direct awareness, and to recognize the asymmetry of time. Then Leibniz's great doctrine of perspectives becomes the very key to the cosmos as a one in many and a many in one. For to direct awareness, no less than to representation, must be conceded gradations in vividness, and, once this is recognized, the importance of inclusion through awareness is seen to be much greater than could otherwise be suspected. If distinct judgmental consciousness, the ability to itemize what one is aware of, is far from coextensive with the range of one's feeling or sheer enjoyment of the environment, then it is not necessary to distinguish between this range and the scope of the environment itself, and the only ground of unity in diversity required for the cosmos is that of dimensions of feeling which participates—in varying gradations of vividness—in other feeling.

The Platonic anticipation.—In the *Timaeus* there is a striking anticipation of the doctrine of the compound individual, and an anticipation which refers particularly to the problem which is least satisfactorily dealt with in Leibniz, the problem of the universe as a whole. According to the *Timaeus*, the universe is an organic body which possesses a mind. The grounds for this view are not specified, except that mind is seen as the only self-moved entity, so that if the universe is a dynamic unity it must be a single mind as well as an organized body. But is it not a little strange that Plato failed to remark that since the universe is a body which contains bodies (ourselves and the animals we know, at least) the very principle of individuality must be the compounding of organisms into organisms?

The conception of a world soul was lost through the obtuseness—if I may be frank—of Aristotle (who, among other blunders, substituted the unmoved prime mover for the cosmic self-mover) and the prejudices, the theological commitments, of the Church theologians. . . . Thus, when cells were discovered—the one clue which Plato lacked—the philosophical bearings of the discovery were not seen. Not the all-excluding atom but the organism containing organisms is the model of reality. (The early forms of the "cell theory" somewhat obscured the living, dynamic, organized character of cells, just as physical atomism still obscures the same character in atoms and molecules.) The germs of this view are apparent in Stoicism, though weakened by a bias against the atomism of the Epicureans—a true doctrine insofar as it emphasized the compound nature of commonsense objects. But the fear of pantheism was a bar to the free development of compound substantialism, which leads naturally to the pantheistic [panentheistic] view of God as the anima mundi, or the mind of nature. It is true that Plato distinguished between God and the world soul, but in the light of Whitehead's illuminating doctrine of the "primordial" and necessary, as contrasted with the "consequent" or contingent, aspects of God it is not hopelessly farfetched to see in the world soul Plato's account of the consequent aspect, and in his ultimate Creator the primordial aspect. This distinction is one of the conceptions which are required to free pantheism—if the old term can still be used for a doctrine so greatly altered—of its well-known difficulties.

Whitehead and the compound individual.—In the "cell theory" or "philosophy of organism" of Whitehead we have nothing less than the first full-blooded, forthright interpretation of the cellular model (passing over the not much less adequate version found in Peirce's theory of the categories, and his doctrine of Synechism, both of which conceptions have advantages not entirely paralleled in Whitehead's system). The theory of the enduring individual as a "society" of occasions, interlocked with other such individuals into societies of societies, is the first complete emergence of the compound individual into technical terminology. [Unluckily, throughout this (and the next) essay I made no use of Whitehead's insight into the primacy of event compared to substance or changing individual.] It is to be emphasized that Whitehead is above all the interpreter of individuality, and of the world of actual individuals as revealed by the inalienable convictions of man and by science. The complexities and obscurities of his writings are partly due to the fact that science shows the actual world to be more complex than common sense could have dreamt of; but there is at least one other cause. Being a mathematician as well as natural scientist, Whitehead has, besides his interest in concrete existence, a vivid sense of the reality of universals. This sense is indeed necessary, as we have already suggested, to a clear understanding of individual actuality, and without it Whitehead could not be the great philosopher of actuality that I believe him to be. But the mathematical universals are only one type of universals, and the study of this type may have led Whitehead to a one-sided view of universals in general. Moreover, he does not seem sufficiently aware of the agonies philosophers have endured, especially in Greece and medieval Europe, in searching for a reasonable form of realism in regard to universals. His knowledge of the philosophical tradition is not superficial, but it seems most profound where that tradition deals most explicitly with individuals. In any case I feel very confident that the conception of organism, of societies of entities feeling each other, compounded of each other's feelings, is Whitehead's primary achievement, no matter what is to be thought about his "eternal objects," his theory of nonindividual entities. Above all, in articulating a philosophy of substance which follows the contours of existence, distinguishes dimensions and degrees of compounding or societal relationship to fit the facts of inorganic, plant, and animal forms, and in showing how this relational structure resolves the antinomies of subjective and objective, experience and thought, change and permanence, continuity and discreteness, internal relations and freedom, Whitehead has, I have no doubt, achieved the major metaphysical synthesis of our day.

Only a few aspects of this synthesis can be considered in the remainder of the present essay.

Internal and external parts.—The human body is a vast nexus or interlocked colony of relatively low-grade individuals, which, in varying degrees, are subject to the control of the human mind. Call the bodily parts a, b, c, etc., and the mind M. Then the relations are these: a, b, c—are mutually dependent on each other, although certain cells (nerve cells) have greatest influence. (Influence is the joint fact of mutual immanence plus the possession by the influencing unit of creative power, i.e., the awareness of unrealized alternatives compatible with the entity's nature to date.) But M has far more influence over any one of a, b, c —say n, than the latter has over it (having vastly more creative power). In this sense the bodily parts "belong" to M, namely as its servants. "Internal parts" simply mean parts in this service relation, and external parts those not so subordinated to the given entity. The difference is one of degree. Of course, as Hegel said, the master depends upon his slaves as well as vice versa, and even God is no absolute monarch, "without body, parts, or passions," but is sensitive to, and in a real sense dependent upon, all other individuals. Whitehead would, I think, do well to adopt explicitly the position that nature is God's body, for by the definition just given of a body this is not a mere metaphor.

It may seem contradictory for two entities each to be part of the other. [I now think it is so, if the "entities" are on the most concrete level, i.e., unit events or actual occasions.] Is not each then less than the other? In a sense yes, for immanence has degrees of vividness or relevance, so that, as in A, B may be insignificant, and similarly A as in B. In-ness, like everything else in a relativist philosophy, is not an all-or-none affair.

In terms of degrees of immanence, degrees of memory, and of originative power, the entire known structure of the world may be interpreted, from space-time as the most general pattern of immanence to the specific character of photons, molecules, plants, and animals. There is literally nothing like it in current philosophy for richness of detailed implications for science. Quantum and vibratory phenomena are explained as the need of low-grade entities for contrast and repetition within a brief memory span. (See *The Function of Reason*.) The degradation of energy is the gradual loss of zest by such organisms due to their incapacity to originate a new pattern and the fact that the monotonous character of their past (from a long-range point of view) is not made wholly harmless by the scantness of their memory, since in the dim recesses of faintness memory retains all the past of an entity.

The much-mooted question of whether quantum uncertainty may be utilized by the nervous system to endow the whole organism with freedom acquires a new meaning in terms of the compound individual. For it is really a reversion to simplicist individualism to try to derive all the properties of the body from the laws of the electronic or molecular level. The point is that cells also are units of action, individuals, and likewise the man himself, and that laws, being modes of behavior, habits of individuals of a given type, must be specific to each type. In the body not merely the arrangement but also the inner natures of electrons, atoms, or molecules are different from elsewhere; for their individualities have been in some [very slight?] degree suppressed or modified by the more powerful individuality to which they belong. Thus the [cell or entire] body can be free, no matter what may be true according to quantum laws; and moreover, it could not be free by virtue of the latter alone. For if its freedom is merely that of electrons, then as has been well said it is freedom of the electrons but not of the body. This objection to some recent attempts to treat human freedom as simply derivative from quantum mechanics and nerve structure is, I believe, quite valid. It is also to be noted that not merely is the body incompletely determined, even to the extent involved in quantum mechanics, but we must also hold that insofar as the body is subject to laws, these are partly peculiar to the biological level. Both new freedom and new order arise at each level of individuality.

The principal weakness of the foregoing doctrine is that it seems to imply the emergence of new laws, not only between physics and biology, but also between physics and chemistry, or between electrons and atoms, or atoms and molecules. Part of the difficulty of detecting such emergence is that we can hardly experiment upon electrons when they are not to some extent under the control of atomic systems, and so with atoms and molecules. In any case the earlier forms of emergence theory, which spoke of certain emergent properties as completely inexplicable, are vetoed by the law of continuity. Emergence and freedom are matters of degree, and hence the laws of lower levels apply to some approximation at higher levels. Mechanism as a method in biology is not to be forbidden. Its claims to be the only method, are, however, opposed by most biologists, at least in Europe (cf. K. Goldstein, *Aufbau des Organismus*).

Compound and composite individuals.—The neo-idealism of Whitehead, his "reformed subjectivist principle," is connected with the distinction between colonies which do and colonies which do not involve a dominating ("personal") unit. Plants and, to a lesser extent, metazoa without brains are of the latter or nonpersonal class. They are individuals only in a slight degree. We might call them composite instead of compound individuals. Thus "a tree is a democracy." To ask how it feels is like asking how America feels, except that "America" is in some ways much more unified. The dualism of common sense is due to thinking of composites as more unified and individual than their parts, whereas the reverse is true. A stone is better interpreted as a colony of swirls of atoms (crystals) than are its atoms interpretable as servants or organs of the stone. The atoms and crystals are the substances; the stone-properties, the accidents. But in the animal body, there is truth almost equally in the view of cells as the substantial realities with the whole body as their appearance or functioning as in the converse view. The animal body and its cells are alive, the stone and its molecules are presumed to be absolutely dead. But this notion of deadness obviously originates from an illegitimate inference from stone-properties to molecule- and atom-properties, whereas the latter are the fundamental ones, by no means directly revealed to the senses which perceive stones. The organism of highly and rhythmically active particles which is an atom [or molecule] is different from the stone in ways which point in the opposite direction from materialism. Only aesthetic principles can account for the tendency toward bold contrast, rhythmic repetition, and perpetual process revealed to startled common sense as the real properties of the stupid, inert, merely passive, and nonrhythmic stone. It is just careless to parody this reasoning as amounting to saying that very small units of matter must be less material than large. Size is not involved, but the principles of perpetual change as compared to the possibility of practically complete rest, at least with reference to the near environment (the earth's motion being clearly insignificant to the stone), rhythmic oscillation as compared to mere motion, immanence of the environment and lack of sharp boundaries, as compared to merely discrete units in a void, and, for all we know at least, origination of unpredictable novelty as compared to absolute repetition of a pattern. To be sure, Newton himself was not wholly on the materialistic side of this contrast. Materialism must be a halfhearted doctrine: only a panpsychist can mean literally what he says.

The best mode of attack upon panpsychism known to me is that which may be made by a logical positivist. The question is how far psychological concepts can be handled in science unless physical equivalents are substituted for them. I have too much respect for this issue to try to dispose of it here. I simply point out that it does not bear unambiguously upon the question of dualism in the sense of a division of the world into sentient and insentient individuals. For all individuals are merely physical systems for "physicalism." Thus this doctrine apparently accepts the law of continuity. But it is not clear whether or not it consistently adheres to it. Not perhaps without significance, too, is the tendency to favor a simplicist view of laws as shown in Carnap's remark that the presumption of positivists is in favor of the view that all laws are derivatives from those referring directly to the submicroscopic level. The societal principle and that of continuity—two aspects of the same thing—can, I suspect, take care of themselves eventually even against this most vital of all current criticisms.

The nonliving societies (of societies of occasions) spoken of by Whitehead are composites too little unified to involve much mutual facilitation between the part-societies.

Eternal objects.—Are eternal objects ingredients in the composition of a compound individual? If so, then what becomes of the unity of the latter? For individuals as ingredients are only relatively distinct from other ingredients; but eternal objects must be absolutely distinct from and independent of any given individuals, since they infinitely antedate the latter. The only way of escape from this antinomy is, I believe, to deny that eternal objects have identical natures as ingredient and as not ingredient in a given individual. How then will they be the same qualities in the two cases? Because before ingression they will be less definite, that is, *more general*. This means that in their eternal aspect they will be completely general, i.e., categories, and that all such specific characters as robin's-egg blue are emergents at a certain date, *created* rather than "selected" out of the primordial potentiality. In this way external relatedness will be limited to the relation of events to their successors. Universals as independent of instances are anticipatory and hence more or less vague. The truth that essences form continua (colors, for example) seems to demand this doctrine, since, by Whitehead's own method of extensive abstraction, continuity is treated as the possibility of endless division, not as a totality of products of such division. Eternally there is just the unitary vague field of quality, not a set of pointlike determinate qualities.

Another advantage of this view is that it avoids the arbitrariness of dividing all entities into sheer individuals, located in space-time, and sheer timeless universals, or into entities which in their natures completely determine their contexts, and those which leave them completely unspecified. Instead of such a dichotomy, contrary to the general principles of the system, which is based on continuity and relativity, we can set up the principle that independence of context varies through all degrees from zero to the maximum, the former limit being that of individuality, the latter that of pure generality,[1] and the intermediate degrees being the more or less specific traits, such as a certain hue of color, color in general, etc. The more specific and determinate the quality, the nearer it comes to requiring a determinate date of emergence and a determinate distribution in space.[2]

God.—The first great problem of metaphysics was, as we have seen, that the universe is a single existent, while it also has as its parts all other existents. The answer to the question, how can this be? is the answer to the question, what do we mean by God? For God is the compound individual who at all times has embraced or will embrace the fullness of all other individuals as existing at those times. He is the only eternal [primordial and everlasting] individual, and the only one whose prehensions of others involve impartially complete vividness for all, wherever they may be in space or (past) time.

How do we know that God exists? The universe must have some primordial and everlasting character, as the ultimate subject of change. The past being immortal, there must be a complete cosmic memory, since the past in the present is memory. The future being predictable, there must be a world-anticipation; for the future as fact in the present is anticipation. Also, action implies the faith that at no time in the future will it ever be true that it *will* have made no difference whether the action was well motivated or ill [successful or not]. This condition is met by the affirmation of a God who will never cease to treasure the memory of the action and of its results.

Finally, as an empirical fact, the world is a unified individual. We say that a stone is less unified than its atoms (or than its crystals). But in one sense this is untrue. For gravitation, light, and other forces intimately bind the atoms to each other. And we say that this does not unify the stone only because much the same forces bind the stone-atoms to the atoms of air and earth and distant stars—to all the universe. In short, boundaries to the unity of the stone are superficial compared to the unity itself. Otherwise expressed, the unity of the stone as peculiar to it is a rather insignificant modification of the general unity of the cosmos. This means that the latter is much more truly an individual than is the stone. That there is no world-brain can be shown to be a necessary implication of the impartiality of the world-individuality. On a priori or metaphysical grounds, this cosmic unity may be conceded a certain absoluteness of impartiality—the righteousness of God.

Positivists will say that at best we are embroidering upon the strict logical requirements. Memory of the past is more than its mere persistence; world anticipation, more than the mere fact that induction is in principle valid; a righteous world-mind, than cosmic order; and so with the rest.[3] But the point is that what "God" adds to these postulates is not mere irrelevant emotional coloring, but the strictly intellectual merit of reducing several first principles to one. Positivism is forever trying to discourage the very search for unity which is science. God is all the first principles as a single principle with an intelligible diversity of aspects. His memory is the past, his plan is the predictable future, his love is his prehension which makes the many individuals one world, his power is the realm of the possible, his enjoyment that of the actual.

This is the first view of God which technically accepts the living, personal, purposive, and therefore temporal, character ascribed to him by most religions, and which treats the relation of God to man as only a special though supreme case of the relation of any individual to any other, namely, the relation of action and reaction, reciprocal inclusion, mutual relevance. God includes us without abolishing our individuality and partial freedom, just as we include cells and electrons. Inclusion [through memory or perception] being made the basis of all relationship, the idea (which troubled William James and many others) that one mind could include another only by a miracle ceases to seem so persuasive.

This is a new cosmology and a new theology, and the symbol of a new era of philosophically enlightened science and religion.

Reprinted from *Philosophical Essays for Alfred North Whitehead,* edited by Otis H. Lee (London and New York: Longmans, Green and Co., 1936), pp. 193-220. All rights reserved. Reprinted by permission of David McKay Co., Inc.

CHAPTER FIVE

Whitehead's
Idea of God

From Plato, Aristotle, and Philo to Spinoza, Leibniz, and Schleiermacher, the great metaphysicians and theologians of over twenty centuries tried to find a rational meaning in the religious idea, the idea of God. And from Carneades to Hume, Kant, Dewey, Santayana, and Russell, some of the acutest philosophical minds have pronounced the effort a failure. Whitehead, for his part, holds the definite and carefully considered opinion that the classical versions of theism are one and all unsound, collectively a "scandalous failure." His idea of God is consequently an intentional departure from most of the philosophical past.[1] Not that he is claiming to be the only philosopher who has understood God! What he offers us is rather the most technically adequate version of a conception of God which a score of philosophers and theologians of great distinction, and hundreds with humbler attainments, have been working out since the fifteenth century, and especially during the last one hundred years. Whitehead is following a trail blazed by some great and many able predecessors (among them Fechner, Pfleiderer, Bergson), but it is only in his thought that their work (much of which may be known to him only indirectly, if at all) comes to fruition in an elaborately systematized philosophy in which the conception of God and the other philosophical conceptions seem as if made for each other, and nothing [or not very much] is mere *ad hoc* concession to some interest or evidence which the general system is not properly adapted to cover. Whitehead's is not the first philosophy to lead naturally and consistently to the religious idea of God, for Fechner's and Ward's philosophies did that; but it is, I think, the first great systematic philosophy to do so.

One must note, however, that Whitehead does not simply brush aside as valueless the work of the classical theists, but rather he sets forth a higher synthesis of the more extreme tendencies of recent theism (as seen, for example, in James) and the older conceptions. According to Whitehead, these older conceptions, in spite of their differences, nearly all involve much the same fundamental error. This is the error into which philosophy generally has tended to fall with regard to most of its problems, the "fallacy of misplaced concreteness." The fallacy takes two forms in relation to God. (1) We may identify God, conceived in terms of value, with sheer "perfection," defined as completeness or maximality of value such that nothing conceivably *could* be added to it, and from which, therefore, every form of self-enrichment, every aspect of process and of potential but unactual value, is absent. This means that the temporal character of value and all contrast between purpose and achievement, as well as all mutual exclusiveness among values (which seems of their very essence[2]) and all relationship to beings whose value is not perfect, must be *abstracted from*, omitted from consideration, in order to conceive the perfect, which must not be contaminated, it is held, by containing any of these things. (2) We may also identify God, conceived in terms of causality, with sheer power or activity, a "cause of all," which is in no aspect of its being the effect of any, an agent which acts but is not acted upon. In this case, too, God is arrived at by abstracting from or omitting one pole of a categorial contrast (or trying to omit it, for unconsciously is it not still asserted?).

A similar abstractness is involved in the concept of God as the "most real being," or "pure actuality"; for of the two polar aspects of reality, actuality and potentiality, only the first could be present in an absolutely maximal reality.[3] Potency must be simply omitted. This is only feebly disguised by the quibbling distinction between internal and "external" potency, as when it is said that, though God is all that he could be, he may not produce all the effects "outside" himself that he could produce. Here is simply another abstract or one-sided idea, this time that of *being* as wholly independent of *doing*. The conception leads to interesting paradoxes, such as that though God actually knows his potential external acts only as potential, potentially he knows them as actual (for they are capable of actuality, and *were* they actual he would know that they were so). In short, his knowledge has a contingent aspect, but his being has no such aspect—as though anything could be more intimately part of a knower than his knowledge and its immediate contents (or does omniscience know indirectly, hence, surely, imperfectly?)!

The two ideas of sheer absolute perfection and sheer causality or actuality represent extremes to which there is in each case an opposite extreme. It is clear that the doctrine, God is the World-Cause as capable of being considered in complete abstraction from his effects, or from the world, has as its logical contrary—*not* merely contradictory—God is the world as capable of being grasped entirely apart from any supreme and independent cause. Between the two opposites there lies a median position which contradicts the extremes only insofar as they contradict each other and retains the characteristic positive features of both. This is the doctrine that God is both a supreme causal factor which can be abstracted from the world of its effects and, in another aspect of himself, the supreme totality of all his effects, and of their effects. That is, God may be conceived (1) as the mere creator, (2) as the creator-with-the-creatures, or (3) as the mere totality of creatures (as not really such). The advantage of (2) is not only that it includes the positive factors of (1) and (3), but that it thereby enables these factors really to be themselves. A creator without creatures is nothing *as* creator, and similarly, the creature as such is nothing without creator. The history of thought seems to show that for every defense of an extreme position such as (1) or (3), there will be a defense, roughly equal in sincerity and ability, of the contrary extreme; so that, unless we can get above the conflict and accord some part-truth to each of the embattled opposites, there is no sane hope of progress toward agreement. Consequently, the burden of proof should be considered as falling primarily upon the extremists, in this case, upon those who assert either radical and complete absolutism or radical and complete relativism, radical and complete independence of God from the world, or his complete identity with it—or even with a part of it, say, with a dream in the mind of man.

Let us symbolize the doctrine of sheer independence as CC, meaning not only that there is an independent or purely causal aspect of God, C, but that there is no other aspect, that independent power describes all aspects of the divine being. Then the opposite extreme may be indicated by WW, meaning not only that there is a world aspect of God, W, but that there is nothing independent of the world in God, nothing but W. Then obviously the median position is CW, indicating that there is an independent factor, which is cause but not effect, and also a dependent or, as Whitehead calls it, a "consequent" factor, which itself has causes. Now if God is sheer absolute perfection, a doctrine which we may symbolize as AA, nothing but absolute perfection, then there is no basis, from the standpoint of perfection, for the distinction, from the standpoint of causality, which CW involves. Simple perfection is—simple, as theologians have nearly all agreed. But suppose perfection has two aspects, one absolute, or A, the other not absolute and hence in some sense relative, or R. Then the C in CW might be the A in AR, and the W might be the R. (In general the partisans of sheer perfection favored CC as against WW.) It is also apparent that as CW is to CC and WW, so is AR to AA and RR. In each case we have a positive synthesis which excludes only the negative or abstract aspect of the extremes.

How can we define R? Very simply. In its generic meaning, perfection, whether as A or as R, is an excellence such that its possessor *surpasses all other conceivable beings*. But A-Perfection means the property of surpassing all others *while not surpassing self* (growth or improvement being thus excluded from whatever aspects of a being are A); while R-Perfection means surpassing all others *while also surpassing self* (permitting, if not requiring, growth in the R aspects of a being). Thus R is a richer conception than A, since it includes the relation of universal superiority to others, which is the only positive feature of A, and includes also the equally positive relation of self-superiority or self-enrichment. The "un-self-transcending transcender of all others" is A, the "self-transcending transcender of all others" is R.[4] Now there is no obvious reason why a being might not in *some aspects* transcend all others but *not* itself, whereas in other aspects it transcended all others than self *and self as well*. More than that, just as cause-with-effect is more intelligible than mere cause or mere contingent phenomena alone, so to transcend self in some respect and others in all respects, to be AR, is more intelligible than to transcend others in all respects and *self in none*, to be AA, or than to transcend *both self and others in all respects*, to be RR. For, as to RR, if self is transcended in all respects, then self has no identity and no meaning; and as to AA, if self cannot surpass itself then it can in no valuable sense involve self-contrast, and without self-contrast self-identity is also meaningless. In still other terms, if there were no abiding standard of growth, growth would be meaningless, and the standard must involve an aspect (A) which does not itself grow but measures all growth, including growth of standards. But, at the opposite extreme, were there no growth there would be nothing for the standard to measure. Measure of growth and growth belong together, in one reality, the perfect, which is both absolute and relative, both static and dynamic, though not in the same aspects of its being. It is this last qualification that has been most sadly lacking in the tradition. It has been too lightly assumed that God's perfection must be all of one kind, without contrast or categorial distinction.

Of course it may be objected that perfection means primarily completeness, the absolute realization of value, and only secondarily and in consequence of this absoluteness the impossibility of self-improvement as well as of being surpassed or equalled by others. But this way of formulating the matter leads to the same outcome. For it cannot be that all dimensions of value admit of absoluteness, and it equally cannot be that none of them do. For some of the dimensions of value are neutral to the contrast between actual and possible reality, and some are not, and the former dimensions imply an absolute maximum, whereas the latter exclude such a maximum; and each of these types of dimension involves the other, so that AR is required if value is to have any meaning at all. Let us take an illustration. The accuracy and adequacy of knowledge to its objects, its truth, is independent of which among these objects are actualities and which are mere possibilities, provided only that the actual things be known as actual and the potencies be known as potencies, that is, in each case, provided that things be known as they are. But the joy, the aesthetic richness, of the knowledge depends in part upon just what things are actualized. For instance, it depends upon the wealth of harmonious contrasts which the objects involve; it also depends, so far as what is known is sentient or perhaps even conscious, upon the degree of joy or sorrow felt by the sentient individuals known, since knowledge of feeling is irreducibly sympathetic, is "feeling of feeling."

Now there can be no absolute maximum of harmonious contrasts, since possible contrasts are inexhaustible and mutually exclusive by the very meaning of possibility as a field of open alternatives.[5] Similarly there can be no "greatest possible happiness of all things other than God." Hence the aesthetic value, and the sympathetic joy, of God's knowledge cannot be absolute. Yet its accuracy and adequacy, its truth, to what is actual and what is possible, at a given stage of cosmic development certainly can be complete, by the very meaning of knowledge. It cannot be that the whole of de facto reality could not be known, such an unknowable whole being meaningless. Indeed, as we shall see, the cosmic whole must actually be known. Hence God's knowledge must be A in its cognitive perfection or truth, and R in its concrete self-value as enjoyment or bliss.

Similar reasoning supports the view that there must be an independent causal factor which, like cognitive adequacy, is abstract and neutral to the distinction between potential and actual, and that there must also be a dependent or consequent factor which is concrete and varies with de facto actualization of potency. In other words, AR-CW [or better perhaps, A(C)-R(W), to show that A and C, R and W, are the same factors considered from two points of view, those of value and causality] is the most promising formula for the divine nature, although the idea it defines is one whose possibilities have only recently been explored.

There is an important ambiguity to be removed from the foregoing analysis. In the assertion that the A(C) factor is independent of or abstractable from the world, "world" is to be taken to mean: this actual world which does exist with just the particular things it contains. C is involved in each and every one of these particulars but itself involves none of them. Yet C, as interpreted through CW, implies nevertheless that there is *some* world, some set of particulars, or other. The world could, so far as C is concerned, and so far as anything is concerned, have been different from what it is, but some sort of world must have been "there," that is, must have been content to the divine knower and effect of the divine cause. Accidents must needs happen, though this or that particular accident need not have happened. Contingent existences form a class which must have members, but not any members you choose to point to. W as the generic factor in all particulars is essential to C, as R is to A, or as variety is to unity. What is contingent is a special form or case under W, say Wm or Wn (really CWm or CWn), the de facto world that now or at some other specified time happens to exist. W requires that there be *some* Wm or other, but not that there be this or that Wm.

We are now ready for the crucial question: Is Whitehead's idea of God a case of AR-CW, or is it one more abstract extreme (such as AA-CC, or AA-CW, or RR-WW, or some other of the eight logically possible cases) involving the fallacy of misplaced concreteness which Whitehead has been at pains to avoid? Certainly his intention is to conceive God in a balanced or concrete way, for he lays down the methodological principle that "God is not to be treated as an exception to all the metaphysical principles, invoked to save their collapse." Rather "he is their chief exemplification."[6] And the metaphysical principles form a set of contraries or "ideal opposites."[7] Every actual entity, including God, is dipolar, and that in several ways. Nothing concrete or actual is merely one or merely many, or a mere cause which is in no way effect, or a completeness which is in no way incomplete or subject to addition, or an activity which is in no way passive, or the mere contrary of these. Of course, neither God nor anything else is in the same sense and respect cause and effect, or active and passive, or good and evil, or simple and complex; but to grant this is not to admit that there either can or must be something actual which is in no genuine sense and respect effect, passive, complex, or evil (God is the "fellow-sufferer," he suffers evil,[8] though he does not commit it[9]). Yet all these unqualified, or not consistently and clearly qualified, negations had been commonplaces, indeed almost automatic reflexes, in theological discussions. They are all explicitly rejected in Whitehead's philosophy, and this is the first time, to the best of my knowledge, that this rejection has been so systematically worked out. (Nicholas of Cusa affirms both poles of the polarities with respect to God, but scarcely shows by what distinctions contradiction is to be avoided. Rather he glories in contradictions.)

According to Whitehead, God and the World may be compared through

> a group of antitheses, whose apparent self-contradiction depend on neglect of the diverse categories of existence. In each antithesis there is a shift of meaning which converts the opposition into a contrast.
>
> It is as true to say that God is permanent and the World fluent, as that the World is permanent and God is fluent. . . .
>
> It is as true to say that God creates the World, as that the World creates God.[10]

The classical procedure was to affirm that God is "above the categories," while at the same time, in order not to have to admit that God is for our thought simply nothing at all, giving certain categories (called "transcendentals") a preferred status as incomparably more true of God than their contraries, or as, in abstraction from their contraries, applicable at least "analogically," though not "univocally," to God and to other beings. Thus, for example, actual being or form as opposed to potency or matter, and one as opposed to many, were held to be descriptive of God. According to Whitehead, the distinction between God and other things (the totality of which he calls the World) is to be treated in a manner at once less equivocal and more complex and subtle. It is less equivocal, for Whitehead commits himself to the application of all contrary categories to God, and in my opinion faithfully carries out this undertaking. (Moral evil is not a category, being absent not only from God but from the lower creatures; yet aesthetic evil is a category and is entirely absent nowhere.) The Whiteheadian procedure is more complex and subtle than the traditional one, because God is contrasted with inferior beings not by the simple method of deciding which among the categories are to have the privilege of applying (even though not univocally) to God, but by showing in what way each of the categories, the entire complexity of ultimate contraries, has its "chief," that is, supreme, instance in God. It is the unrivalled excellence of the activity-*and*-passivity, the unity-*and*-complexity, the being-*and*-becoming, yes, the joy-*and*-suffering, of God which elevates him above all others, actual or conceivable. Whitehead's God is as much, nay more, the supreme being as is the God of the Thomists. The difference is that Whitehead so conceives being that it can really have a supreme instance, without equivocation, and if by analogy, then an analogy that does not play favorites among the irreducible dimensions of existence upon which all analogy depends.

It might be objected that at least "supremacy," or being the "chief" instance of the categories, as itself a category which, rather than its contrary, "inferiority," or "being surpassed by another," must be favored in relation to God. But this is the exception that our rule is able readily to account for. The contrast between the being that is better than all others and these others is the contrast between a by definition unique individual, and a mere class of individuals. Of course to be the supreme being is peculiar to God. But by the same token supremacy is not a category, analogous to actuality as opposed to potency, or unity as opposed to complexity, or being as opposed to becoming. Moreover, we shall find that in a real sense even the supreme being includes inferior being, though it is not any the less supreme over it for that.

It is true that Whitehead objects to "metaphysical compliments"[11] to God, and thus appears to suggest that God has been too highly thought of, is not really "supreme" over all conceivable beings. Nevertheless, I think his position is better expressed by saying that in the attempt to praise God people have unwittingly talked nonsense (emptied their categories of meaning) and nonsense is doubtfully classified as praise. Only in one sense is it possible, according to Whitehead's philosophy as I understand it, to overpraise God. At any stage of the cosmic process there may be possibilities of value for that stage greater than those actually achieved in it, because of the unlucky or even perverse actions of the creatures. All does not occur for the best. This means that God's concrete being is not all that it might have been as "inheriting" that stage. But on Whitehead's principles no God is conceivable who would not thus depend for part of his value upon the actions of the creatures. Thus, though God is at any time less than he (but only he) might have been, he is not in his generic property (as he is at all times) less than he generically might be; for, to be subject to being sometimes less than is, at those times, possible is implied in the only generic nature that any God *could* have. In still other terms, God's realization is less than it might have been, because all realization, realization as such, is essentially social, and hence in its concrete degree dependent upon other beings. Thus there are no "limitations" in God except those the general possibility of which in the perfect being is part of the meaning of any conceivable perfection.

We have already implied an affirmative answer to our question: Is the God of *Process and Reality* describable as AR-CW? We have now to document this answer.

Primordial and Consequent Natures

That Whitehead's God is not AA is easy to prove. For "all realization is finite, and there is no perfection which is the infinitude of all perfections."[12] Moreover, the Consequent Nature of God is said to be relative, incomplete, and in flux.[13] Nor is God CC, for he is to be conceived "as requiring his union with the world," and Whitehead criticizes the classical theologians for supposing that though God is necessary to the world, the world is not necessary to God.[14] On the other hand, Whitehead's God, taken in one aspect, really is A and is C. For the Primordial Nature is "limited by no actuality which it presupposes," and is complete, perfect, infinite.[15] That is, God is unequivocally A and C, though not AA and CC. Is he AR and CW? He is certainly A plus a relative aspect, and he is C plus the world as internal to his complete nature.[16] Thus to show that he is AR-CW we need only prove that the relativity ascribed to him is relative perfection and not ordinary, imperfect relativity. Now since God contains in "everlasting imperishableness" all actual values, from the moment of their actualization, and combined in the utmost harmony of which they are capable,[17] there is no conceivable way in which any individual (personal-order society) other than God could equal, not to mention surpass, him. For the content of the other individual, if and when it exists, must be fully contained in God, so that the two could not be distinguished except as the other failed to contain some value that was contained in God. Thus God is the self-surpassing being who in all possible circumstances surpasses all others, that is, he is R-Perfect.

When it is said that the Primordial Nature is complete, yet "deficient" in actuality,[18] the apparent inconsistency is only apparent. For "the unlimited conceptual realization of the absolute wealth of potentiality,"[19] *as* such realization of the potential, is superior to any conceivable conceptual realization or awareness of potency that could be distinguished from God's. It is complete in its kind or dimension, the dimension of "mentality" or abstract realization of value. But it does not at all follow, a long tradition to the contrary notwithstanding, that God must be complete in concrete dimensions as well. Nay, it follows that he cannot be. For potentiality could be neither complete nor incomplete, it could be nothing, were there a complete actuality, a full realization of potency. Inexhaustibleness is of the essence of potency and the presupposition of actuality. Possibilities are in part mutually incompatible, they are not always compossible, and, as Whitehead says, theologians have been strangely reluctant to face the implications of this truth.[20]

It might be thought that if God is CW, both the supreme cause and the supreme totality of effects, he must be the pantheistic, all-inclusive substance, responsible for all evil, the "supreme author of the play," and the "foundation of the metaphysical situation with its ultimate activity," against which Whitehead protests.[21] Does he not say that God is "in the grip of the ultimate metaphysical ground,"[22] the "creativity," which is repeatedly distinguished from God and never identified with him? In all these ways it seems to be implied that there is a causal factor, a C, which is beyond God. This is a delicate point, but I think the answer is, No. First, the creativity is not an actual entity or agent which does things: it is the common property or generic name for all the doings. Second, the internality of the world to God's concrete or consequent nature has nothing to do with a reduction of all activity, all creative "decision," to God's own activity or decision. For there are two ways in which activity may be contained in a given actuality, (1) as self-decided by that actuality, and (2) as contributed by the self-decisions of others. "Recipience," "patience," tolerant prehension of the activity of others, is essential to concrete being, whether that of God or of anyone else. God has all activity within himself only because he accepts the activity of others as such and enjoys it within his own "immediacy." God appropriates the actions, the decisions, of others, he does not decide just what they are to be. We are told in the most unequivocal language that God's influence upon others is not decisive to the last degree of determination.[23]

This solution of the problem of evil is the oldest of all (cf. the Book of Genesis), except for the fact that scarcely anyone before Whitehead ever made an adequate and honest place for it in a comprehensive metaphysical system (Varisco, Ward, and Fechner are perhaps exceptions to this statement). The problem is how a genuine *division of power*, hence of responsibility for good and evil (implying a possibility at least that all of the evil, as well as some aspects of the good, may derive from creaturely decisions) can be reconciled with the ascription of all the wealth of actuality to God. To do this we must have general metaphysical principles whereby actualities can be *contained in other actualities yet retain their own self-decisions*. Now, according to Whitehead, it is true that every actuality as a whole is an act of self-decision. But it contains parts which are decided by others, indeed are constituted by the self-decisions of others (in the first-mentioned actuality's past). The synthesis is free, but the content synthesized is in part derived from others. In Aristotelian language (but not in Aristotelian doctrine), actualities are, through their form, matter for each other's form. This is the social nature of reality. To be decided in part by others is essential to being as such.[24] To enjoy a decision it is not necessary to make it, but only to make a further decision as to just how the first decision is to be enjoyed in relation to other actualities, that is, it is only necessary to "objectify" the first decision within one's own immediacy. If God were "pure actuality" in the sense of simple perfection, AA, then to enjoy a decision he would have to make it. The *actus purus*, the form containing no others as matter, the activity without recipience, was a precise way of denying the social nature of God, of denying absolutely that God is love, as Spinoza almost consistently perceived and the Schoolmen made it a point of honor not consistently to perceive. Also, as Whitehead points out,[25] the notion—which theologians first hit upon in the doctrine of the Trinity—that personalities can be literally immanent in each other can be at least as validly applied to relations among the creatures and between the creatures and God; though of course the creatures' receptivity for each other and for God is subject to certain imperfections, involving particularly the relegation of most of the included content to a low or negligible level of awareness, or distinctness of consciousness.

When Whitehead says that creativity in general is wider than God, he is simply pointing out, as I take it, that not all decisions are God's self-decisions. He is not denying that all decisions are in some manner enjoyed, possessed, by God. Even we enjoy many decisions that we do not make, particularly the radically subhuman and, in our awareness, not individually distinguishable decisions of the bodily members, such as cells or molecules. Creativity is thus, I suggest, the abstraction which leaves out of account the duality of decisions as self-made and as made by others. Thus all creativity belongs to God *either, but not both*, as his self-decision *or* as his uniquely adequate way of being decided by others. All this only amounts to saying that existence is social and that there is a supreme, hence supremely social, existent—in which double assertion all great truths are contained with a fullness from which men (apparently dazzled, in Plato's image, with excess of light) have fled as though it were the most baneful of errors.

We have now to ask how far the distinction between A (or C) and R (or W) coincides with Whitehead's distinction between Primordial and Consequent Natures, or as I shall say, PN and CN.

PN is described as the conceptual envisagement of eternal possibilities, and as such is absolutely perfect, A. But this is not the only A aspect of

God which Whitehead recognizes. For the divine awareness of all actual occasions as so far occurrent, his enjoyment of the total past of the universe, is perfect in its adequacy to that past, and equally and unsurpassably so at all times. With each new stage of the universe, there is more for God to know, but he knows each and every stage, as it is actualized, quite perfectly, or "without the qualification of any loss either of individual identity or of completeness of unity."[26] Is then God simply omniscient in the old-fashioned sense? Yes, on two conditions.

(1) "Knowledge of all things" means, of each thing as it is, of the actual as actual, of the merely possible as merely possible, of the future as future, of the past as past. For Whitehead there is a future, even for God, not because God is in advance ignorant of future events, but because, so long as they are future, objects of knowledge are not events, are not fully individual and determinate entities. There is nothing in the future for anyone to be ignorant of, except those more or less determinate outlines of probability or possibility, those impure potentials, which distinguish the future both from the determinate past and from the pure undecidedness of the eternal potencies. These outlines of the future are known to God just as they, at any time, are, so that he is entirely without error or ignorance in regard to them. This doctrine is at least five hundred years old, but apparently no great philosopher saw its importance before Whitehead.

(2) Though God's knowledge is at all times, and so primordially, free from error and ignorance, and thus cognitively absolute, A, yet there is a sense in which it perpetually improves upon itself, namely, in richness of content and so in aesthetic value. As future possibilities gain determinacy and become actual events, God's knowledge, without the slightest increase in adequacy to its content, realizes the aesthetic value involved in the *new contrasts* which the new content presents, both in itself and in relation to the old. For Whitehead, the value of truth consists in its contribution to harmony, unity in variety; but the harmony due to the truth correspondence between knower and known is only one dimension upon which the harmony of knowledge must be measured.[27] There is also the unity-in-variety of the object itself, which becomes, through the correspondence, the possession of the subject. Furthermore, there is no such thing as absolute or maximal unity in variety, since every definite variety excludes others. Apart from process, there would be but one out of all possible overall aesthetic patterns for the content of God's knowledge. Through process, the wealth of patterns can be inexhaustibly increased, though it can never become absolute.

But not only is God at all times unsurpassably perfect in the accuracy and adequacy of his knowledge, both of the possible and of the de facto or actual (though he is ever growing in the resultant aesthetic enjoyment), but he is also at all times unsurpassably perfect in the adequacy (goodness, wisdom) of his purposes and decisions. He "saves all that can be saved," and he exerts a "particular providence for particular occasions"[28] (James's "piecemeal supernaturalism"), by furnishing all but the last element of determinateness to the subjective aims of the actual entities. Now we are given no suggestion that any other conceivable being could surpass the quality of these divine functions, or that God himself is any more adequate in discharging them at one time than another. Thus there is aesthetic but not ethical or cognitive improvement in God, aesthetic R-Perfection and ethico-cognitive A-Perfection.

It follows that if the PN is that which God primordially or at all times is—and otherwise it seems a confusing phrase—then the description of PN as "conceptual" is inadequate. PN is at once conceptual, volitional, and perceptual. It is in fact the *common element of all the successive conceptual, perceptual, and appetitive states of the divine life*, abstracting from the differences between these states. This common element is abstract, and so it is *known* by conception, but it is equally a quality of perception and of will.

With nondivine individuals no literally primordial character is possible, since these individuals have had a genesis. But there is a quasi-primordial feature of every enduring individual, the individual quality which a man, say, has had during all his life as a person. This seems to involve a relatively fixed style of both conceiving and perceiving, as well as of volition. Only God has an absolutely fixed and ungenerated general style or self-identical character, an abstract element of strict invariance individual to him. The PN is this element of mere identity, apart from all differences in the Divine Life. It is true that identity has meaning only in relation to difference and really includes difference; but we may distinguish between difference as such, as a generic and hence identical abstract factor, and this or that individual, concrete difference. Now the CN is this peculiar identity of difference or change as such. It and the PN mutually require each other. But there is a third something which contains both of these abstractions with a contingent addition, the de facto individual difference, the concrete partly novel divine state of the given now. Thus we have (1) the static perfection of PN, which is a definite quantum of value, namely, absolute or maximal value, and, as necessary to this perfection but applying to other dimensions of value, (2) the dynamic perfection of CN, which is not a definite degree or quantum of value, but the *generic property* of (3) a *class* of possible values, this property consisting in the values being always superior to those possessed by any being other than God, and also superior to those possessed by God himself at any earlier time, as well as inferior to any values that he may possess in the future. The primordial or static perfection includes the law that there shall be a consequent or dynamic perfection. The law that there shall be change in the form of enrichment is itself unchanging, unenriched. We have, then, to distinguish between the generic property of having a consequent state, and the particular state that God in any given now may have. It is to be remembered also that when we refer to God we ourselves are always in some consequent state, say CNm, which contains not only the entire generic or abstract divine nature, PN-CN, but also some individual de facto concrete phase of that nature, PN-CNm. The impossibility of deducing any particular PN-CNm from the PN-CN is thus no difficulty. But we can deduce the necessity that there be *some* concrete state, PN-CNm or PN-CNn or PN-CNo, etc., and that each such state be followed by a successor; and this deduction is not useless, for it guarantees that there will be a future, that planning is not futile. The deduction consists in drawing the consequences from the negative outcome of the effort to find any basis of meaning in experience, however imaginatively extended, for the notion of the mere abstract or generic factors as entities simply apart from any instances. One may abstract from *each* instance but not from *all* instances. Another instance will always do, but none at all will not do. (This was Aristotle's insight, I take it.)

Abstraction from the concrete proceeds backward in time and depends upon memory [in a broad sense], as Plato saw. Today need not have followed yesterday, although *some* today must have followed yesterday, and similarly with yesterday in relation to its predecessor. Thus we can abstract from any finite slice of the past, however large, but not from all the past. As Whitehead says, the primordial nature is not before or apart from but *with* all process, every stage of which is a contingent successor to its presupposed predecessor.

Thus we have the following structure of the divine life:

PN-CNn as containing PN-CNm, its predecessor,
    as containing . . . etc.
PN-CNo as containing PN-CNn as containing PN-CNm . . . etc.
PN-CNp . . . etc.
etc.

Each stage is the cumulation of the earlier, and contains of the later only an approximate outline, plus the law that there shall be *some* individual event or other of which the outline will be approximately descriptive. (See below, pp. 83-88.) The certainty that this law will be fulfilled is based on the omnipotence of God, if by this old term is meant that he is absolutely equipped with the power and the will to bring the fulfillment about somehow, to prevent the world from collapsing into chaos or empty monotony.

Since any given PN-CNm state could have been otherwise, we must conceive a disjunctive series, PN-CNm1 or PN-CNm2 or PN-CNm3 . . . , as the total set of [sets of qualities] PN-CNm might have had, granting its predecessor. Suppose, then, PN-CNm1 has actually occurred; it is an interesting question whether PN-CNm2 and so on are to be regarded as . . . determinate, or as more or less indeterminate segments of a range of possibilities in which, as possibilities, nothing quite so definite in qualities as an actual event is present. Of course there must be the possibility that the indeterminate may become determinate, as well as the law that *some* indeterminate segment of possibility shall be individually determined. But the possibility of further or individual determination need not itself be individually determinate. This is the question of the definiteness or otherwise of eternal objects or pure potentials. It has a certain bearing on the question of the conceptual character of the PN. If eternal possibilities are fully definite items, then God's concepts need never change, and his entire conceptual being is fixed forever. All that can change (or give place to new ones) are his physical prehensions and with them his hybrid prehensions of the impure potentials as relevant to a given state of the cosmos. The hybrid prehensions will change, however, only in their physical constituents, and the impure potentials will be simply identical with certain eternal objects as selected for a given occasion by the physical prehensions. If, on the other hand, impure potentials are more definite than anything to be found in eternal possibility, then God's concepts must become more determinate with time, and thus it will not be true that the conceptual aspect of his being is completely primordial, just as it is not true that the physical aspect of his being is completely derivative. (What is not derivative is the law, the general how, of his derivations, his unique style, whose functioning had no beginning, of adequately prehending actualities.)

It is to be understood of course that any PN-CNm implies a set of world-members, of creatures, as existing in it. Since in this fashion PN-CNm embraces ordinary imperfect things, there is no need to attribute ordinary imperfection or ordinary relativity, r, to God himself, except precisely as properties of *his* parts. Just as a small part can belong to a large whole, so it is clear that the imperfections of the parts are not as such and identically imperfections of the whole. What *is* true is that the whole must be R- and not merely A-Perfect. (For there can be no greatest possible number, or an absolute variety.) Consequently, we need not consider the ideas of God which are derivable by adding r to A and R. AR makes room for all the r's there may be, whereas mere A would make any r factor strictly superfluous, irrelevant, meaningless.[29] The interesting thing is that whereas so many writers have seen that there might be difficulty in conceiving finite evils to exist as such, if there be an in all ways simply perfect or best being (in the best or only possible state of itself), far fewer have seen that it is equally difficult to make sense out of finite good as out of finite evil, assuming AA. Neither finite good nor finite evil can have anything to do with sheer maximal good. God as AA could not impart significance to finite values, whether positive or negative. The problem is to enable the finite to contribute to the "best" being, without demanding, what is impossible, that the contribution should, either alone or with whatever supplementation you please, effect an absolute sum. No sum of finites can be absolute. It can very well, however, contribute toward making something R-Perfect, superior to all that is not itself, and through progress superior even to itself.

There is a relation of this to the Russellian theory of types. There can be no "all" which is absolute being, the all of all possible totalities. But there can be an all which nothing other than itself can surpass, since anything other than itself will, to exist, belong to the "itself." The cosmos must be such an all, if we admit that any possible entity is possible only because the cosmos might produce it, either within and as a part of itself, or as a state of itself as a whole. The unity of this whole is involved in its parts, since their very existence is their role in the cosmos as one, as *the* cosmos. Thus the correct treatment of *all* avoids the two extremes of AA and rr or mere relativity. As at all times the complete possessor of all that at those times exists, the cosmos must have an A aspect, for there are no degrees of complete possession. But since there will be more to possess at one time than another there is, also, an R factor. AA and rr (or atheism) are the twin absurdities between which philosophy has tragicomically swung for over two millennia.

Arguments for God's Existence

It is Whitehead's contention that "metaphysics is a descriptive science," that direct experience, intuition, is basic and proof is secondary. So far, Whitehead agrees with Bergson. The groundwork of all existence is present in all instances of existence, hence in all experience, and the task is to see it there. Argument can only rest upon some part of the groundwork that happens to be more clearly discriminated. Still, insofar as some aspects of the metaphysical situation are more readily observed than others, at least in a given state of culture, personal or social, argument may be in order. And Whitehead does offer what might with some qualification be called "proofs for God," even though he also declares that "nothing like proof" is possible. God is, according to him, that aspect of the metaphysical situation which, though involved in the other aspects, is less immediately apparent and obvious (at least to ordinary nonreligious experience) than they, and insofar is in need of indirect evidence.

To the question, Why after all is there a conception of God in Whitehead's philosophy? the answer is twofold. First, Whitehead is not without religion. Second, his categories, adopted at least as much for other purposes, require God as their "chief" and indispensable exemplification. In saying that God must not be invoked to save the collapse of the categories by making him an exception to them, Whitehead is not denying that the categories, however well chosen, would collapse without God, but he is saying that they must require God, if at all, as their supreme instance, not as an exception or a violation of their requirements. There can be no obligation upon categories to render God superfluous, unless the possibility of atheism is axiomatic. (Since Whitehead believes in the unconsciousness of much that is in experience in the form of feeling and impulse, he is not committed to accept at face value the claims of various persons to "believe" in a godless world.) Categories are obligated to describe the world in terms of their exemplifications, and if they can only do this on the admission that there is a chief example of their meaning, that fact is insofar a proof that such an example, a God, exists, unless another set of categories, at least equally adequate for other purposes, will function without a supreme example.

How do Whitehead's categories require a supreme example? There are as many answers as there are categories; for they all require God. (1) Possibility implies a supreme and primordial ground, (2) actuality an all-inclusive actual entity, (3) the transition (creativity) from possibility to actuality a supreme creative agent, (4) memory [prehension] a highest type of retention of elapsed events, (5) purpose [subjective aim] and love a highest or perfect type of purpose and love, and (6) order a supreme ordering factor. (3) is Whitehead's well-known argument for a "principle of limitation" or concretion. (1) is the argument from the "ontological principle"; (2) is found particularly in *Modes of Thought*, and is given no title; (4) is the doctrine of everlastingness, not presented so much as an argument for God as a consequence drawn from accepting his existence, but capable of becoming an argument; (5) and (6) are found here and there throughout his [later] writings.

(1) Possibility is either a property of existent things, or it is independent of all existence, a self-sufficient realm of essence, as Santayana says it is—though at the same time substituting essence for possibility and thereby advertising that he is not really solving or even facing the question of possible quality, any more than of actual quality, but is talking about something nobody ever encountered, that is, a quality as it would be were it neither actual (a datum in a real experience) nor even capable of being actual. Only qualities that at least *might* get into existence concern us, and the only more than verbal notion anyone has ever set forth as to what would make nonactual things possible is the notion of "power," the "I can," as an undetermined but determinable aspect of an existent. Only what exists has the power to create further existence, and it has this power because what exists [a society] is not complete in all aspects but has an element of futurity, or a principle of self-transcendence, of being potentially what it as yet is not. But if the only existents are ordinary imperfect things, and if, as it seems reasonable to suppose, these things have not always existed, then when they came into existence they did so as determinations of determinables already existing, and the ultimate power involved must lie back of all such nonprimordial and secondary things. "The general possibility of the universe must be somewhere" is the summary of this line of argument.[30] If possibility is meaningless without existence, then it cannot be that all existents are contingent, for this is to say that the being of possibility also is contingent, that it might have been that nothing was possible—precisely the implication of Santayana's doctrine, since had nature not existed (and its existence is said not to be necessary) there would have been nothing capable of actualizing essences, which are not self-actualizing. The conclusion of the argument is that there is a primordial power *whose nonexistence is not a possibility, since possibility presupposes its existence.* Its reality being the ground of alternatives, its nonreality is not an alternative. This is the old argument from contingent being to necessary being, with the difference that it is not concluded that the necessary being is necessary in all its aspects, but only that any contingent aspects it or other things may have presuppose one aspect of itself which in all possible times, places, and instances necessarily is. What can this necessary aspect be? We experience potentiality as the way in which experience involves the

future in the present, in the form of more or less determinate purposes, undecided as to the precise value which is to be actualized, but determined to actualize some value or other. This involves universals, ranges of value, and a function of deciding at a given moment upon *a* value within such a range. Personality is the only clear case we know of such a combination of universals and decisions. To say the necessary, primordial power is a primordial personality, in its essential character an ungenerated, indestructible unity of subjective aim, appetitions, mentality, and acts of fiat, is simply to give the only answer we can to the question, what is the noncontingent basis of contingency? In the last few remarks we have expanded (1) to include (3), the argument for a principle of limitation.

As to (2), what can it mean to say of an occasion that it actually occurs in a world in which other actualities also exist? To stand outside the occasion and say, "it exists," is to refer it to a *common measure or register of existence* by reference to which other things also exist.[31] This measure cannot be the thing's own solipsistic or private self-awareness; for then existence would have no common or public meaning, and to say many things exist would be to say nothing.[32] Nor can the measure be the imperfect sort of social awareness that ordinary things may have of each other, for then there is no criterion to decide between the imperfections of their views of themselves and each other. To refer to "existence" as a public meaning is to refer to a register on which, with infinite exactitude, everything is recorded just as it "really is," on pain of its not being really anything. Since actuality is essentially, for Whitehead, an affair of value and feeling, the register of existence must be something infinitely sensitive to shades and varieties of feeling.[33] All is clear if we assume an all-embracing "tenderness," or sympathy, which appropriates all feeling as soon as occurrent, not by robbing it of its selfhood, its self-decisive character, but by enjoying this character with infinite "patience" or tolerance. The standard of existence must also be the standard of value, for nothing can really measure what we are that cannot measure what we are worth to ourselves and to each other. It must be fully conscious, for the unconscious cannot answer, point for point, quality for quality, to the conscious, or even to the contrast between the conscious and the un- or semiconscious.

As to (6), it is perhaps Whitehead's favorite argument. The only empirical basis for order, the only answer to Hume, that Whitehead finds is in such factors as immediate memory, anticipation, the sense of conformation to past emotions and purposes and to the feelings flowing to us from the body, and the necessity for aesthetic harmony among these factors if the enduring self or personal society is to have any richness of content. Order is drive toward harmony in the relations of past, present, and future, of self and others immanent in self. It is aesthetic teleology. Now if there is no cosmic seeker of harmony, there can be no reason why the various seekers of harmony should have the pure luck to succeed in assisting rather than thwarting each other in the search. They have only limited knowledge of each other's needs, or of their own needs, and indeed, they would have no standard by which to recognize each other as realities. Local order can in some minor way be in the hands of local orderers, local aesthetic drives; but cosmic order, presupposed by all lesser orders, can only be safe, or anything but doomed, if there be a unitary cosmic aesthetic drive, that is, a cosmic love which seeks beauty everywhere it can be attained, and guides the general direction of cosmic change so that the right balance of novelty and repetition shall in general be secured. The laws of nature are not merely "imposed" upon dead matter, nor merely immanent trends in local agencies, nor mere descriptions of uniformities observed (they would then give no assurance as to the future).[34] They are immanent, but this immanence is given a cosmic reference by an element of imposition, of interfusing of ideals more or less unconsciously derived from the one whose subjective aim effectively surveys the cosmic whole. This is not the usual argument from design. For it holds, not that the order of the world is so superior that it must have a superior orderer, but that if we did not take a cosmic order unconsciously for granted we would not be able even to say "world" or to know anything at all, even about disorder. To believe that there is a cosmos is to believe in a cosmic individual whose content of integration is in part the variety we see.

That the general trend of physical nature seems to be toward a state of minimal activity or a "running down" (second law of thermodynamics) shows that the ultimate creative aspect of reality is not accessible to the physicist, not that there is no such aspect. Moreover, the running down of a type of order is a familiar aesthetic phenomenon, as we see in the history of the arts. Each general style has its day in art, and then undergoes decline, loss of appeal and zest, until some new order, through exploration "along the borders of chaos" as Whitehead says, is arrived at. It ought not to be that the present style of natural activity, the pattern of the present cosmic epoch, should last forever. With the inexhaustible realm of possibilities not utilized in that pattern to draw upon, why should the cosmic artist adhere forever to one design?[35]

And if the physical world in general is running down, life on this planet is a partial exception, there being no evidence that the ascent of life is a mere example of the laws of quantum mechanics, but every reason to think it is partly contrary to those laws (though not in gross physical degree, the issues of life involving small amounts of energy, physically regarded). In life we see a creative force—Whitehead agrees with Bergson here—of which low-grade physical realities are only a sort of minimal and in a manner retrograde expression. They are there chiefly to serve, and to pass away when their service is done.

(5) Since the basic structure of reality for Whitehead is the social integration of occasions, it is not surprising that he argues for a cosmic, supreme, and in certain senses perfect sociality. Only because there is a cosmic society with personal order (though Whitehead does not use this expression in this connection), a supreme love, whose integrity is presupposed as the measure of all lesser orders and of all disorder, can we conceive the various societies as more or less integrated, or as in any way comparable to each other, or able in general to survive in each other's presence.

When a society disintegrates, this is not a disintegration of the cosmos, but a rearrangement of its integrity, without which nothing would have any definite character in relation to anything else. Integrity is not indeed the only value, since richness of content is also a value. God seeks richness of enjoyment in his creatures generally so far as guidance of their free decisions (by determining the limits within which the freedom is to exist) can produce such richness. For his own richness of content is [includes] the total richness of theirs. He loves them quite literally as himself, for they furnish parts of himself and his happiness through their own happiness.[36]

The argument from everlastingness I shall consider in the next section.

Everlastingness and Futurity in God

Whitehead has not always written as though the principle of process applied to God. He has called God "nontemporal," and has contrasted him with "the temporal world." He has never, I think, said that God has a past, present, or future. And in one passage he has stated that for God there is no past.[37] The context of this last remark, however, indicates that what is meant is that the primordial conceptual awareness of eternal objects is not derivative from any antecedent concrete awareness, since the divine conceptual awareness must have been already involved in any concrete awareness. As for "nontemporal," the definitive declaration is surely the passage which describes God as in one sense nontemporal and in another sense temporal.[38] We must, I think, also emphasize the fact that it is in Whitehead's three most recent books that the temporal aspect of God is most clearly and vigorously affirmed, so that there may have been a change in Whitehead's belief since he wrote *Science* and *Religion*, a change in the direction of greater consistency with the Principle of Process.

Is there a past for God? It is said that in God occasions never "perish," and in *that* sense nothing is past, is gone, for God. But it does not follow that there is no order of succession in the divine life, which is most expressly stated to be "fluent." It is indeed not the case that succession depends essentially upon perishing, upon the fading of immediacy as events cease to be present events. As twenty centuries overlooked, and Bergson was one of the first to realize—though only in his somewhat cloudy, "intuitive" fashion—the order of succession depends rather upon the logical difference between retrospective and prospective relationships.[39] The later event prehends the earlier and so contains it, but the converse is not true; and this one-way relationship remains even when both earlier and later events are in the past (or when—it is all the same—there is a new present), no matter how fully their original immediacy is preserved. Obviously, it is not because of fading or perishing that earlier is contained in later, though later is not contained in earlier. It is rather *in spite of perishing*. Were loss of immediacy the last word, how could the faded event in its nonfaded vividness, as it was when present, be contained in the new present? Yet such containing is the theory of succession under discussion. It is the reality of the new *as added to that of the old*, rather than the unreality of the old, that constitutes process. The denial of perishing in God, so far from removing succession, is required to rescue it from partial if not complete destruction. For us, much of the past, that which has been, is "as though it had never been," except for profoundly unconscious prehensions, and these cannot be construed unless there is some consciousness whose clarity registers and measures their content. It is adequate awareness which measures inadequate, not vice versa. Thus for instance the Primordial envisagement of eternal objects is necessary to make our inferior envisagement of them possible. And similarly, in the CN, "succession does not mean loss of immediate unison," and this preservation of events as they are when they occur is just what gives them a definite status in the "past," as x has a definite place in "x as a part of y," where y is the later, richer, more determinate entity. This is that higher mode of becoming which men have tried vainly for centuries to conceive when they held that all is together in God, yet not static or inactive or dead.

The poetic majesty of the conception of unfading everlastingness of all occasions in God (down to the de facto present) should not blind us to the simple, cogent reason for the idea. It is almost comical to see critics (including Santayana) object to the immortality of the past as a fantastic, incredible, gratuitous idea, while these same persons—Mead being almost the only exception known to me—lightheartedly assume the immortality of truth, however detailed and trivial, about the past. Indeed, they usually go further and assume the eternity of truth, its completeness above time altogether, thus rendering time an illusion of which the real content is timeless. Such critics substitute for the simple and consistent idea of Whitehead and Bergson the following paradoxes: (a) They suppose a world of truth which is, item for item, an exact duplicate of the past, in one-to-one correspondence with its determinations, however detailed. This duplicate or truth world lacks of the actual past no determinate character, but only an ineffable something called actuality. (b) They suppose that truth is *real now* as involving a relation of correspondence with an object which is not real now. Relation-to-the-past is there—save for the past. Relation-to is there, we should say. If we add to these paradoxes the almost universally accompanying one that (c) truth about past, present, or future is said to be timelessly complete in all eternity, although that which it is about is either incomplete or at least seems to lose its distinctive character of process if it be supposed complete, we have three appalling demands upon credulity, or ability to believe nonsense. It was indeed partly to avoid such absurdities that Bergson adopted his view of the cumulative character of time.

But perhaps it will be thought a paradox that the past should, in present experience, be still immediately given. I have elsewhere on several occasions explained this to mean that the past involves universals of which later events are instances, and in such fashion that the instances imply their universals but not the converse. Every event contains more or less determinate desires, expectations, fears, purposes, hopes, and these involve generality, indetermination as to the exact details which may fulfill or disappoint or somehow be relevant to them. The planned or feared event as outlined in the plan or fear is never so individually definite as the event which comes to pass at the time in question, and this greater definiteness of the subsequent event remains exactly that, no matter how complete the preservation of the earlier event. Indeed, it is only if the preservation is complete that the precise indeterminations of the past in its hopes and fears can be retrospectively seen for what they were when present. On the other hand, the fulfillment or disappointment, felt as such, of a purpose or hope includes the memory of the purpose or hope, plus details not foreseen in the anticipatory state and not contained in it as preserved in memory, as to how things actually "came out." Clearly logic allows the asymmetrical relationship required. A can be in B although B is not in A. In fact, there would otherwise be no distinction between general and particular; for the general is that which does not imply other things (unless they are of equal generality), whereas the particular contains the general as an abstractable feature. Why should not this asymmetrical structure of universal-particular be essentially an aspect of the structure of time? Time either is or is not essential to existence and to all being. Many who think it is thus essential reject the only theory of time that does justice to its basic place in being as the key to the interrelations of the categories.

The foregoing doctrine can be expressed as the contention that the cause is never "equal to the effect," the latter always being the richer; the former, seen retrospectively, being a reduction of the latter to an abstract or incomplete version of itself. The subject is always "superject," always an enrichment of existence, even of God, and it involves that which is enriched, but not conversely. This *is* succession. When Whitehead views PN as a causal factor implied by all actual entities but requiring none of them in particular, he is consistent with his first principles. But those are deceiving themselves who, like Spinoza and Jonathan Edwards, wish to conceive God as C, as existing and intelligible in himself alone, and at the same time hold that all things follow without qualification from his [will or] nature (Spinoza in a sense makes a qualification, but it is equivocal), or that it is the function of a cause to necessitate its effect. Independence *means* asymmetrical contingency (or asymmetrical determinism, it is the same thing), the noninvolvement of the effect in the cause, or it means nothing. There are no degrees of necessity. If my hat requires God and God requires my hat (at least as an illusion or "appearance"), the logical status of the one is as dependent or independent as that of the other. Whitehead has escaped this old trap, and has done so by "taking time (and freedom and memory) seriously."

There are three questions concerning the temporal structure of God which I should like to put to Professor Whitehead. In doing so I am in danger of revealing my lack of scientific knowledge, but I hope at least that the questions will have a definite meaning.

1. Must there not be a cosmic present, in spite of relativity physics, the de facto totality of actual entities as present in the divine immediacy? As Parker and Bergson have said, the inability of human beings, by signaling methods, to determine a unique cosmic present or simultaneity need not

prevent God, who knows things directly, from experiencing such a present. Since God is not spatially localized, it appears that he must intuit all occasions wherever they are as [just after?] they occur in one state of experience. But then can it be without qualification true that contemporaries are causally independent, nonimmanent in each other? Since they are all immanent in God, and he in turn immanent in them, must they not be immanent in each other? For, since God is not spatially separated from things, it seems no definite lapse of time can occur either between his prehension of them or theirs of him. There can be no transmission with the velocity of light from an event to the divine observer, or from the divine process itself to the creaturely events. (There is a somewhat similar problem about the relation of the human consciousness to brain-cell events.)

2. If there is a divine present, distinguishable from both the divine past and the divine future, it will, I take it, be an "epochal" affair, not a mathematical instant, nor yet containing infinite divisions, but a unit actually undivided yet potentially divisible (such that it might have been divided, or might have been part of a longer undivided epoch). What will be the length of this epoch? I should suppose it would be identical with that of the shortest creaturely unit or specious present, since the perfect perception (physical prehension) will make whatever discriminations are necessary to follow the distinctions in the things perceived, no more and no less. The longer units will then be experienced by God as overlapping several of the shorter, and therefore not absolutely undivided, taking account of the immanence of the shorter in their prehensions. But this involves problems of synchronization that inevitably baffle my lay mind.

Whitehead says that the consequent nature shares with each actual entity its actual world, that is, the totality of things definitely in its past. But God shares worlds not just with each but with all actual entities not definitely in the cosmic future, that is, with all really "actual" entities, since future entities are nonactual, indeterminate, potential.

3. Is the world-process, as everlasting in God, without beginning? Then the totality of actual occasions is an actual infinity. I have no objection to this, provided, as I hope—and in spite of Kant, Renouvier, and Parker—the idea of the actually infinite is meaningful. If the totality of immortalized actualities is infinite, then the enrichment of God through each new occasion is the addition to a realization already infinite. This too, I take it, is not fatal, since either (a) the order of the infinity might increase, or (b) if the number of elapsed events did not increase, the class would, since new members are added and none lost. (a) is, as I understand from

mathematicians, not compatible with the epochal theory of time. It seems that (b) [suggested to me by Bertrand Russell] must be the solution. And I suppose the addition of new contrasts to everlasting reality can enrich it aesthetically without effecting a numerical increase in the contrasts already there.

Personality, Substance, and Event in God

The Absolute-Relative or AR conception of divine perfection is that God is the self-transcending transcender of all others except self. Self-transcendence presupposes the notion of self. But the unit of reality in Whitehead's thought, it might be objected, is not the self or enduring individual or substance but the occasion or event. Self is apparently a secondary notion, in fact a certain sort of "society" of "its" occasions or states. It seems to follow that the self-transcending selfhood of God must also be a secondary matter, whereas in consistency Whitehead is bound to assert that God, at least as PN, is an absolute necessity of existence.

The difficulty is, I believe, largely verbal. Whitehead is not essentially or without far-reaching qualifications committed to the view that occasions are more fundamental than enduring individuals.[40] First of all, nothing is more fundamental than the unvarying totality of eternal possibilities; and these would be nothing apart from the self-identity of God as PN. Secondly, to belong to a society with personal order, that is, an enduring individual or substance, is one of the two chief ways in which an occasion is enabled to possess richness of contrast in its content, the other consisting in its enjoying social relations with members of personally ordered societies other than its own. Mere occasions which did not belong, directly or indirectly, to any person or substance would be the impossible case of occasions with no significant content, a case excluded absolutely by the necessarily existent goodness of God, the cosmic orderer.[41] In addition, occasions that failed to belong to at least one personal society, namely God, would have no place in temporal order, would not really be occasions, events. For the unity of time is immanent in occasions, which are successive to each other only because each contributes to the value of the next, and substantiality is constituted by the particularly prominent strands of this contributiveness or immanence, and the divine substantiality is the only adequate or perfect measure and ground of temporal unity.

What Whitehead definitely rejects in substantialism is [includes]: (1) the idea that it is merely an accidental property of some kinds of substances that they involve accidents, occasions, process; (2) the idea that substances cannot (or at least, need not) have each other as accidents, cannot or need not be immanent in each other;[42] and (3) the idea that the unity of substance is an absolute, all-or-none affair. (1) would imply that there might be a substance which had no accidents and was not in process; (3) would make the most fragile and imperfectly integrated self as much a self as God. According to Whitehead, (2) is, as he once remarked, the foundation of immorality. Those who accuse Whitehead of dissolving personal identity[43] (and thus damaging our ethical conceptions) might bear in mind that what he really does is to assert the *equal* importance of interpersonal relations, and also to assert the absolute meaninglessness of substance apart from change.

I wish, however, to go farther, and to maintain that Whitehead can more truly conceive God as a self-identical substance than the old substantialism could. For when it was a question of God, traditional doctrines really came closer to the idea of a state without substance than of a substance without states. Where all distinction between substance and state is eliminated, if any meaning survives it is more like the idea of a single occasion, which as Whitehead points out is "immutable," than it is like an enduring individual which identifies itself in the midst of successive states, which is therefore precisely not immutable but changing, and therefore remains also itself as that same changing individual or endurer of accidents. On the other hand, Whitehead, who seems to take states more seriously than substance, really does view God as an enduring individual with a unique and indeed perfect form of self-identity. God is the self-transcending transcender of all, not the mere state of complete value. In other words, he is a self-contrasting and therefore in a significant sense self-identical subject with an ever partly new superject, not just a single non-self-related or barely "simple" state of being. Without self-contrast, self-identity is meaningless and substance degenerates into a mere state, subject into a mere object. So far from true is it that Whitehead fails to do justice, in relation to God, to the real meaning of substance.

But, some will ask, is Whitehead's God personal? A person in ordinary language is at least what is in some degree *conscious* and *individual*. Now Whitehead makes it very plain that his God is conscious, taking CN as well as PN into account. The individuality of God is also evident enough. The individual is the *determinate* or decided (except as to its future, and even that is relatively decided) in contrast to the multiple indecisiveness of mere potentiality, and it is the *integrated* in contrast to the "democracy" or even looser organization of a society of societies when the former society is without personal order. Now the concrete being of God is definite and is not the equivalent in actuality of the entire realm of possibilities. [The absolute God (AA) of the tradition was, on the other hand, more or less admittedly nonindividual, for it was the complete actualization of potency, or it was a completeness "beyond" potency and actuality.] Also the concrete being of God is asserted by Whitehead to have pre-eminent unity, surpassing that of any other individual. So what is there of personality that God could fail to possess, and possess in a superlative degree?

Is God, then, the "personal order" of the inclusive society of societies, implying that the universe is God's body? Whitehead does not say these things in so many words, but he says things from which they are deducible, by his own definitions of the terms of the above question. Personal order is raised to the highest potency in the immediacy of the past as unfadingly everlasting in God, and in this order the cosmos is contained. Moreover, the definition of body applies literally to God, if suitably generalized to cover a supreme case. For the body is simply that much of the world with which the mind, or personal society, has effective immediate interactions of mutual inheritance, and over which its influence is dominant.[44] Such is God's relation to all of the world, and therefore all of it is his body. This has none of the degrading effects that giving God a body is supposed to have; indeed, it is only a way of saying that God's social relations with all things are uniquely adequate, that he really and fully loves all of them, and that they all, however inadequately or unconsciously, love him. It scarcely needs saying that to have a body is not to be connected with lumps of mere dead insentient matter, "vacuous actuality," there being no such thing for Whitehead, or perhaps for any philosopher who competently and honestly faces the destructive analysis of this concept which modern philosophy has effected. Nor is it true for Whitehead that lesser organisms within a mind's organism are absolutely controlled by that mind, deprived of all decisions of their own, or that what the parts of the body decide for themselves the dominant mind decides for itself. Hence creaturely freedom and God's nonresponsibility for evil are compatible with the view that God is the personality of the cosmic body, the totality of societies inferior to that personal-order society which is the mind and life of God.

The Principle of Concretion

It is somewhat unfortunate that Whitehead's view of God was chiefly associated, for some years, with the phrase "principle of limitation" (or of concretion). This is an inadequate description of his view, and that in three ways. (1) God is at once the principle of abstraction, of unbounded possibility, *and* of concretion, of limited realization of possibility. The eternal possibilities which require limitation by divine fiat are themselves divine concepts.[45] (2) God is not merely a principle or set of principles; he is the concrete actual entity whose importance has the universality of first principles. (3) God is not the only agent of abstraction or of concretion, but he is the "supreme" agent,[46] the only agent equal to a principle in the scope of its action. Every subject-superject is an effector of concretion and contains the envisagement of possibilities. But God is the only such agent whose functioning is presupposed by all existence throughout all time, the only strictly cosmic agent.

Possibilities do not themselves decide which of them is to be actual.[47] This would be a contradiction, since it would make the unselected possibilities impossible. Further, actuality cannot in advance decide upon its future stages, since futurity in its distinctive difference from pastness means a certain indecisiveness in what is future so long as it is so.[48] Hence the "selection" of a given possibility for realization can only be a free act in the present occasion, which is self-creative.[49] No reason can be given from which such a free act can be deduced, although that there be some such act or other following upon any given moment of process is a deducible necessity from the nature of reality as process.

Thus we understand when Whitehead says of God:

> His existence is the ultimate irrationality. For no reason can be given for just that limitation which it stands in His nature to impose.... No reason can be given for the nature of God, because that nature is the ground of rationality.... There is a metaphysical need for a principle of determination, but there can be no metaphysical reason for what is determined.[50]

This is the metaphysical basis of the methodological truth that matters of fact are not knowable a priori. Metaphysically necessary truth is abstract and embraces of concrete facts only the requirement that there be some such facts. The whole truth is metaphysical plus empirical, and this is so even for God. Whitehead is denying Spinoza's notion that all things follow from the necessary essence of Substance, and Leibniz's notion that all things follow from God's goodness plus the superiority of this world over all possible worlds. Leibniz never did tell us intelligibly how some one set of possibilities could be better than all others. Deduction must assume something more definite and particular than a mere "what is possible is possible." Creation is the dance of Shiva of which the Hindus speak, not the drawing of a conclusion. There is an unbridgable gulf between reasoning, which turns upon universals, and action, which is always individual. By reasoning upon universals some conclusion as to the *sort* of thing to be done may be reached, but what is done will be an individual instance, not a sort, and the leap from the sort to the instance will not be reasoning but sheer fiat. After the instance is given, then the next decision will have to take account of it. Thus, as Whitehead says, reason presupposes creation. What is reasonable depends upon what has been done, including that in what has been done that is more than reasonable.

When Kant said that artistic rules are deduced from genius, not the acts of genius from artistic rules, he was unwittingly suggesting a theory of process superior to that furnished by his own philosophy, according to which events must conform to absolute rules. It is rather events that furnish the basis for the particular, approximate rules that are relevant at a given time.[51] The cosmic creative genius is the ground of all definite laws, and no antecedent law implies the particular laws which the creative acts from time to time express and, for some limited period, establish.[52]

It is true that in *The Function of Reason* Whitehead says that reason is the organ by which orderly novelty is introduced into the world. Reason balances the need for contrast and the unexpected against the need for harmony of the new with the old. But "reason" here refers, I take it, to the total act which includes reasoning in our human case, and in the cosmic or divine case includes that part of reason which is the awareness of possibility as such. But it is clear that the particular orderly novelty is not as it were deduced or necessary.

Evil and God's Power

Is God an efficient or a final cause? He is an efficient cause because he is a final cause, and vice versa. He furnishes their subjective aims to the creatures (open to their further determination as to details). This furnishing is effected by the hybrid prehensions which the creatures have of God's conceptual prehensions.[53] (This is a return to the doctrine of Augustine, Matthew of Aquasparta, Malebranche, and Spinoza, that we see truth in the divine ideas.) Now prehensions, whether physical or hybrid, are the bridge over which efficient causality is transmitted. But what is transmitted in the hybrid prehensions which we have of God is an aim, that is, a final cause. God controls by "persuading." The persuasion is, up to a certain point, irresistible, but only because we love God with an immediate love or sympathetic prehension which is our very being, and can therefore at most be distorted rather than destroyed, while we persist at least.

God's persuasion of us is balanced by our persuasion of him. He prehends our prehensions, and the particular subjective aims which he furnishes us are made what they are partly by his participation in our own previous decisions.[54] God literally feels our feelings, our desires become elements of desire in him. Our decisions indeed cannot become his decisions, as though he decided them; and this means that our ethical evil cannot be made God's ethical evil. Ethical evil prehended in another becomes aesthetic evil in the other. God suffers our evil acts (he also enjoys them, so far as we do) and he suffers their consequences in others, as we often do not.

But is God positively righteous? No, if this means, Does he reward and punish with mathematical exactitude, "though the heavens fall?" And the heavens would fall, for it is not possible that God should serve any absolute law of reward and punishments and also get on with the business of cosmic prosperity and beauty.[55] God is perfectly good, but with the goodness of love, not of legalistic justice, which is a secondary device of goodness. And love, as Whitehead reminds us, is "a little oblivious as to morals," if, that is, by morality is meant a set of rules for determining the distribution of sweet and bitter according to "desert." Existence is social, and it cannot be that what an individual enjoys or suffers should follow exclusively from his own good or evil acts or be exactly fitted to these. The goodness of God consists in this, that he never thwarts any desire, however perverse or trivial, without himself sharing fully in every quality of feeling of pain or sorrow that the thwarting involves in the creatures. Thus God is the "fellow-sufferer who understands."[56] He does what has to be done to maintain the social beauty of the cosmic system, and its enjoyableness for most of the creatures; and he does not do it coldly or from without, but as one who is within the tragedy as well as within the triumph of life.

To such a view Santayana has objected that it is strange that God, who has been working through all the past, should have brought the world at last to the state it is now in.[57] This writer even suggests that the devil could as well say that he tolerates good for the sake of evil as God can say that he tolerates evil for the sake of good. Now, first, there can for Whitehead be no question of gradually eliminating evil from the universe, for the causes of ever-new evil must be operating in the present as in the past, since they lie in the same element of free-decisions-plus-social-inter-dependence upon which all good also depends. Increased opportunities for good also mean increased opportunities for evil, as all can see in human history and in any conceivable history. What counts is the surplus of good, the good of existence on the whole, not only for God but, as part of his good, for the creatures generally or in the main. Now the total value which the travail of the past has harvested, and the deepest meaning of "progress," is not to be seen by taking a cross section of the present, in attempted abstraction from the immortal past. It is the total or real present as in God, all existence down to the latest increment, that is metaphysically progressing toward ever new and greater richness of contrast and harmony. The rate of this progressing is not fixed by fate or deity, but is always something to be decided, in part, by each and every creature. What is not to be decided, even by God, is that progress, in the sense and direction explained, there shall be; for this is the "necessary goodness" and perfection of power of God, which lie beyond the "accidents of will." The rate of progress is greatest when the creatures (a) do the best they know or can guess as to how to contribute to it (avoid ethical evil), and (b) are lucky in their guess. It is a question of luck, for each is largely ignorant of what others are doing, and God can only set limits to the amount of harm which bad guesses can do, he cannot rigorously eliminate the harm while leaving the creatures their essential measure of freedom.

In the second place, God does not "secretly commission the evil to appear, in order that the good may assert itself." Evil is not primarily there so that the good may have something to vanquish. Evil arises automatically in connection with the pursuit of good. Evil requires no contriving, just as to miss the target requires no skill. But is God's skill then limited? No, but the target is a self-moving one, and the exact direction of its movement is incalculable; hence the outcome of the shot depends partly upon chance. This lies in the conditions of existence, any possible existence, and does not limit God by comparison with any conceivable being.

Granting that evil does arise, God does wring some good out of it.[58] Yet it is good that is to be pursued, not evil, even as means to good. Monotony and suffering are the two rocks which the ship of being, aiming at beauty and love, must ever seek to avoid, and the only reason for steering toward either rock is to correct a drift toward the other. The destruction of interest through monotony is just as great a danger as suffering and hatred. It is part of Whitehead's insight that he sees this so clearly.

God and Eternal Objects

Occasions are ingredients of process that are immutable but not primordial; eternal objects are ingredients of process that are both immutable and primordial. Enduring societies are ingredients of process that are neither immutable nor, with one exception (God's life as a personal society of divine occasions), primordial (although primordially there are some societies or other). Societies are mutable factors in process. But there seems to be a fourth type of entity, the impure potentials, the selection of pure potentials or eternal objects which are realizable in a given society, which conform to the style of feeling and subjective aim characterizing such a society. Like their societies, impure potentials belong not to all time, either forward or backward, but to a certain stretch of time. It is true that like societies they are immortal in the sense that their having been belongs to the everlasting content of being, but if their societies cease to [acquire additions] to the series of occasions constituting them, then the impure potentials are no longer capable of further actualization in the manner peculiar to these societies.

Now there are two ways of conceiving the relation of impure to pure potentials. Either the former are mere selections among the latter, or mere arrangements of them with respect to gradations of relevance and with respect to positive or negative prehensions, or the mixed potentials are really creative determinations without which potencies would be determinable rather than determinate or wholly definite. If all the "forms of definiteness," each perfectly definite in itself, are eternally given to God, it is not altogether clear to me what actualization accomplishes. True, it removes contradictions among possibilities; but if contradiction does not interfere with definite envisagement, again there is some difficulty to see what need there is to remove it.

Whitehead does say that the eternal objects have indeterminacy as to their mode of ingression, but there is perhaps some obscurity as to what this qualification involves.[59] Granting that there must be some eternal measure of quality, some set of ultimate variables or dimensions, such as "intensity," "complexity," "joy," "suffering," is it necessary that these variables involve all possible values as distinct items, for instance all the possible "lines" or "points" on the color-solid, all possible ways of *subdividing the continuity* of quality? Or is there a process of "extensive abstraction," or something analogous, by which subdivisions are inexhaustibly created in the course of the creative advance of the world? Then, though any actual set of qualities would be infinitely far from exhausting possibility, for it would have reached no limit of subdivisions and would be confined also to certain portions of the dimensions subdivided, yet no item of the actual qualities would be antecedently contained in possibility, and thus actualization would really add something, namely, definiteness.[60] Whitehead would doubtless insist, with Santayana, that mathematical ideas at least must be regarded as definite prior to any particular embodiment.[61]

(The very idea of "*continuity* of quality" seems to imply this.) But mathematical ideas, as Whitehead has often remarked, are abstract or general. We say that every pair is, as pair, equivalent to every other—pair of apples, pair of virtues; but a determinate color is not a class name in such fashion. "All the reds I could not tell from this red" may yet as reds all be slightly different, in saturation, hue, or tint (meaning by these terms attributes of sensation, not of physical stimuli, conceived quantitatively), and it is not clear to me why these differences must be eternally given to God as distinct items.

It would not follow that, as Santayana has suggested, choice between alternatives would no longer be possible.[62] For such choice need not operate among eternal possibilities exclusively, but can involve those determinations of the ultimate determinables which have already been achieved in the past. A painter can decide between using red and green in a given part of his picture, since he has seen red and green before, but it follows neither that red and green are eternal nor that the exact red-sensation which his painting will give him, or someone else, will duplicate perfectly any previously experienced quality. Each moment of time will add a little to the definiteness of qualities, even as envisaged by deity, but only a little.

On any showing there is a division of potentialities into two radically different levels: the level which contains the categories, those utterly general dimensions of reality of which Whitehead's philosophy gives the most complete description yet set forth, and without which as at least implicitly involved nothing at all can be conceived; and the level of specific qualities, from which it seems possible really to abstract entirely and still have meaning. Whitehead seems to be trying to deduce the specific from the generic, to show that the primordial nature of existence involves all species of quality. Is this any more credible than that all things follow from the nature of substance? It seems that either "red" is a category, as general as "process," or it is not completely general, and then we have to consider whether or not it is the law of generality that the less general should be contingent, should be external to the more general.

Of course, that there be some species or other must itself be a category. Specificity in general may be eternal, though no given species is so.

There is this advantage in restricting the eternal to the categorial universals[63] (and to God as envisaging and always *somehow* applying them). This is that the enduring subject of states (or self-identical individual) might then be given a somewhat more secure status. The enduring self might be constituted, in one aspect, by its impure potential, its own peculiar potency of becoming as a type of quality not to be found in eternal objects. (The other aspect of self-identity would be the immanence of a thing's history in its present being, by which the Whiteheadian enduring individual has a *concrete* identity woefully lacking in the older substantialist philosophies.) It sometimes seems to me that the semblance of not having enough substantiality in his societies of occasions is due to Whitehead's ascription of so much specific identity to the eternal objects as belonging to the divine self primordially, leaving only "selection" among these for the identities of lesser selves.

If arithmetic and pure geometry follow from the categories of logic, as *Principia Mathematica* seems to show, then mathematical ideas must be regarded as eternal objects, even if my suggestions be accepted. As a mathematician, Whitehead may perhaps have been unduly influenced, as in a somewhat analogous connection he thinks Plato was,[64] by the atypical character of mathematical properties, their extreme abstractness and generality. It also does not appear to me that his idea of God, or of most other subjects, would be injured—perhaps it would be clarified and strengthened—if one eliminated the idea of *eternal species*, while retaining that of eternal highest genera, including the genus of specificity as such.[65]

I should like to close by expressing the conviction that the chief obstacle to a more general appreciation of the greatness and truth of Whitehead's philosophy is not any defects it may contain, but that greatness and truth itself. Most of us, to think with any clearness, must drastically oversimplify reality. Every page of Whitehead shows that his power to grasp complex relationships and his familiarity with diverse aspects of life and the world as disclosed in science and experience are greatly superior to that of most of us teachers and writers in philosophy.

Reprinted from *The Philosophy of Alfred North Whitehead*, Library of Living Philosophers, vol. 3, ed. Paul Arthur Schilpp (Evanston & Chicago: Northwestern University Press, 1941), pp. 513-59.

CHAPTER SIX

Is Whitehead's God
the God of Religion?

Reflections suggested by Stephen Lee Ely's little book, The Religious
Availability of Whitehead's God: A Critical Analysis *(Madison: University
of Wisconsin Press, 1942). Although I cannot accept the author's
objections to Whitehead's doctrine, I find the expository portion of the
book an admirably clear and largely accurate simplified account of
Whitehead's system.*

According to Professor Ely, the Whiteheadian God is neither omnipo-
tent nor benevolent, and so is hardly the God of religion. Whitehead, he
contends, deals with the problem of evil only by giving up *both* of the
religious concepts which are at stake in the problem. Is this so?

If by all-powerful is meant "having all the power there is as one's *own*
power, so that all decision is one's own decision," then God is not
all-powerful for Whitehead. But is he for religion? The moment it is
admitted that man has freedom, that he decides at least something of what
happens, it is implicitly or explicitly admitted that some power, however
little, is man's and not God's. It will not do to say that the power is
delegated; if delegated, it is not kept. All that is kept is the power to set
limits to (perhaps even to terminate) the exercise of the delegated power.
But these limits measure the extent to which power is *not* delegated; they
do not contradict the necessity that if anything at all is delegated then not
everything is kept. If, however, it be further argued that God *might* have
kept all the power, and therefore it is all really his, then Whitehead would
say that neither philosophy nor religion justifies the notion that God had

the choice between creating and not creating free beings other than himself. Theologians, but not the prophets, tell us that God might have refrained altogether from creation. True, the notion that God acted from necessity and without freedom in creation is not religious; but it is one thing to say that God was free to create or not to create just *this* world (as much of it as depended upon his power, abstracting from creaturely decisions), and another thing to say that he was free not to create any world of free creatures at all. Necessity may have constrained him to do something—though it is no constraint, since he could not have wished to do nothing—but there may have been no necessity to do just what he did.

What, then, does religion mean by almighty? Is it not that God has "all the power over all things which is compatible with the delegation of some power to each thing in accordance with its level of being"? That is, omnipotence, in the only religiously sensible meaning, is *the ideal case of power assuming a division of power*, the maximal concentration of power that permits distribution of powers among a plurality of beings.[1] Now, for Whitehead, this is the only form of supreme power that is philosophically intelligible. For a being that had all the power would either exercise it over nothing at all or over the powerless, that is, really over nothing, if it be true that "being is power." The most perfect conceivable power is power over something that has power, and thus the maximal case of power cannot be all power as the power of one being. Whitehead does not "limit" the power of God as compared to some conceivably more powerful being; he merely points out that there is a social element in the very idea of power, an element of interaction with other power, that must be retained in forming the conception of the being whose power is the logical maximum or perfect case. In Whitehead's terms every occasion is in some measure self-determining, and in some measure passive, receptive, toward the self-determinations of others; each occasion, by "prehending" or feeling others, accepts their self-determinations as part-determinative of its own being. This applies also to the occasions which constitute the concrete or "consequent" nature of God. He allows us to determine parts of his own life, and he *cannot* decide just what this determination shall be; for that would conflict with the social character of being and of power, including the being and power of God himself.

Whitehead's distinction between God and "creativity" is taken by some to mean that there is a power beyond God's power. This seems to be an error. Creativity is not a power, but just power, and to say that there is power distinct from God's is to say that the creatures have some power of their own.

But is not God's power limited still further by Whitehead's apparent denial of creation *ex nihilo*? If the temporal process has always been going on—and we are not told of a beginning—then at all times God has had to take account of previous creaturely actions. However, this is only to concede, for every moment of time without exception, a "limitation" which, on the usual view (if taken honestly), must be conceded for every moment of time but one (the first). Also, whereas the usual view attributes to God creative action with reference to a finite past only, the alternative holds him to have been creative during an infinite past. Thus the alleged extra limitation (the absence of any first moment, untrammeled by previous acts of the creatures) is atoned for by a surplus in creative achievement of infinity over finitude. As as for the question, "Which is the more religious view?" has anyone proved that Genesis, for example, derives its religious value from the assumption, hardly explicit in the text, that God's forming of the cosmos as we know it was *not* preceded and influenced by earlier creative acts, each resulting in its own temporary universe—and so on without beginning?

Professor Ely notes that, though Whitehead holds the "primordial" aspect of the divine nature to be infinite (since it contemplates the infinity of all possibilities as such), he refers to the consequent nature as "finite." However, if I am right that Whitehead ascribes no beginning to time, then there must be for him an infinite aspect even of the consequent nature, since this involves a perfect memory of all the past and hence contains a numerical infinity of remembered events. The finitude will be in the set of new events entering the divine life at a given stage and further in the fact that even an infinite series of past events will not be "absolutely infinite," in Spinoza's terminology, for many possibilities will not have been actualized—just as the even numbers are an infinite set and yet the odd numbers are omitted from that set. To be infinite in the mathematical sense is not necessarily to be everything possible.

In view of the foregoing considerations, I suggest that Whitehead denies to God no power and no infinity which religion need claim for him. Theologians like to render themselves dizzy by such phrases as "absolute" and "infinite," but this intellectual pastime—"paying metaphysical compliments to God," Whitehead calls it—is not particularly religious. (Professor Ely, I am glad to note, is aware of this, yet at certain moments, in the heat of argument, he forgets it, or underestimates its significance for his problem, the religious character of Whitehead's God.) The "perfection" ascribed to God in the Bible is plainly enough moral and practical or dynamic, not mathematical or unambiguously static and metaphysical—as though the Scriptures had been intended to fit mechanically into the theologian's game and to warrant any sense he happens to read into such terms as perfect, immutable, and the like.

But is Whitehead's God benevolent? Whitehead seems to think so. He says of God that "love, which is partial in us, is all-embracing in him."[2] He speaks of the divine "tenderness" which "is directed toward each actual occasion, as it arises."[3] However, the author we are discussing seeks to show that Whitehead cannot really mean what these two passages seem to say.

First of all, he reminds us of the passage in which Whitehead states that God "in his primordial nature, is unmoved by love for this particular or that particular." But to say that God, in his primordial aspect, does not love this or that particular is not in the least to deny that God, in his total reality, including the "consequent nature," may love all particulars. (This is, in grudging fashion, conceded by Professor Ely.) The primordial nature is God in one abstract aspect in which he is viewed as setting the most general purpose of the universe, apart from any particular purposes for particular times and places. Even the most general purpose does refer to particulars in a general way, though not to "this or that particular." The most general aim is, "Let there be, at each moment, *some* particular values or other, and as great a total of them as possible." For, in Whitehead's view, actual value is always particular, and the only reason the primordial nature does not involve love for this or that particular is that it does not involve awareness of particulars but is that aspect of God which is concerned only with unparticularized potentialities, with the possibilities for particular values rather than the values themselves. It is in the consequent nature that there is awareness of concrete particulars and love for them, "the particular providence for particular occasions," "the love of God for the world."

However, it is claimed that, according to Whitehead, God does not really value the creaturely occasions or experiences for their own sakes but selfishly or as "at best but instruments of God's joy." To support this, Whitehead is quoted as saying that "depth of satisfaction" in the creaturely experiences is for God "an intermediate step towards fulfillment of his own being."[4] Intermediate step is equated by Professor Ely with mere instrumentality. This seems to me to betray a tendency to make the most and more than the most of any words in Whitehead that can possibly be made to support the critic's thesis. When a phrase in Whitehead flatly affirms the divine love, and there are many that do, every effort is made to explain it away; but phrases that even seem in the least to lean in a contrary direction are taken as though they were well-nigh definitive assertions of divine egoism. (I hope I do not fall into an opposite form of the same unsound procedure, but at least I may neutralize the exaggerations.) All I can see Whitehead to be saying here is that we contribute to God's values by enjoying values ourselves, by constituting a part of his satisfaction through our own. Whitehead says that "the function of being a means is not disjointed from the function of being an end. The sense of worth beyond itself is immediately enjoyed . . . in the individual self-attainment."[5]

Just what would divine altruism be if it is not that God finds his joy in that of his creatures? The good man is at least one who is made happier by the happiness of others than by their misery. You may object that a man should not make this reflexive happiness of his own the motive of action but should be moved directly by the happiness of the other. But still I ask, what is it to be moved by the happiness of the other if not to find some happiness in it one's self? However, in the purely human case, it is only very incompletely that the happiness of the other becomes a part of one's own happiness. We never fully enter into the other's happiness, and we may die before it is achieved. But God, who perfectly "prehends" all events as [or just after] they occur, always fully and identically possesses (and ever remembers) our happiness as an element in his own. Hence in him, and only in him, it is literally true that altruism and self-interest coincide. His altruism toward me is a part of his self-interest, without being any the less altruism. Omniscience means just that—that good done to others is bound to be fully enjoyed by self. For whom, then, is the good done? For the other as included in self and for the self as including the other. The latter expression is more adequate, in that the self in this case includes all selves, so that the necessary adjustments of interest between creaturely selves is in this way allowed for.

I repeat, what could the divine love be if not such an inclusion of the interest of all as elements in the self-realization of God? To expect God not to benefit by any benefits he bestows is to deny his omniscience; or it is to claim that a loving being could fully know the joy he produces in others and remain unpleased by this as well as untroubled by their sufferings. Again, if it be said that God, like the good among us, should view his own happiness as a "by-product" not to be deliberately sought, while he seeks the happiness of all other beings, I reply that whereas man has too little consciousness to go around, so that he must "forget self" if he is to remember others, God is not similarly limited, and there is no need for him to be naïve about his own interest, especially since the creatures have as much need as he can have that he should preserve and enhance his own all-sustaining life, which, Whitehead says, "floods back into the world" at each moment as inspiration in the depths of our being, where we feel ourselves as contributors to the general good, which is shared between all things (according to their several abilities) and God.

To me it seems obvious that only a mere machine that blindly passed out benefits could conform to the notion of a benevolence that had nothing to gain from the success of its services to others. And a will perfect in knowledge as well as goodness could have no means of distinguishing between success for others and success for itself, for either success could only be the maximizing of values in the beings known, since these values form the content of the divine value.

Still, you may say, may there not be emergent values of the divine experience as a whole which might perhaps be greater if something were sacrificed in the values of the included elements, the creatures? For instance, perhaps it would be better for the whole if some parts suffered, and thus afforded the whole aesthetic contrast. Does not Whitehead say that in God's way of experiencing our sorrows their evil is "overcome" and that evil "becomes a stepping stone in the all-embracing ideals of God"? So the suspicion is voiced by Professor Ely that God may even seek human suffering for his own ends. However, there is practically nothing in Whitehead to suggest definitely that God does anything more or less than get the most good possible out of such creaturely evil as he cannot prevent (without a greater evil, such as an undue curtailment of freedom in the creatures). Wise and good men always make the best of things, even evils, and there can be no egoism in this unless it is done at the cost of diminishing the good of others. In Whitehead's view there is bound to be suffering, because of conflicts between creaturely freedoms. Moreover, suffering for Whitehead is not the only evil. The lapse into negligible value through tedium is no less to be opposed, since it threatens the destruction of all values whatever. Now God is concerned to avoid tedium not only for himself but (it is part of the same thing) for others. To prove egoism or cruelty in God, one must show that he has more to gain from creaturely suffering, as alternative to boredom, than the creatures and less to gain from creaturely happiness. It is as though a man were to have more to gain from the ill-health than the health of his own bodily cells, by health meaning vitality and intensity, as well as internal harmony, in the life of these lesser beings. Or as though a man able to choose, aware of all alternatives, and too well endowed himself to envy another, were to prefer, for his own happiness, that those with whom he associates should be in misery.

Even could one make a case for cruelty in God, it would still not be clear that it was egoism. For if God needs something, then all would have a need for him to get it. Apart from God we are nothing, in Whitehead's philosophy. What we, in the depths of our being, live for, our "insistent craving" is "that zest for existence be refreshed by the ever-present, unfading importance of our immediate actions, which perish and yet live forevermore."[6] Death, the noncoincidence in us of self-interest and altruism, and the fact that we forget, and thus lose, much of the values of life almost as fast as we achieve them, make it impossible for a man genuinely to live simply for himself, taken in abstraction from something more comprehensive and more permanent. The only rational purpose a man can have is to realize himself and his fellows as ends which are included in a greater and more lasting end, and by virtue of this inclusion serve in a sense as means—though a sense easily misunderstood if means is construed as mere instrument instead of as integral part. We are means only as ends, intrinsic values self-realized. If, then, our ultimate inclusive end does not wish us well in the same sense as we, when true to our best self, wish ourselves well, there is a contradiction in the system. One ought to try to interpret the system as consistent, and I suspect it can very fairly be done.

One thing is clear. To take the phrase "God 'overcomes' evil" as showing that Whitehead thinks God makes it to be no longer an evil that evil has occurred is to contradict many other things he says concerning the reality of evil. Amazingly enough, Professor Ely quarrels with Whitehead, in other places, for *not* securing the sheer cancellation of evil. Granting, says our critic, that the evil is overcome for God, for us it remains that we have suffered. The creatures are but "tiny fragments of a pattern that they cannot ever appreciate." Well, we cannot fully appreciate the pattern of the world, since we are not God. And that part of the pattern that comes after our death, perhaps we will never know in detail at all. But not being omniscient, not being divine, is bound to have its limiting effects according to any theology. And, at least, we can have some dim sense of the world pattern as it is now; and if the pattern as it turns out after we are no longer living is perhaps not destined to be our possession, does it follow that we cannot accept it as fulfillment of our aim? Is self-interest all our interest? If Professor Ely really means this, then indeed he can never understand Whitehead, scarcely a line of whose metaphysical and theological writings has been written without some reference to the social character of motivation. Can we care for posterity, including later phases in the divine life, *only* if we are to be there through personal immortality in the conventional sense? (Professor Ely does not discuss immortality in this sense.) Is the demand for an absolute reward, an absolute coincidence of self-interest and altruism for us men, really a high religious attitude? An ignorant being is bound to work good and ill upon others without fully possessing the good or ill himself. Virtue for such a being is to perform deeds calculated on principle to result in good for others, whether or not there be reward. He who says that belief in the divine enjoyment of a richer life than ours, to which our own can contribute, and which in turn will contribute to lives of creatures yet to come, can be no consolation to us for the trials of existence is simply denying that we can genuinely love either God or man. If, at the same time, it be urged that God ought not to have any regard for his own interest, but should practice sheer altruism unrelated to his own self-realization (whatever such altruism might be) on the ground that otherwise God will "not be good in our sense," then the argument seems more tortuous than convincing.

It is possible to imagine a conflict between altruism and self-interest in God if one forgets that God has to love all as well as each. He never has to choose, I should suppose, between his own interest and that of "others," for these are related as whole and parts; but he does face terrible conflicts between the interests of this other and that other or between this element and that element of his self-interest. This, as Professor Ely well says, is the tragedy of God. Free beings cannot be coerced or infallibly persuaded into harmony among themselves, and the resulting discord is within God, not external to him. He suffers as well as enjoys our lives, and thus, Whitehead says, he is "the great companion—the fellow-sufferer who understands." When, therefore, it is complained that God fails to remove the fact that we have suffered, part of the answer is that he himself has suffered too. Of course, he has had this suffering in a larger perspective, but that means suffering on a vaster scale as well as enjoyment on a vaster scale. True, the total character of God's life may always be overwhelmingly joyous, as ours is not always. But this does not mean, according to any cogent evidence I can see in Whitehead's system, that the suffering is not real as such or that God is glad we suffered and thus compelled him to suffer, except so far as, for us as well as for him, there was perhaps no alternative at the time that would have avoided the evil while involving equal good—equal escape from boredom, for example. But the free creatures are sure constantly [often?] to miss better alternatives.

Another criticism of Whitehead is that God, in making our lives portions of his own, deindividualizes us. It is held that God could not "merge me and my values into an indefinitely immense system and still claim that I have maintained *my* individuality and my values." Again, "my achieved individual values may be eternally the means, immortally contemplated by God, but he sees them as part of a system. Their individuality, even for God, has perished." This seems to amount to affirming that the many cannot really "become one" while remaining themselves, or that Whitehead's doctrine, not just of God, but of everything, is untenable. For the whole system is built on the theory that individuality can include other individuality as such, literally have or "prehend" it. Individuality thus is opposed not to inner complexity but to lack of integration of this complexity. This is the doctrine of individuals within individuals which I have called the idea of the "compound individual," and there seems no doubt it is Whitehead's. One proof is that for him all actual value is particular, and hence if we became values for God only by losing our individuality, then by just so much would we fail to contribute to his value. It is also an aesthetic fact, I think (and Whitehead frequently appeals to this fact), that the more individually differentiated and integrated the parts in an aesthetic whole, itself well integrated, may be, the more rich the individuality of the whole. That is why the drama at its best is such a superior form of art. And God is the being whose capacity to appropriate other individualities into himself without deindividualizing them is uniquely perfect. It is only we who must, in a sense, "abstract" in prehending other occasions as data in our own experience, if not by totally excluding anything of them as individuals, at least by relegating them largely to a position of faint relevance in the background of our experience, the "fringe" (James's term) rather than the focus. But God prehends things, we are explicitly told, "without loss of immediacy," that is, with their full individuality as relevant and conscious datum. Thus the "final end [is] . . . in the perfect multiplicity of the attainment of *individual* types of self-existence." [7]

It seems remarkable that Professor Ely sees confirmation of the suspicion of divine egoism in the fact that Whitehead says beauty is more fundamental than truth and that even goodness is the aim at beauty. For beauty turns out, when we look at Whitehead's definition, to be his explication of what others call happiness. For he says it is the mutual adjustment or harmonization of elements in experience, avoiding the two extremes of tedium and painful conflict. Thus to say that the aim of the universe is beauty is to say it is happiness. God seeks the happiness of each creature as element in his own happiness. Clearly this is not aestheticism in any sense in which there is conflict with ethical considerations. The ethical side comes in through the social character of being, which makes the aim at beauty an aim not just for self, and also makes it include, as a supreme form of beauty, the beauty of companionship and generosity.

Says Whitehead, in his latest utterance (published apparently after Professor Ely had completed his manuscript):

> The ascription of mere happiness, and of arbitrary power to the nature of God is a profanation. This nature . . . is founded on ideals of perfection, moral and aesthetic. It receives into its unity the scattered effectiveness of realized activities, transformed by the supremacy of its own ideals. The result is Tragedy, Sympathy, and the Happiness evoked by actualized Heroism.
>
> Of course we are unable to conceive the experience of the Supreme Unity of Existence. But these are the human terms in which we can glimpse the origin of that drive towards limited ideals of perfection which haunts the Universe.[8]

God's happiness is tragic and heroic by virtue of its sympathetic sharing in our sufferings. Professor Ely's interpretation seems to be close to the profanation of attributing mere happiness to God. Indeed, by suggesting sadism, Professor Ely carries the profanation further.

Perhaps what is implicit in our author's critique of Whitehead's doctrine is the notion that a benevolent God should bring us eventually into some heaven where we would no longer encounter evil at all. Presumably the evil of knowing that we once fell into evil must then become wholly a good. What this means I scarcely know, and I doubt that religion at its best demands it. There may be personal immortality in the traditional sense—Whitehead's philosophy seems to leave the question open—but even so we would still really have suffered, and furthermore we would presumably suffer throughout our endless future, if it be true that tragedy arises from freedom. Is freedom to vanish in heaven? And if tragedy does not arise from freedom, then surely the problem of evil is insoluble!

Although it is not "personal immortality" in the usual sense, the form of immortality Whitehead's system insures us is in a way more clearly personal than the conventional form. For it is the perfect preservation of our actual life on earth, just as it took place from the inside, in the imperishable divine experience, which, having once received our experiences, never allows their vividness to fade. Thus our entire earthly personality is undying, even though perhaps we are given no post-terrestrial experiences linked by *our* memories to the earthly ones. After all, it is not too easy to see how the same human or quasi-human nondivine personality is to go on *forever* accumulating new experiences and yet remain self-identical—in any significant sense the same person. The finitude of our type of being seems appropriate to the finitude of our lives. If, however, it would be possible to have significant finite self-identity through an endless life, and if this would mean more valuable experiences than could be achieved in any other way, then Whitehead's God would, it seems, have reason to bring it about. The whole matter is difficult enough, for natural theology at least—whether Whitehead's or another's.

A last objection to Whitehead's theology is that it is hard to tell how much in it follows rigorously from his system, as based on secular experience, and how much must be derived from special religious intuitions. Whitehead has sometimes spoken as though not much religious character can be imputed to God by a purely secular philosophy. It appears, however, that he has in recent years come to feel more than at first that such terms as "love" in relation to God have a good technical foundation. The theory of the "consequent nature" of God, at first neglected or half-developed, has in fact, as I believe, made this inevitable. True, in *Process and Reality* it is said that nothing like proof as to the nature of God is to be looked for. But in a still more recent work it is urged that in philosophy generally proof is essentially secondary to intuition. My own feeling is that to attempt to separate the God of Whitehead's system from the God of love which he certainly does at times speak of would serve no purpose and would weaken both the systematic and the religious aspects of his philosophy. For example, Professor Ely sees no reason in the system why God should preserve all achieved values in his own being. But God, even the god of the system, does things for the sake of value, and what would be the value of dropping values once realized? I believe nothing but trouble would result from such an assumption. Similarly with God's "superjective nature" by which, as enriched by the world, he in turn passes back into the world to share this enhancement. What is this but the general systematic principle of Whitehead that actualities acquire relationship to other actualities by prehending them, feeling their internal content? It would be an arbitrary exception if the creatures did not prehend the consequent nature of God, an exception which would, I think, wreck the system no less surely than it would spoil its religious value.

A quotation from Whitehead may help us to summarize his doctrine. In the "Ingersoll Lecture on Immortality," he says:

> This immortality of the World of Action, derived from its transformation in God's nature is beyond our imagination to conceive. The various attempts at description are often shocking and profane. What does haunt our imagination is that the immediate facts of

present action pass into permanent significance for the Universe. The insistent notion of Right and Wrong, Achievement and Failure, depends upon this background. Otherwise every activity is merely a passing whiff of insignificance.[9]

Only theism can explain what is meant by achievement, can unite the sense that we are self-ends with the sense that we live not only for others but for something that neither our death or forgetfulness nor the death or forgetfulness of the human race can ever simply cancel out and reduce to nonentity. If the achievement of life is living, then it is our living itself that must be added to the universe as a value once for all; and only a love that savors the living of others as part of its own achieved being can enable ignorant, forgetful, and mortal beings to realize a public and lasting end through their own self-realization.

Reprinted from *Ethics* 53 (April 1943): 219-27. Copyright©1943 by The University of Chicago Press.

Whitehead's
Philosophy of Reality
as Socially Structured Process

There are two basic attitudes in philosophy, and always have been. These are: the minimalistic, skeptical, or positivistic attitude, on the one side; and the maximalistic, speculative, or metaphysical attitude, on the other. According to the first, the aim of philosophy is to rid us of illusions, confusions, and unverifiable statements, leaving us with only those forms of knowledge which are *clear* and *testable* by interpersonally convincing evidence. In our day, this means that we are left with science (whose success becomes an unexplained miracle, in that any inquiry into a principle of order in the world is rejected as metaphysical) together with the irreducible core of commonsense beliefs by which we obviously must be guided in actual living, whether we admit them in words or not. According to the contrary attitude, the aim of philosophy is to do full justice to all aspects of experience, even those which, perhaps, can never be made entirely clear and obvious, or put to any unambiguous test such as will convince every intelligent person. In men with this attitude the greatest fear is not that they may be unclear, or adopt beliefs with insufficient justification, but that they may miss the full meaning or nature of life by confining attention to the superficial aspects which, for that very reason, are the obvious ones, and the ones upon which general agreement can be secured.

The issue was once put whimsically by Whitehead, in a comparison between himself and Russell: "Bertie says that I am muddleheaded; but I say that he is simple-minded." There you have it. To men of the Russell type, the Whiteheads always appear muddleheaded, and just as surely, to men of the Whitehead type the Russells appear simple-minded. Whitehead once heard Russell discourse on "value." Russell, it appears, had suggested that Pavlov's conditioned reflex experiments furnished our best clue to a theory of value. Whitehead rose and remarked: "There is a lost dialogue of Plato's on The Good, and I have often wondered what could have been in that dialogue. Now I know: when one of Pavlov's dog's mouth waters, that is the good!" Russell was thinking: how can "the good" be made a clear and controllable idea? Whitehead was thinking: controllable or not, let's talk about the good, in all its subtlety and depth, and not something else.

There may well be an ultimate dilemma here for the human mind: if you want clarity and agreement, at all costs, the price may be that you will do little justice to the complexity and hidden depths of experience; if you want adequacy to this complexity at all costs, the price may be that you will not be able to maintain a high standard of clarity and intersubjective confirmability in your thinking, speaking, or writing.

Of course, one may aim at a balance between the desire to be clear and the desire to be adequate to the richness of experience. This indeed was Whitehead's aim, and I think he came measurably close to achieving it. Still I fear that he had to sacrifice something of clarity—at least, of easy, obvious clarity. His works are difficult. I am confident, however, that no other philosopher of comparable clarity is more profound, more nearly adequate to the full meaning of life, and that no other philosopher of comparable adequacy is more clear. In our century and for our century, there is, in my opinion, no serious rival to the Whiteheadian philosophy, as an expression of the maximalistic or speculative aspect of the philosophic enterprise. This conviction is not due, in any simple way, to early conditioning. Before I had paid much attention to Whitehead, and before he had written his more speculative books, I had written a doctoral thesis, followed by two years of study in Germany, and had reached some of the main outlines of the philosophy to which I still adhere. But when I came to Whitehead I found in him a coherent system containing most of the significant ideas which I had detected as scattered fragments in various twentieth-century philosophies, or had arrived at in my own reflections.

It is easy, I think, to see that the rather widespread neglect of this philosopher is largely coincident with the almost equally widespread neglect of speculative philosophy itself. The arguments given for this antispeculative attitude are relevant almost exclusively to types of speculation very different from Whitehead's, and thus they do not justify the neglect of his works. One reason for the neglect has been that many of his later works, in which alone the system is made explicit in anything like its full scope and depth, were for a time out of print. Now, with the publication of a comprehensive anthology of his writings, embracing a number of important selections from these unobtainable books, that difficulty is in part removed.[1] The aim of the selection is to present the essential Whiteheadian ideas, without duplication. This has been quite well accomplished, in most respects.

I take the occasion of this publication to suggest some outlines of this system of "Speculative Philosophy" (Whitehead's own term). I shall not adhere closely to Whitehead's terminology, but shall put the ideas in my own way. [In doing this I may be making explicit some points which are only implicit in Whitehead, or developing—I hope in a reasonable way—some of his principles, e.g., the ontological principle, also categorial coherence.]

The speculative question is this: What ideas are strictly universal, not special cases of more general ideas? Is "matter" universal, with "mind" a special case; or vice versa; or are both special cases of some third notion? Again, is "becoming" a special mode of "being," or is that which simply is, but does not become, a special case or aspect of that which becomes? (In this dichotomy, at least, there can hardly be a third term, for a thing either becomes or does not.) Still again, is value a special kind of fact, or is fact a kind of value; or are both instances of something neutral to this distinction? Or finally, in the contrast between what is "relative," i.e., made what it is by relations to other things, and what is not thus "constituted by relations," which is the more universal conception?

Some philosophers deny that such questions as the foregoing need have an answer. For, they say, mind and matter, for instance, might be equally ultimate, and there may be no third something of which mind is one special kind and matter another. However, Whitehead would argue, one cannot justify dualism in this fashion. For, granting that there is mind *and* matter, what is the "and," the togetherness of the two? It is either material, or mental, or some third sort of thing not yet accounted for. Whichever way you answer, at least one of the two—mind, matter—is reduced to a special case. For in the totality "X and Y," X is one aspect or constituent and Y the other, yet the togetherness is itself one entity. Thus there is something, the togetherness of mind and matter, which is either material, or mental, or some third sort of thing; and if this togetherness is material, then mind is only one part or aspect of matter; if it is mental, then matter is only one aspect of mind, and if it is neither mind nor matter, then both of these are but aspects of some "neutral" kind of something.

Let us make this question more concrete. In actual experience, mind and matter are together, namely, in our experiences. If we know matter at all, we somehow perceive it. But we also perceive mind, for at each moment we are aware both of physical things *and* of our own experiences, feelings, thoughts, desires, and so on. Thus both minds (I use the word "mind" to refer to the reality of experiences) and bodies are together as things given in human experiences. Every experience has an aspect of sense perception, and also an aspect of self-awareness, or awareness of experience itself. The latter includes, or perhaps consists, in memory—in part "immediate memory," the sense of just having felt or sensed or thought a certain something. Thus our abstract argument about "together-ness" is no mere play on words. An experience *is* somehow a unity of "physical" and "psychical." But experience is just what we mean by the "psychical." So it seems that the universal concept is that of mind rather than of matter.

Materialists sometimes say that while matter or the physical is observed, mind, soul, or the psychical is not. They forget that "observed" is a psychical conception! A camera may take a photograph, but it observes nothing, for it asks no questions and seeks no knowledge. Through the camera, men may observe things. Also, memory is a sort of observation of past experience, as sense perception is of inanimate objects.

Here then we have the first two Whiteheadian doctrines: first, in all dualisms, one of the two terms (or else still a third term) must be the inclusive one which describes the togetherness of the two; second, experience contains the togetherness of itself and matter, and hence the latter is somehow an aspect of experience. (It is not solely an aspect of *our human* experiences; that is another question, to which we shall return. However, it *is* an aspect of these experiences, whatever else it may be; and this illustrates the inclusiveness of experience in a special case.)

Let us now add a third point. It is always possible to state a dualism in such a way that there can be no third or neutral term, so that the togetherness (what Whitehead calls the "coherence") of the two concepts must be describable without going beyond them. Thus if, instead of "mind" and "matter," we say, what feels, senses, remembers, desires, or thinks, and what does none of these things, then anything either does or does not perform one or more of these actions or functions. Now the materialists say that some physical bodies feel, desire, and so on, and some simply do not. Very well, what is the togetherness of the bodies that feel and the bodies that do not? Is this togetherness itself felt and constituted by feeling, or is it a mere property of things which do not feel? But surely a thing without feeling cannot contain both things with and things without feeling! For then it would contain feeling after all. The inclusive reality must have all the positive properties of the included realities. It follows that the final concept here is that of the sentient, not of the insentient. The latter is included in, and somehow is a special case of the sentient. We shall see what this means presently.

Let us first consider some additional dualities. Does that which is real by virtue of becoming, or that which is real without becoming, include the other? The answer is that, since a totality with some new items is a new totality, even though it includes other items not new, while an old totality must consist only of old items, therefore the becoming of novelty, rather than mere being, explains the togetherness of the two. Being is an aspect of creative becoming, not vice versa. Thus the Philosophy of Process is not the result of an arbitrary preference for becoming, but of the simple logical insight that given a variable, X, and a constant C, then the togetherness of the two, XC, is a variable.

Thus variability is the ultimate conception. (If you say there is no variability, then you destroy the contrast upon which both concepts depend.) To derive constancy as a special case or aspect, we have only to remark that even to speak of X as one variable through its variations is to refer to an aspect which is fixed throughout. To create the new we not only do not have to have exclusively new items, but we must not. For things wholly without anything in common could not even be compared. However, the point often overlooked here is that the common element is contained in the diverse realities as a "common denominator," an abstraction, while the concrete as a whole is the diverse, not the common. Being, as identical, is in the becoming of the new, not vice versa. From successive events, we can abstract what is common; but each event is more than any such common denominator of itself and its predecessors.

Take again the duality, "fact" and "value." In any actual value there are facts. We can enjoy only the situation we are in, the facts we have on hand. We may supplement these facts by dreams, but the facts enter into the value of the total experience, nonetheless. Values are enjoyed facts. But also, no known fact is less than an enjoyed (or suffered) fact. For mere neutral registering of the valueless must be left to cameras. It cannot be the action of living animals. Thus "value" is essential to fact, since it alone expresses the relation, actual or at least potential, of fact with experience.

Finally, take the relative and the nonrelative. How can the nonrelative constitute the togetherness of itself and the relative? Such togetherness must contain relations and be in part constituted by them. So we see that relativity, not absoluteness, is ultimate. "The Absolute" is only an aspect of the relative, not vice versa. How can this be conceived? Quite easily. The absolute is whatever all alternatively possible relative terms have in common. Again we confront the idea of a common denominator, an abstract constituent which enters into diverse concretes. For Whitehead, every event is itself an absolute with respect to later events. For it is that to which every later event must relate itself as causal condition or predecessor. What we do now is thus (looking forward) an absolute, for subsequent actions must conform to this present act, must contain it as constituent of *their* past. On the other hand, *it* does not have to conform to subsequent actions, for these do not exist as yet. Relativity is retrospective, not prospective; present events are absolute only so far as the future is concerned; they are relative to the past out of which they arose, with which they had to conform as best they could.

Is there anything which is absolute in *every* regard? Whitehead says, yes, there are aspects common to all possible events, regardless of date. For instance, all have the property of being events, and of being retrospectively relative and prospectively absolute. These two properties are themselves common denominators of all relations among events, and so completely absolute. All such common denominators ("eternal objects") have their togetherness in what Whitehead calls the Primordial Nature of God. This is strictly absolute, in that all possible relations involve it, while it is neutral to the differences among these relations. It is the Absolute of absolutes, the only perfectly absolute thing, neutral to *every* relational alternative.

But unlike most philosophers, Whitehead asks the further question, is there a Relative of relatives, a term eminent among relative things as The Absolute is among absolute things? It seems there must be, since the final togetherness of absolute and relative things must itself be relative, for reasons already indicated. So, while the Primordial Nature of God may unite in itself all that is wholly absolute, something else must unite this with all that is relative. There must be an all-inclusive relative thing. This is called the Consequent Nature of God. "Consequent" means relative, made what it is by relations to all other things. It is consequent upon these, and it constitutes their final togetherness. Since the relative includes the absolute, the Consequent Nature includes the Primordial Nature. The former is not merely the Consequent Nature *of* God, it *is* God; while the Primordial Nature is not God, but merely a nature which he has. However, one may distinguish three things: (1) there is the Primordial Nature, the absolute constant or abstract least common denominator of process; (2) there is, as an aspect of this, the *constant requirement* that there *must always be* something more concrete, which itself is not constant or absolute, but partly new at each stage of process; (3) there is the actual concrete state of the given moment, God-now as constituting the togetherness of the world-now. Just as "now" is a "token-reflexive" or context-dependent word, denoting a new date each time it is uttered so is "God now," denoting the actual state of God which is inclusive of the actual state of the world. A philosophy of process denies that there is any totality of reality to which nothing can ever be added, and which can be labeled once for all as *The* Universe or *The* Real. What we have to do with is always *our* universe; and our forefathers' universe lacked some of the features of ours.

In such a philosophy the old notion of timeless omniscience is taken as self-contradictory, for there is no fixed totality of "all process" for such a purely eternal knowledge to know. Rather, process is in itself unfinished and inexhaustible. This does not exclude an ideally adequate and comprehensive knowledge; for the universe now is a totality (I cannot consider here the difficult question of the relation of this to relativity physics) and hence it can be totally known; and when there is more to know, the new totality can also be totally known. It is arguable that this contains all the real value that there was in the old idea of a purely eternal or timeless omniscience, without the troublesome paradoxes to which it led, for instance, how the temporal things eternally known could fail to be equally eternal as terms of the eternal cognitive relation of knowing them.

I wish now to try, in brief outline, to clear up the question of "mind" and "matter," discussed earlier. Whitehead is not the kind of idealist or subjectivist who denies or doubts the reality of the physical world of organisms, minerals, planets, stars—the spatial system with which physics, astronomy, and biology deal. His point is only that we can form no conception of the *nature* of the physical except in terms of the nature of experience. For the unity of our experience is the unity in which everything is initially found, and only by abstraction from or analogy with this unity can we understand *any* concrete unity. For instance, take the unity of present with past, which is implied in the idea of causality. A thing arises out of conditions and its nature expresses its origin. But no amount of staring at the things we visually perceive exhibits such a relationship to the past. What we see, colored surfaces, tell no tales of origin. We can infer origins because we remember cases in which *this* happened when and only when *that* had previously happened. But this is knowledge from memory, it is not seen in the thing we are looking at now. But let us consider our self-knowledge, our awareness of our own experiences. Each of these experiences involves at least some memory of preceding experiences. And here memory is not merely a means to enable us to infer knowledge of connections between present events and past ones; memory here *is* a connection of present and past. For present experience *is* a remembering experience, and if its memories had been otherwise, it would have had a different quality as experience. [It is also a perceiving experience, and this relates it to the past. What this and the next paragraph should have discussed is prehension, as common to memory and perception. See the next chapter.] This is not proposed as an inference, but as a description of what we experience. To remember having just been very angry is to feel now the emotional disturbance and intensity of the anger, even though we may have begun to change our attitude toward one of forgiveness or even amusement. Memory imports quality from the past into the present. But one cannot visually see present quality as containing reference to past quality. The conclusion is that awareness through memory of the nature of experience is a more profound approach to reality than mere vision, which as Whitehead says is "superficial." There are forms of life, even men, without vision, but none wholly without [perception or] memory. Memory is our chief clue to the relativity of events to their conditions in previous events. Memory *is* something in the present conditioned by the past.

To form a notion of what in inanimate nature connects events with their conditions we face the alternative: *either* we try to generalize the notion of memory [and perception] in every possible way, for instance so as to allow for vast specific differences between various levels and types, such as human memory, canine memory, amoebic memory, molecular memory, atomic memory, protonic memory—or we refuse to employ the idea of memory, generalized as much as possible, as our clue to connections among events. But then we shall find that we have no other clue. We have thrown away the one key which we possess. Philosophers who do this tell us that there is no key, and therefore there can be no lock, no secret to lay bare. There is indeed no *other* key, but since these philosophers say nothing about this one (I could give forty cases with only slight research), I must regard them as begging the question.

What Whitehead is saying then is this: when we really understand psychological conceptions in their full generality we shall also understand the principles of biology and physics. For there is no lower limit to the psychological problem. Amoebae react to stimuli, and this is what we mean by perception, as seen from the standpoint of the external observer. But molecules react too, and so do all the primary individuals in nature. Cameras, as we have remarked, do not perceive, but their "reaction" is mere shorthand for the behavior of their molecules. You may argue that this is also true of amoebae or human beings. But in the case of human beings we are conscious of the unity of ourselves as active. And the amoeba makes upon an attentive observer an impression, which the camera does not, of acting *as one*. So do molecules when we "observe" them intellectually, in terms of our best physical knowledge. Thus the way is open to extend the psychological interpretation as far down as you please; or to stop short where you please. What is not a matter of choice is this, that if and where you stop short, that point will mark the limit of your understanding of the nature of things, in this sense, that whatever is not interpreted psychologically will be understood only in terms of spatiotemporal relational structures, with no possibility of conceiving the natures of the entities which serve as terms for the spatiotemporal relationships in question. What we see, besides such structures, are only colors, but these, as remarked above, tell no tales about their relativities to the past. They have no causal character that can be discerned.

Whitehead's philosophy, in sum, is a philosophy which makes process and relativity the inclusive conceptions, and which makes experience as such the universal form of reality; but it regards *human* experience as merely one of a vast variety of kinds of experiences making up nature, with a supreme form of experience constituting the all-inclusive Consequent State of God, the constant character of all such states being the Primordial Nature of God. This last is the eternal Ideal inspiring all process, including the process of divine experience itself. It is roughly what Aristotle called "God" (*Theos*), but which for Whitehead is only an abstraction from the concrete divine Process.

One technical conception is too central to be omitted even from this bare sketch of a subtle and complex philosophy. It is the notion of an "occasion" or "actual entity." This refers to a least unit of process, a unit-becoming, or quantum of process. For, according to Whitehead, becoming is not continuous but discrete. We have only a finite number of experiences between waking and going to sleep. Each has the length of one "specious present," perhaps a twentieth of a second. But this time-length refers only to an average for human experiences. Birds, living more rapidly, with higher bodily temperatures, probably have a shorter present, and reptiles or fish, at least in cold air or water, one considerably longer, while on the atomic level there must be unit-becomings, "experient occasions," thousands or millions of times shorter than a twentieth of a second.

The word "actual," in "actual entity," is carefully chosen. A unit-event does not "exist," for it is not common sense to use this word for events. They occur, or are actual. The word entity is also carefully chosen. One cannot say "thing," for in common speech things are houses, trees, planets, and the like, and these "exist" by virtue of a series of events embodying a certain character. The *existence* of "things" is the *actuality* of events with the special characters connoted by the things in question. If the same house-character pervades a solid sequence of physical events visually observed or observable, we say the same house exists during the time of the sequence. What is observed is precisely the persistence of the character and the solidity of the sequence, that is, the absence of temporal gaps, at least for our perception. The "thing," the house, as observed is nothing, according to Whitehead, except the character as in the sequence. And I think Whitehead can safely defy anyone to observe anything more. Thus when we examine the matter we see that Whitehead's technical term, *actual entity*, is highly appropriate, and could not easily be replaced. Mere "event" would not do, for in common speech this term is used for such topics as the outbreak of a war, the signing of a contract, and so on, and these involve, for Whitehead, a vast number of actual entities or unit becomings which happen to share or somehow exhibit an overall pattern of special interest to the speaker or writer. Whitehead wants to refer to a much more definite concept. "Unit-happening," "quantum-process," "unit-event," could all be used, but actual occasion, or actual entity, have the merit of giving expression to the doctrine that actuality is the basic concept in this philosophy, not existence. For if certain events are actual, then certain "things" or persons will exist; but to assert the former conveys *more*. Thus, granting that Churchill exists, we can still ask, *how* does he exist, as sick in bed, in good health, sleeping, walking, talking, reading, etc.? But if we know the sequence of actual entities currently embodying the Churchillian character, and prolonging the sequence constituting the Churchillian life, then we know the answers to these questions.

This is the first fully articulate doctrine of "reality" (meaning that which is opposed to fiction or mere fancy) as inclusively process. Beings are finally in happenings, not happenings in beings. Aristotle and Leibniz worked out the best versions of the two possible ways of trying to conceive the alternative: happenings are in beings. The choice, for all the future, lies among these three possibilities. With respect to this issue, you cannot, I am inclined to think, substantially improve upon these men, you must choose among them. In two thousand years, there have been only these three. The rest are merely vaguer, or more confused, in their ways of saying what one of these philosophers says. Personally, I have little doubt that Whitehead's way substantially includes what is sound in the other two, while the others are unable to state with comparable effectiveness certain additional things which Whitehead is able to say. The speech habits of everyday life according to which, for instance, every time from this organism there issues the word "I," the referent is the same person, traceable to birth in June, 1897, in a small town in Pennsylvania, are translatable, so far as I can see without remainder, into terms of Actual Entities, with their relativities, sequences, more or less abstract identities, memories, "objectifications," or "prehensions," of their predecessors, their "personally—or impersonally—ordered societies" (linear or nonlinear sequences), with the "defining characteristic" of each society (what every member inherits from its predecessors). By such notions, Whitehead carefully provides for the ordinary ways of speaking of things and persons which persist through change.

Leibniz's view is rather different. He holds that a man, at any time, and just in being himself, includes all the events, experiences, acts, of his entire life, so that from the first moment the man existed, all that "was to happen" to him was already somehow in his individuality. Thus becoming is wholly contained within being. But then does anything really become? If the future is entirely real now, how is it future? Aristotle is too close to common sense to say such a thing. But what then does he say? Nothing clear-cut, but something subtle, complicated, never fully defined, concerning matter, form, essence, privation, accident, and so on, in the midst of which the elementary question gets lost: Is being in what becomes, or is what becomes in what simply is? Leibniz and Whitehead share the honor of alone dealing directly and sharply with *this* question. But whereas Leibniz defies common sense, and in the end leaves all concepts problematic in meaning, since what may qualify the man later really, it appears, qualifies him now, and thus now and later are confused, Whitehead takes the only remaining way out, and regards "the man" as a persisting character qualifying events, rather than the events as characters successively qualifying the man. This has the merit of expressing what we observe. For no one observes his later experiences as qualifications of the "self" which was given in earlier experience; *that* self was and is qualified only by the earlier experiences. Thus the self as really possessing all the experiences, present and remembered, is a new total reality each time it is referred to. It is a novel creation. "I" is then a token-reflexive sign, one getting its particular meaning from the occasion of its use. "I was born in Pennsylvania" refers to a common character of all the sequence of events leading up to the present experience in which is the conscious use of the word. Here we have a predicate ("traceable to birth in Pennsylvania") common to all members of the sequence. But "I have just had a new idea" refers to a predicate unique to recent members of the sequence.

There are many gradations between the two extremes. "I" sometimes refers to the identical individuality always there from 1897 until now, with the properties included in this identity; but often it refers to an individuality which has not existed nearly so long, and to properties emerging with this new individuality. What then is the togetherness of the two, the old, long-persistent self, and the new self? Leibniz gave one of two possible answers: the old, original self possessed and possesses everything. But this is paradoxical. Surely it is the new self which inherits the original self, in memory possessing it, so far as memory is effectively achieved, while only the latest experience, with its unity of awareness, its "I," is the final subject for all the predicates now true of "me." That me which my parents identified when they gave me a name as a child did not contain my present thoughts as its properties in any way whatever, and if it did not contain these thoughts, then to say that it now nonetheless "has" them is to assert that novelty can somehow be insinuated into an identity. On the contrary, insert the least novelty into something, and to that extent it becomes a new total reality, for xy is a different totality from x as not containing y. Accordingly, what you are really saying is that, while there is a new totality, what is not new in it is more important than what is new. But granting that, it remains true that it *is* a novel actual entity, and that the subject of both the old and the new predicates is the new subject, while the old subject still has only the old predicates. The believer of my childhood notions cannot possibly *be* the believer of my contradictory adult notions. That childhood believer can never be other than childish throughout all future time.

Evidence that Whitehead's theory is not an idle rearrangement of words can be seen by considering how it alters one's view of death. Common sense here gets into trouble, and those philosophies which leave the ambiguities of common sense unresolved get into the same trouble. Common sense inclines us to suppose that *either* the ego must go on to new experiences after death, *or*, as the only alternative, death is the outright cancellation of one's personal reality. Until death, one goes on existing, and there is seemingly no problem of permanence, and then abruptly—the end, unless one wakes up to find oneself in heaven or hell.

But this is a confusion. The self of my childhood experiences already has perished, humanly speaking, except so far as it is retained in the depths of the memories of my more recent selves. And all my selves have perished, with the same qualification, except the latest actual present self, the believer of what I just now believe, and feeler of what I just now feel. Thus far more than 99 percent of my personal actuality has already perished! Millions of experiences, each with its own qualities, are now telescoped into one latest experience, and otherwise are (on the human level) almost as nothing. Death merely removes the (vastly) less than 1 percent; it is thus not the essential problem of immortality at all. The primary question is not that of "survival" but of whether the pale persistence of past actual entities in present human memory is all that there is, or whether there is a more excellent form of memory by which past actuality is fully possessed "forevermore." Thus our real permanence must be in the Consequent Nature of God.

Take another issue, that of self-interest and altruism. Most philosophers have said: I love myself because, after all, I *am* myself; but that I should love others is either a mystery, or it means that I see in them contributors to my own welfare.

Thus our natural selfishness is given a metaphysical ultimacy which makes it awkward to express the empirical facts according to which people are almost as ready to neglect their own future advantage as to neglect [that of] other people. The only self one *always* in a sense loves is the self of the present or the very near future; otherwise the interests of all future selves, whether called by one's own name or another's, have to take their chances of receiving or failing to receive attention. Self-interest, in the calculating sense, involving foresight, is really one kind of altruism, a kind of generosity or sympathy of a present consciousness for a future consciousness. Whether or not, then, this future consciousness will bear my name or be associated with this organism now typing is a secondary matter which I may, or may not, be taking particularly to heart. By adopting this view we deprive selfishness of metaphysical inevitability and clear the way for the operation of empirical influences making for a good balance between provision for the personal and for the nonpersonal futures, unconfused by dogmas of self-love as coinciding with self-identity.

Thus, in two crucial cases, we see that the issue is not merely technical or verbal, but has human importance of a quite obvious kind. These are not the only illustrations of this importance. In interpreting quantum mechanics, biology, religion, any subject, a philosophy of process, as socially structured, can make valuable contributions.

Concerning the present anthology, I have two comments to make. First, anyone who seriously wants to understand what Whitehead means by "God" should supplement his reading . . . by studying also the final chapter of *Process and Reality*, which is devoted to this topic. Whitehead is reported to have said that this chapter is the best thing he ever wrote, ...

Reprinted from *Chicago Review* 8 (Spring-Summer 1954): 60-77. Minor passages have been omitted, as indicated by ellipses.

CHAPTER EIGHT

Whitehead's
Theory of Prehension

In the metaphysics of the twentieth century—and there is such a thing—Whitehead occupies a position like that of Leibniz or Spinoza in the seventeenth century. Whatever defects there may be in the philosophy of Whitehead, I regard his theory of "prehension" as one of the finest contributions ever made to epistemology.

The word "prehension" is created by dropping the first syllable from "apprehension." Prehension is a part or aspect of the more or less complex whole which is an act of awareness. It is the element of pure givenness in this act; experience as the having of an object. An experience for Whitehead is a unitary event or process termed an "actual entity" or "occasion." Every concrete thing which is given to or prehended by an entity is a prior event or actual entity, or a group of such entities. Contemporary events are not, strictly speaking, prehended, nor are occasions subsequent to the act of prehending. Thus memory and perception are alike in that the object of both is in the past. This assimilation of perception to memory is a highly original element in the doctrine.

The temporally prior entities which are given of course cannot depend for their reality upon being given to this or that particular subject, since the earlier does not depend upon the later. The subject-object relation is external, or nonconstitutive, for the thing given or prehended; on the other hand, it is internal or constitutive for the subject prehending. A particular subject could not conceivably be that subject, that momentary experience, without prehending just the things it does prehend. This is what Whitehead means by "causal efficacy" or "conformation." The present occasion is just a certain way of prehending its past. Hume is here flatly contradicted. Events are "distinguishable" but yet not "separable"; for, granted the later event, the earlier ones which it prehends could not have been otherwise. Causal efficacy is thus not a merely mysterious link between earlier and later; it is the fairly obvious truth that there cannot be prehension of X without X, and since prehension cannot be creative of its antecedent objects, they must be furnished to it by the actual past. Finally, not only does the present prehending subject require a certain past, but that past required, not indeed this particular subject, but still, some suitable subject or subjects capable of prehending that particular past. To be prehended by a particular subject is never essential to a thing, but to be prehended by *some* subject able to do the appropriate prehending is essential. This is a quasi-Berkeleyan element in Whitehead. To be is to be destined to be perceived. Why is this asserted? Because: (a) to be present is to be destined to become past, and (b) in this philosophy, being past and being object for some subject are held to be indistinguishable. Experience shows us no other equally concrete way of having-as-past besides prehension.

It is amazing how many questions are answered at one blow by accepting the doctrine of prehension. Are there *internal* relations of events to other events? Yes, for so far as events prehend others, they are constituted by their relations to these others. Are there *external relations*? Yes, for so far as events are prehended by subsequent events which they do not themselves prehend, they must be independent of these; also, so far as events, being mutually contemporary, are without prehensions running either way, there is mutual independence. Is there causal *connectedness*? Yes, first, because the occurrence of events strictly entails that of those events which they prehend; second, because process is bound to go on, and subsequent events must have enough in common with their predecessors to be suitable prehendors for these, in order to objectify, or "pastify" them (so to speak). Finally, is there any freedom of indeterminacy in reality? Yes, and in all cases, since events never strictly depend upon or imply their precise successors. And here Whitehead furnishes perhaps the neatest, strongest argument for freedom ever proposed. The subject prehends not one but many prior actualities. (Otherwise the world would have temporal but not spatial structure.) "The many become one and are increased by one." A single new actuality contains as its data the previous many actualities; but how could the many unambiguously prescribe their own unification into a new unity? There must be an emergent or creative synthesis, to constitute not merely *that* but *how* the many are made into a new one. Determinism, I suspect, cannot get around this difficulty. The *that* is necessary, causally fixed, but not the *how*.

Thus, Whitehead's view of givenness not only solves certain epistemological problems; it also gives an answer to Hume's skepticism about causal connections, and yet it avoids the contrary extreme, absolute idealism's denial of contingency and freedom. In a single conception it explains the spatiotemporal structure of the world, the possibility of knowledge, and the reality of freedom. It is, in my opinion, one of the supreme intellectual discoveries.

Note on Whitehead and Aristotle

Whitehead's most explicit comparison of his view as a whole with Aristotle's as a whole is made when he says that Aristotle had a theory of becoming, to which he has added a theory of perishing.[1] The future is involved in the present as "potentiality"; both authors agree on that. But how is the past involved in the present? Surely not as potential! How then; as actual? Or is there a third mode? "Perishing" is the realizing of the past in the present as immortal actuality. In ordinary cases, such "objective immortality" is radically deficient or abstract; it fails to do justice to the vividness of the past. But in the divine objectification, justice is done.

Several critics argue that entities which have "perished" cannot survive to enter into the constitutions of new entities. However, to perish, in this technical sense, is not to be "annihilated," or even changed into a diminished reality; for entities "do not change." The entity completes its decision, and hence it cannot reconsider and re-enact the latter; indeterminacy "has evaporated," and the finished entity is then accepted by the next synthesis as a datum. To perish and to become objectifiable by new entities are the same. Hence they cannot interfere with one another. "Perish" is a metaphor here, and has proved a dangerous one. The self-completed entity is used as datum in subsequent syntheses—that is the whole story.

Reprinted from *Actas: Segundo Congreso Extraordinario Interamericano de Filosofía*, 22-26 July, 1961 (San Jose, Costa Rica: Imprenta Nacional, 1962), pp. 167-68.

CHAPTER NINE

Whitehead's
Generalizing Power

Whitehead came to this country at the rather advanced age of sixty-three. He had, until then, not taught philosophy, though he had studied it, and his books on scientific subjects were in some respects notably philosophical. But now he was brought to Harvard by the imaginative Chairman of the Department of Philosophy there, James H. Woods, to teach that subject. When he read the cablegram inviting him, he said to his wife, "To teach philosophy—something I have always wanted to do." He quickly plunged into intensive reading in the history of philosophy, and at the same time into the elaboration of his own speculative ideas. He also looked into the past and present state of philosophy in this country. William James appealed to him a good deal; he admired Dewey and Santayana; he came to know something of Peirce, whom he had previously encountered as a mathematical logician, but scarcely as a speculative philosopher. How far American thought influenced him one can only guess. What I believe can be shown is that if he had known our intellectual history thoroughly, he could have claimed to present in his own system a fusion of some of the most positive aspects of our tradition. Certainly he felt at home among us. In a letter, he told me that he thought that the future of philosophy depended far more upon this country than upon Europe, which he said was hopelessly entangled in outmoded traditional ideas.

What are the positive aspects of American thought of which I just spoke? First, from the beginning, our great thinkers have generally been theists. Santayana and Dewey, to be sure, are exceptions. Second, belief in the reality of human freedom has been prominent. True enough, very early in our history the grim theologian Urian Oakes and later Jonathan Edwards were theological determinists: God in eternity decides all things, including our sinful acts and their punishments. However, this view did not remain characteristic of American thought. More and more the belief was asserted that absolute determinism, theological or otherwise, is absurd. The future, by its very meaning as future, is in the making, not settled already or eternally, and we genuinely participate in its settlement, moment by moment. Here William James, Charles Peirce, W. P. Montague, John Dewey, and others have approximately agreed.

A third feature of American thought has been belief in the primacy of mind in reality. Edwards, Johnson, Emerson, Royce, Howison, were metaphysical idealists; James was strongly tempted by panpsychism, though he could not quite make up his mind on the issue. Peirce was a convinced panpsychist. It must be admitted that, beginning with Santayana and Dewey, a good many materialists or dualists have been influential in our midst.

A fourth feature is the gradual shift from philosophies of being or substance to philosophies of becoming or process. Even in Edwards this tendency can be seen. James analyzed the self into a sequence of states in each of which there is a new subject which thinks and feels, rather than a simply identical subject thinking and feeling throughout life. Peirce's analysis points in the same direction, as does Dewey's and at times even Santayana's. In this tendency American thought has found its way to a view which was first clearly formulated two thousand years and more earlier by the Buddhists, with their "no-soul, no-substance" doctrine.

In Whitehead these four characteristics of our tradition are present in elaborately systematic and yet eloquently imaginative form. What distinguishes him from other American thinkers, except perhaps Peirce, is above all his Leibniz-like power of sweeping, yet clear-cut generalization, a power greatly intensified by his scientific training. For it is in modern science that the art has most successfully been cultivated of generalizing without falling into mere vagueness or ambiguity. This power of clear generalization is what chiefly separates Whitehead from Dewey. Thus, for instance, Dewey holds that feeling and thought are sheer exceptions in nature, in spite of the truth that we have no reason to think that any but relative differences separate man from the other animals, and these even from atoms. Also, Dewey's concepts were too narrow to enable him to formulate a reasonable view of religion, however hard he tried to do so. The true empiricism, said Whitehead, will not try to invent an absolutely different concept from that of experience, with its aspects of feeling, memory, love, freedom, and so on, in order to explain the nonhuman, but will generalize these aspects so that, though we can only dimly imagine how, they will cover all possible forms of individual existence, not only from particles to man, but even from man to God. It happens that I reached some such view before I knew anything of Whitehead.

Whitehead's "philosophy of organism" might perhaps better have been called "the societal philosophy," for "society" is a more central technical term in it than "organism." Whitehead's belief is that, just as biology in some respects teaches us more about the general features of nature than physics, so sociology and social psychology, generalized like biology to cover all levels of life (and they all do have social aspects) can teach us more than mere biology. What is the logic of this procedure? One seems to be "explaining the lower by the higher," thus the inorganic by the organic, and the inferior levels of the organic by the superior. Many accuse Whitehead, therefore, of reading the emergent aspects of life downward, as though they had not emerged at all. But he knows what he is doing and why. He holds that nature is intelligible if, and only if, the specific traits which emerge are special cases of more general principles which do not emerge but are found all the way down. Yet if we try to discover these principles first or chiefly in the lower levels of reality, we are doing it the hard way, with little likelihood of success, and this for three reasons, all of which were urged by Whitehead. First, we ourselves are at the top of the scale of things on this planet, and we have means of knowing ourselves additional to those by which we know the lower creatures. Human experience we know by the direct route of memory, especially immediate memory; how one has just been feeling, thinking, and perceiving. All other individual forms of experience we know less directly, or at least less definitely.

Second, although the general principles of nature must of course be expressed even on the lowest levels, it is the very meaning of "lowest" that the principles are there expressed in lesser degree, and this means that they may be harder to detect there. Suppose for instance that atoms have some spontaneity, or freedom of decision between alternatives: they certainly can have very little of such freedom, compared to the higher animals, and this would partly explain why for so many centuries it was thought that atoms had no freedom at all. The denial of freedom, thus apparently justified, was then often extended to the human body, viewed as a highly complex system of atoms, and only that. This whole procedure was fallacious.

But now we come to a *third* reason for looking to the higher levels for our explanatory principles. The lowest levels of nature are not disclosed to the senses in their individual constituents, such as bacteria, molecules, and atoms. Our senses are adapted primarily for dealing with individuals of roughly our scale of magnitude, and our perceptions lump billions or superquintillions of atoms together as though they were merely one thing. Biologically this is appropriate, since a single atom, molecule, or cell has in general practically no importance for our animal welfare.

The three reasons add up to the conclusion: if you want to know what the general principles of individual existence in nature may be, you must look first and chiefly to the higher and the highest individuals, not to the lower. You must then take pains so to generalize the principles you discover that they will explain also the lower levels. Then and only then can you safely consider man as merely a superior member of the system of natural things, reversing the order of explanation, using the lower to illuminate the higher.

Let us look at this process of generalizing the traits found in man. First, take the concept of freedom. For two thousand years theologians and philosophers had attempted to deal with creative freedom as but a special or exceptional case of something else, such as causality. Whitehead makes the daring leap, less clearly outlined already by Lequier, Fechner, Bergson, [Peirce], Berdyaev, and a few others, of making creativity itself the universal principle of reality and causation. Not just God creates, not even just God and man, but every concrete unit of reality has its own special kind and degree of creativity. To be is to create. One argument for the doctrine is a simple logical one: deterministic causality is an absolute negation, implying the zero of creative power; surely such a zero is not a general principle, but an extremely special case, or perhaps a mere limit of thought. By contrast, the notion of creativity is a relative concept, with an infinite range of possible degrees, since an activity may be more or less free or creative, more or less productive of unpredictable novelty. Given this notion, we can treat the apparent determinism of inorganic nature as due to its extremely limited or slight degree of creative power. From this standpoint, the traditional view of man as free, while the lower animals are taken to be simply unfree, is as arbitrary as the Cartesian view that only man feels or thinks, while the other animals are mindless, insentient machines. Animal feeling and thinking is of course on a much lower or simpler level than ours, but it is there. So with freedom. Freedom in trivial details—just which instant does the cat meow, or make this or that motion with its paw—is one thing; freedom such as man possesses to fashion ideals, plans for a house or a city, designs for living, religions, or scientific theories, is a vastly different thing. Animal freedom is inferior simply because it concerns inferior matters, slight and trivial details.

Similar reasoning prevents us from denying freedom absolutely even to atoms. Science recognizes no absolute distinction between life and nonlife, and is less and less inclined to do so as it advances in its grasp of the structure of nature. Can it avoid the conclusion which Whitehead draws that the only way to make the presence of freedom intelligible is to universalize it into a cosmic category, applicable to all individuals, from particles to man, and also to whatever superhuman entities there may be?

But now we come to a problem. If all individuals make their own decisions, act with a certain spontaneity, what prevents universal conflict and confusion? Can all things freely conspire together to make an orderly world? Each adjusts to all the others; but one cannot adjust to chaos. Hence the notion of "mutual adjustment" presupposes the solution of the problem of order, and does not furnish it. Suppose, however, that each individual adjusts, not simply to others more or less like itself, but to one supreme free agent; then, since all reflect the influence of this one agent, they are thereby put into a certain degree of conformity to each other. The supreme agent decides the outlines of the world order, this decision the lesser agents accept; what is still left for them to decide is by comparison trivial. As lower-animal freedom, or still more, atomic freedom, is trivial compared to human, so is all worldly freedom compared to God's. All creatures, indeed, have genuine freedom, both for good and happy results and for unhappy ones; but the choice between world-order and chaos [not even God has that choice], or one world-order and another, is not theirs. That some results of the creatures' choices may be unhappy is a risk which has to be run if there is to be any world at all. For in this philosophy, to be is to be free. The creator has to *create creators*, for nothing can exist which is wholly uncreative, unfree.

Since our freedom is genuine creation, in eternity God cannot know our actions, for in eternity there is no such thing to know. Creation is step by step, not once and for all, in a single eternal fiat. Yet God does know our actions, not indeed in eternity, but rather, in a kind of divine supertime. Whitehead expresses this by distinguishing between the Primordial Nature of God and his Consequent Nature. His Primordial Nature is God in eternity, knowing only what is itself eternal, his own ideal or system of ideals for the creation. The Consequent Nature is God in "flux," progressively enriched by his knowledge of the progressively created and in part self-created creatures. It is God as inheriting the world, or as the ultimate posterity, the only everlasting and adequate heir of all achievements, and thus the final measure or judge of their importance. It is really God as supreme Creature, and not just supreme Creator.

This view harmonizes well with another feature of much American philosophy, the belief that the social structure of reality is fundamental. Royce had a social theory of reality; and so did Peirce. One way of expressing the point is to say that love is fundamental. Peirce invented the term "Agapism" for such a doctrine. In Whitehead, perhaps more than in any thinker who ever lived, the old saying, "God is love," is given its fully generalized interpretation. If the supreme reality is essentially the supreme form of love, everything other than God must be some sort of love on an inferior level. Thus, for instance, according to Whitehead, each momentary experience is bound to the past by some sort of "sympathy" for past experiences, those of oneself and, to some extent, of others. Also, the mind-body relation consists, from our side, in our unconscious but vivid sympathy for the feelings of the bodily cells. Even the power of God over the world is the love of the creatures for God (as Aristotle said, but never worked out systematically), and this love is due to and directed toward the supreme love which constitutes God himself. This supreme love is not the mere beneficence, the mere passing out of benefits, which is all that some theologians seem to have meant; Whitehead sees God as having actual sympathy for the world, as feeling its feelings and sharing its thoughts. In this way we "enrich the divine life itself," as Berdyaev (independently) held. And we love God just because we can thus enrich his life; or, as was said long ago, we love him because he first loved us, but also and equally because he will love us when we can no longer love ourselves; somewhat as our cells may be imagined to love us because we never, while we live, cease to love them, and thus we largely sum up their real value. We are as cells to the cosmos. Whitehead once called his view, a "cell-theory of reality."

Besides the need for a supreme form of freedom to order the lesser forms, Whitehead has several additional reasons for introducing the idea of God into his philosophy. One reason is the following. Like James, Royce, and Santayana, and apparently unlike Dewey, he finds absurdity in the idea of a humanity perishable, both individually and as a race, and yet the highest form of mind in existence. Our experiences, he says, are but "passing whiffs of insignificance," unless our joys and sorrows in some way enrich the universe throughout all future time. James said something similar. The long-run goal of living cannot be the grave, nor yet conventional personal immortality (for which Whitehead sees no evidence, and which, for still other reasons, does not solve the problem as he sees it). Nor can the goal be merely our human posterity, which may die out, or at any rate fail to receive any proportionate benefit from our having lived, a benefit capable of expressing our sense of the importance of our lives as we live them. The goal must lie in some value we can contribute to an imperishable reality, capable of correctly appreciating our achievements, the intensities and harmonies of human and all other experiences. This reality can only be a divine consciousness, completely aware of all that has occurred.

So far we have seen Whitehead generalizing the ideas of mind, freedom, society, and immortality beyond the usual limits within which these ideas have customarily been considered. Let us now consider other topics in a similarly universal light.

Our experience discloses to us what we call things and persons, and it discloses these as existing in changing states. Thus we seem to have two basic categories, things, including persons, and states or events. But how are things related to events? Apparently in two absolutely diverse ways: there is the event in which a thing or a person first begins to exist at all, and there are the events which merely prolong this existence through time. The first event produces the thing, the others do not. Aristotle called the first "substantial change," and the other a mere change of accidents. But which is the fundamental kind of change, or is there a third kind which explains both? Some have argued that the basic change or becoming is the acquirement of new states by some really fundamental substance or substances in nature, perhaps the atoms, or the world substance as one. But then the basic substance or substances could not be created, for this would be another sort of becoming, and so creation would be ruled out by definition. There are other objections, which I must pass over. There is, however, a view which is able, without these difficulties, to exhibit all change as in principle one: this is the view of Whitehead; also (but did he know this?) of universal Buddhism. According to this doctrine, the basic change is simply the becoming of ever-new events. If certain events, forming an apprently unbroken chain or sequence through time, exhibit some notably persistent characters, we speak of the chain as the history of the same thing or person, otherwise not. Thus all change is made intelligible as the becoming or creation of events. Thinghood, including personality, is a special case of this, where continuity through events obtains to a high degree.

Such is Whitehead's or the Buddhists' view. Events or states are the primary logical subjects which have predicates, and in one and the same sense of the word "have," meaning, "are essentially qualified by." If a certain event had had a single predicate otherwise, it would have been a different event. Does this mean that there is nothing accidental? Not at all. For it is always accidental that *this* event occurred, and not some other. Yet, whatever event occurs it will, as that event, have the only predicates that *it* could have had. The commonsense distinction between what Smith is as Smith, and what he is accidentally, can easily be expressed in the language of events. For we identify Smith as a chain or sequence of events or states, this sequence exhibiting persistent traits without which we should not recognize Smith as himself; it also exhibits characters which we do *not* demand for this identification. Just what we so demand is a relative matter, partly settled by convention.

We have considered some cases of Whitehead's habit of generalizing beyond a dualism which many other philosophers were unable to transcend or clearly explain: such as the dualism of free versus unfree; or the dualism of substantial change versus change within a self-identical subject. Let us take still another instance of this generalizing power. Most philosophers admit two forms of concrete experience, memory and perception. Which is fundamental, or is there a third principle that explains both? We are seldom told even that there is here a problem. Whitehead knows that mathematics, physics, and biology have progressed because they have never been content simply to accept a handful of separate principles, but have always looked for a higher principle to unite the others. Whitehead also knows that memory and perception have at least this in common that both relate us primarily to the past, rather than to the present. It takes time for light or sound to produce in us a perceptual experience. It is amazing how few have seen that this alone should lead us not only to question the absolute distinctness of the two principles, memory and perception, but also to look chiefly to memory for the clue to their common nature.

To be sure, both perception and memory appear to depend not only on past events, but on the present state of the nervous system. However, we need not admit that in either case the nervous state in question is absolutely in the present, for why not suppose it is rather the state which just occurred a fraction of a second ago? Whitehead sees reasons for taking this view, for locating the neural conditions both of memory and of perception in the immediate past, rather than in the absolute present. In that case, both forms of experience are related to the neural state as memory is to its object, namely as present to past. Thus all concrete experience may be viewed as memorylike, whether we wish to call it "memory" or not. Memory in the ordinary sense may be called "personal" memory; perception is then "impersonal memory," experience of the nonpersonal past.

We can now see a further reach of generalizing power. If the dependence of experience upon neural conditions is like that of memory upon its object, then causal conditioning, in this one case at least, is identical in principle with memory. So here we have a clue to Hume's problem of causal connection. The present depends upon the past as memory upon the remembered: to remember something is to be an effect of that something. As Whitehead puts it, generalizing as usual, "causality is physical memory." So we have gone not only beyond the dualism of perception and memory, but also beyond that of concrete experience and causality. All are aspects of one thing, memory in its personal and impersonal aspects. Consider (this is my own example) the first experience of a human infant or embryo: as the first experience, it can have no personal memory whatever; does this mean that it has nothing like memory? This is the sort of absolute exception or singularity which no mathematician or physicist is content with if he can avoid it. And we can avoid it. The infant in his first experience has no *personal* memory, since by definition there is no earlier event in the sequence taken as constituting his history for him to remember; yet the infant can perfectly well have nonpersonal memory, for example, concrete experience of the just previous state of his own organism. The infant begins his sentient life by remembering, that is feeling, how his nerves were just stimulated. Of course he has no concept of nervous state, only a feeling of it. Still, we thus avoid the monstrous singularity that a first experience should be shut up in the present, void of internal connection with its prior conditions, whereas experience in general is essentially a response to such conditions. Only some such view as Whitehead's has anything like so neat a way of avoiding this singularity.

We are not yet done with the generalization of memory. God, too, is thought of as a rememberer. Whitehead never used the word "memory" at this point, but he uses what in his system are equivalent words. God is forever "prehending," that is, remembering perfectly what has just happened in the world, and also he remembers what he has just remembered, and so on and so on, and thus the entire past of the creation is completely summed up and immortalized in God. The simplicity and clarity of this view seem to me sublime. It gives reality a means whereby it perpetually sums itself up, and preserves its achievements. "O death, where is thy sting, O grave, where is thy victory?"

Of course divine memory is not just another case of memory. It is different in principle from ours, as theologians have always said God's knowledge was different from ours. But the difference can be derived from the universal principle itself, and does not make God a violation of the principle. Memory either is or is not mixed with failure to remember, with forgetting. All our memories are adulterated with forgetting. This means that it is *our* memory which in a sense violates the principle of memory. God's memory is sheer memory; he simply does not forget, or fail to remember anything.

In most philosophies of religion, God appears as the great exception, the great singularity. Insofar, the scientific urge toward generalization might seem to argue against theism. And in a sense of course, the being which is "exalted above all others" must be radically exceptional. But in Whitehead's philosophy it becomes clearer than in perhaps any other that what is singular about the divine reality is precisely its rigorous universality, the purity with which it expresses, and in this way coincides with, the ultimate principles of reality. Tillich says, "God is Being Itself"; Whitehead could say, God is Process Itself, in its various aspects. For instance, as we have seen above, God is memory itself, unqualified with forgetting, memory always coextensive with process so far as already actualized. Tradition had said, God is the cause of which, without exception, every other thing is effect. Whitehead also can say this; but equally he can say, God (in his Consequent State) is the effect of which, without exception, every other thing is part-cause. In this way, the old difficulty is removed that, whereas causes as we know them are always also effects of prior causes, the supreme causative agent was held to be, not at all the supreme, but the zero, case of effect: a concrete, active reality to which, however, no cause can contribute, thus either something quite outside the chain of cause-effects, or the no less monstrous singularity of a first member of the chain. This singularity is eliminated by the doctrine of the Consequent Nature (better, Consequent State) of God. God as Consequent is no less rigorously universal in his manner of being effect than God as Primordial is universal in his manner of being cause. Each state of the consequent nature is supreme effect of *all* before it, and supreme cause of *all* after it, and yet it is an ideally integrated actuality.

Has Whitehead everywhere carried through this magnificent program? There are several difficulties, of which I shall consider but one here. If, in philosophies of being, God is Being Itself, in a philosophy of creativity should he not be Creativity Itself? Yet Whitehead refuses to say this. Why? I think because he has his attention upon a possible misunderstanding. If we identify divine creating with creating in general, then it seems that the creatures can have no creativity of their own. To avoid this, and to avoid making God the selector of the detailed goods and evils of the world,

Whitehead distinguishes between God and creativity. Yet there is a sense in which even for him this distinction is not final. All actual creativity is *either* God's own creative synthesis, *or* it is a datum for his creative-synthetic action. It is either a divine "subjective form" or a divine "objective form," either a divine contribution to the creatures or a contribution divinely received from the creatures. So the apparent deviation from the principle, no mere singularities, is apparent only. God is the individual with absolutely universal functions: universal action upon others, universal passivity or reception of the action of others, universal memory, universal perception, universal cause, universal effect, universal sympathy, universal consciousness of all things.

If the higher realities exhibit in greater degree the universal principles, must it not be the strictly highest reality which exhibits the principles in their full meaning, and in this sense is coincident with that meaning? Thus God in his eternal aspects is no mere case under the categories, nor yet a mere exception to them; rather he is the categories in their pure or unqualified meaning, as fixed characteristics of an individual life within which there is a duality of perfect and imperfect cases, the former always including the latter, since the inclusion by an actuality of antecedent actualities is itself a category expressed without limitation only in the Universal Individual, who alone survives every other and so comes to have each among its own antecedents. I believe that the unique intelligibility of theistic philosophy can only in some such way be made manifest. But much work remains to be done if this program is to be carried out in all of its implications.

I have scarcely a shadow of doubt that Whitehead is close enough to the truth and to the sound philosophical method to deserve serious attention. But no philosopher is exempt from criticism, which, together with speculative daring and the sense for the realities of experience, is the life of philosophy.

Reprinted from *Proceedings of the American Catholic Philosophical Assocation*, vol. 35 (1961), pp. 163-71.

CHAPTER TEN

Whitehead and
Contemporary Philosophy

...There are two ways in which we may come to look favorably upon the views of a living philosopher. One way is to be exposed, at a tender age or state of development, to a philosophical teacher, master, authority, under conditions which protect the student from serious encounter with modes of thinking incompatible with the teacher's. The other way is to undergo the philosopher's influence only after, or along with, intimate reaction to fundamentally different philosophical attitudes, and after one has achieved some clarity as to one's own experience of reality and value. Or again, it is one thing to derive philosophic individuality largely from another person and a different thing to recognize a certain congruity between one's thinking, already firmly individualized, and his. Of course, there is no absolute difference here, but a considerable relative one. It happens that I was never in the usual sense a "pupil" of Whitehead's; also that long before knowing anything of his work I had already reached some basic philosophical convictions grounded upon explicit reasons in whose force I still today put some trust. And before (in 1925) becoming a colleague, and for a semester an assistant, of Whitehead, I had been exposed for nine years to the influence of many other philosophers, for four of those years to a powerful group of teachers at Harvard, and for two more to Edmund Husserl and several other distinguished European professors. Simultaneously with the exposure to Whitehead came the more detailed influence of Peirce, the study of whose manuscripts occupied most of my time during the same three years. The main effect of Whitehead was to reinforce and crystallize into a technical doctrine a vague sense already acquired that reality on its most concrete level is process not "substance," creative becoming not mere being, and also to clarify another vague notion that what is usually meant by "personal immortality" is probably beside the point, since the divine immortality, and our oneness (in some sense) with God, is the proper solution to the problem of the transitoriness of life. Whitehead's "objective immortality" was a lucid explication of this notion. But the basic beliefs: that reality consists of feelings, that these are essentially "social" (in Whitehead's language, cases of "feeling of feeling"), that there must be a supreme, all-inclusive mind, which is somewhat misconceived both in most theologies and in historical pantheism, that the future is open and in process of determination, that there are new facts from moment to moment, and even new divine cognitions, that process is all-inclusive—so much I already thought I knew, thanks to influences, experiences, and reasonings too complex to touch upon here. And of course, similar ideas are either stated or, in some passages at least, implied by Peirce. But Whitehead was the only living thinker who seemed to have an adequate grasp of these matters, and also the only one in whom I could find the sort of systematic clarity and comprehensiveness that we admire in Leibniz. I still see no rival to him in our time, or in the nineteenth century, in this latter respect. . . .

One sign of [Whitehead's] increasing influence is the appearance of four books, within as many years, dealing with Whitehead's philosophy.[1] Of these, I find the work by Leclerc a useful and largely sound introduction; in the other three, especially Christian's book, I can recognize certain merits. As Popper keeps telling us, the rational method in general is that of free criticism. Therefore, if Whitehead is important, he ought to be criticized. We should be looking for indications that he is, in this or that respect, mistaken. Also it is vicious to be so critical of criticisms of a favorite author that one would, if successful, protect him against exposure of his weaknesses. However, criticism of an author who dealt in a comprehensive way with the central scientific and philosophical issues of our time, with much technical knowledge and immense imaginative daring, must fulfill exacting requirements if it is to be of much value. Most of us are at a disadvantage here, and I suspect that this is not the least of the reasons why so many writers have been ignoring Whitehead of late. I confess that, on grounds well stated by Leclerc,[2] I have regarded the general approach taken by Lawrence in his book as rather unpromising and have therefore not reckoned in detail with his criticism; though I presume Leclerc is right in thinking the job rather well done, asssuming the type of approach.

The book by Christian is admirable in style, organization, and lucidity; moreover, in most respects I find that he grasps Whitehead's meanings well. However, he imputes to Whitehead a few conceptions which he admits are not obviously in the text, and which I believe were not intended, unless perhaps in moments of partial absentmindedness on Whitehead's part. These concern chiefly the meaning of "objective immortality," or the "immanence" of actualities in subsequent actualities prehending them, and the sense in which God is conceived as infinite and perfect. I think we have here intelligent and beautifully argued (partial) misconstructions, an attribution to Whitehead of the author's own convictions (as I gather). Be that as it may, this is a fine and interesting book.

Also interesting, though in a rather different way, is the largely critical study by Mays. Here, despite some penetrating *aperçus*, especially concerning the relations of Whitehead's philosophy to mathematics, misinterpretation is almost pervasive; or else I do not know at all what Whitehead meant. The book is ingenious, and at some points illuminating; and for all I know, there is some justice in the author's objections to Whitehead's way of arguing from the physics which he knew—essentially that prior to Heisenberg and Schrodinger; for, as Whitehead admitted, he was unable to keep up with the subject after he began his teaching at Harvard and plunged into intensive study of the history of philosophy. Certainly Mays is right to this extent, that if one interprets physics as does Bridgman (the chief authority cited), the way to Whitehead's metaphysics will not be altogether clear! But Mays's failure to grasp various important aspects of Whitehead's thought will, I am confident, be apparent to close students of his writings. Think of reading *Process and Reality*, including (apparently) Part V, and then writing,[3] "It is difficult to follow Whitehead when he says that 'the consequent nature of God is conscious,' but it is questionable whether he means by this more than that we are consciously aware of the concrete world in perception." Only gross confusion or blatant dishonesty could have led Whitehead to try to express any such obvious truism by the ten pages or so of eloquent writing devoted to the Consequent Nature, not to mention various passages which implicitly say the same sort of thing. And no one so confused or dishonest could have written those majestic pages.

It would be more reasonable to say that Whitehead is the first great systematic philosopher who does mean it when he says that God is conscious; i.e., knows the world to be such and such (although it might have been otherwise) and knows that he knows this. It is the older theologians who seem not to mean what they say when they attribute "knowledge" to deity. For knowing, being aware of, are relational properties or states, and Aquinas takes pains to tell us (and he is only saying more sharply what many had already said) that relations between the world and God are not relations for God. In other words, the world is perhaps known by God, but God does not know the world! Whitehead deliberately avoids this paradox by attributing relativity, intrinsic related-ness, to God. There are divine "physical prehensions" of the world. Mays[4] mentions this, but takes it to mean something[5] it could not honestly mean in this philosophy. Yet only through such prehensions can deity, or anything else, be concrete or "actual." The Primordial Nature, Whitehead expressly and repeatedly tells us, is by itself a mere entity of reason, a mere abstraction from the divine actuality.[6]

The attempt of Mays to make a certain phase of theoretical physics the source and essence of Whitehead's philosophy is in my opinion less correct than Leclerc's view that Whitehead is trying to solve certain traditional problems of metaphysics and epistemology, or than the suggestion of Lowe that "sociological" phenomena, the broad distribution of societies in nature, constitute the more important source of his beliefs.[7] But as the two authors just mentioned fully realize, the matter is more complex than any single account of this sort. As Lowe has put it, "Whitehead is aware of almost everything." The philosopher himself once told his students that (I quote from memory), "as physics is the interpretation of our external perceptual experiences, so metaphysics is the interpretation of our religious experiences." Nor is it correct to say, as Mays in effect does,[8] that these religious experiences were taken to be essentially our reactions to order in nature, or to permanence as constituted merely by order. (See the surprising exegesis at the top of p. 63.) Any careful textual examination will show that the permanence which religion is thought to be most concerned with is "objectification by the physical prehensions of God" (to Mays evidently mere circumlocution for ordinary physical prehensions), since these are the only experiences free from "negative prehensions," or from the "abstractness" whereby the vividness of achieved values drops down and down, in "physical memory," until in the end the values must be wholly lost, or fall as close to zero as you please, were it not for the divine "love" which "tenderly cherishes" them everlastingly.

Whitehead was a very honest writer. He may sometimes have got "mixed up"—who doesn't?—but he always tried to say what he meant. When he said "love," he did not mean something very different, such as the "extensive scheme," with which[9] Mays apparently identifies the Whiteheadian God. Here, as at several other points, Mays has an ingenious thesis, valiantly carried through against considerable textual odds, concerning what Whitehead might have meant, had he been a very different sort of man and philosopher—for instance, intellectually more simpleminded and morally more complicated—than he was.

It would be less than fair not to add that Whitehead's exposition of his natural theology was sufficiently defective (a fact of which he was aware) to make it impossible to find a trouble-free interpretation of all that he said on this subject. One is forced to suppose him mistaken, or at least ill-advised in his choice of words, in some passages. But on Mays's interpretation at least ten pages of his author become gibberish, and many others by implication needlessly puzzling. And Whitehead has been quoted (I forget by whom) as saying that the final chapter of *Process*, which includes the ten pages spoken of, was the best essay in his writings; an evaluation in which I incline to concur. Is it so paradoxical that it should also be true that there are some grave defects in the exposition? Where thousands of gifted minds have earnestly sought to arrive at a rational conception of deity and, according to Whitehead, have not succeeded ("traditional theology is a scandalous failure"), is it to be expected that the feat could be accomplished for the first time, in a great systematic philosophy, without blunder or blemish? Whitehead said once that he felt that his thought about God was "very vague," but that others would be able to clarify the matter.

I will say in passing that I deem it a serious slip by Whitehead to have termed the *Primordial* Nature of God an "actuality." This taken literally is just what it cannot be, in the system in which every actuality is a unit-becoming in its concreteness. But it can be shown that there are reasons for the slip; that the confusion was rather natural.

Perhaps it has been unfair to take Mays's treatment of the theistic aspect as sample, since here he is at his weakest. But there is in his book a general trend toward oversimplification, both of Whitehead's views and of the problems he was trying to solve. To evaluate the criticisms, one must check carefully with *Process and Reality* and *Adventures of Ideas* (in all earlier works Whitehead was groping toward his philosophy; only in these two works was he free to expound it). One must also remind oneself that an attempt to develop an explicit doctrine cannot be discredited by showing that if we fall back into some much vaguer notion, the definite difficulties of the more explicit view disappear. Of course they do, and so do its advantages.

When, for example, Mays says[10] that human experiences do not interact with "molecules," because the latter are not concrete particular entities but abstract general conceptions useful in interpreting our concrete experiences, he is really declaring either for phenomenalism, or for something like naive realism, without telling us how the difficulties of any more explicit development of these positions are to be dealt with. For instance, are cells not particular realities either? And where do we draw the line between actual particulars and mere concepts? Whitehead has his way of dealing with a host of problems; there may be a better way, but merely to remind us that, as Whitehead himself was very fond of emphasizing, the concepts of physics are highly abstract, can hardly suffice to show the needlessness of his doctrines. Whitehead had things to say early in his career about this very way of seeking to banish the problems of a scientific cosmology.

I

Although, as the books we have been discussing seem to evidence, there is increasing interest in the philosophy of Creativity (a better summary description, perhaps, than "philosophy of organism"), it cannot be denied that this philosophy meets with great resistance in some quarters, especially outside the United States. Let us consider some of the reasons for this. We cannot undertake to cover all the important reasons.

Positivism.—The conviction that synthetic propositions can only be empirical, and that nonsynthetic propositions can only be linguistic, seems to imply that either Whitehead was engaging in scientific guessing, unjustifiably extended beyond its observational base, or he was merely setting down some verbal stipulations, with some emotive, especially religious, associations.

Dogmatic Pluralism.—In spite of the great vogue of the dilemmatic argument just sketched against any such metaphysics as Whitehead's, certain views which seem at least as hard to defend against that argument pervade current philosophical writing, and constitute a principal obstacle to a genuine encounter with the philosophy of creativity. The Russellian reiteration of Hume's thesis that distinguishable events are "separable," each event being devoid of internal relatedness or logical dependence upon any other, is extremely common; although if it is not metaphysical I wonder what would be. Is it analytic? Ayer says flatly, yes.[11] In that case, it appears that something besides language and its contingent rules is at stake in the analytic. According to Whitehead's own language, events "prehend" certain other events, and this implies that they depend logically upon these others. Moreover, since this concept of prehension is held to be of universal relevance, presupposed in all more special conceptions, a language in which it were really analytic that no event could depend logically upon any other would, for Whitehead, be incoherent.

Dogmatic "Naturalism" (Materialism).—Another view which is quite as problematic, whether taken as empirical or as analytic, but which causes many philosophers to dismiss Whitehead practically unread, is the belief that the emergence of mind out of non-mind is almost axiomatic. Whitehead's dismissal of the concept "matter," except as an abstract way of viewing sequences of "experient occasions," or concrete units of "feeling of feeling"—his "panpsychism," to use a term which, for perhaps sufficiently good reasons, he avoided—is felt by some to furnish almost ground enough for rejecting his entire system. They *know* (I have talked to them) that atoms and electrons do not feel, or in any way consist of feelings of any sort. Or at least, they know that this *might* be the case and that Whitehead can have no sound reason for applying the psychical terms universally. I have also talked to some scientists about this, and I find them less sure that a view like Whitehead's is mistaken or unreasonable. Some well-known scientists, in fact, hold such a view (e.g., Julian Huxley, Pierre Teilhard de Chardin, Sewall Wright, Ralph Gerard), and the rest mostly leave the question at one side as not, at present at least, a scientific question. It is not physicists or biologists, but philosophers without any special rapport with physics or biology, who have told me that panpsychism is not worth discussing. If the question is indeed a factual one, it appears that certain philosophers have discovered facts hidden from science, as well as from many of their fellow philosophers.

Is it perhaps analytic, or apparent from the mere rules of language, that not all of nature could consist of some form or manifestation of mind in the form of feeling? Then here, too, we seem to learn about more than mere words from analytic necessities. It must be understood that Whitehead knew as well as anyone that to say outright, "Everything feels," would be to make the term "feeling" useless. But this he by no means does say. Abstract entities (e.g., triangularity) obviously do not feel, and in his system such entities are taken as "real," though of course, not as "actual." Also chairs and stones do not feel, though they are held to consist of processes whose unit-becomings are sentient. I should like to meet the person who can show that this theory is analytically false. And if the question is empirical, then it is worth remarking that science is not so treating it. What scientist as such stands up to be counted on the question, Where is the lower limit of feeling in the plant-animal series? or even is willing to say that there is or can be a lower limit? And quite a good many are ready to be counted as denying such a limit. They, or some of them, do this not on a factual basis, but rather as a result of conceptual analysis. For they agree with Whitehead that the notion of a sheer absence of mind or feeling from any part of nature is probably a meaningless one. What criterion of such absence can be proposed?

There are indeed criteria for saying that certain particular entities "do not feel," that is, are not singular subjects of feeling. For instance, it is reasonable to doubt (as even Leibniz did doubt) that trees feel, for, as Whitehead picturesquely puts it, "a tree is a democracy"—not so much a singular as a collective entity, like a swarm of bees. He is here speaking factually, and I know competent scientists who would agree with him. But it is a distinct question if a tree-cell is, in a similar sense, a mere "democracy" of molecules; and if it is, still some level is implied on which dynamic unity *is* found. (For the disunity of the whole is relative to the unity of certain parts.)

Carefully reasoned criteria for the total absence of feeling from a portion of nature, both as a whole and in its constituent parts, have not been formulated. Until they have been worked out, the conception of "mere matter" has not been given empirical meaning. I do not anticipate that they can be worked out in such a way as to justify the conception. But the problem is being dealt with far more by dogmatic proclamation or innuendo than by careful reflection. Whitehead, however, reflected upon it, over much of a long lifetime. So did Leibniz, Peirce, Clifford, and many another who reached much the same conclusion as he. My own conviction that reality is indeed an "ocean of feelings" (Whitehead's phrase) was reached at an early age, without conscious reference to any philosophical writer or teacher, and was based, as I know from conversation Whitehead's was, upon an attempted analysis of immediate experience, where alone reality can be encountered. He found, as some of the rest of us have found, that no mere surd to feeling is ever given, but only certain sensory qualities whose affective character is, to be sure, less obvious than that of some other qualities, but (as I tried to show in my *Philosophy and Psychology of Sensation*) is nevertheless detectable. There is here an appeal to observation or intuition, and someone is a poor observer. The question is, Who?

Determinism.—Not much can be made out of Whitehead's philosophy by anyone who is unalterably convinced that the concept of absolute causal regularity (classical determinism) even makes sense. For in Whitehead's language, whose first principle is that of creative process, determinism can enter only as a limiting conception which could not be literally realized in any world. Hume (and many of his followers) believed that causal regularity is at least logically capable of taking an absolute form, and that we actually have good observational grounds for regarding this possibility as realized. Today, not many would say so, in the face of the evidence that laws, so far as knowable, are probably all of a statistical character. Thus Hume was mistaken in regarding his determinism as an empirical proposition. Is it then analytic? Some have thought so, but they, too, are few today. I cannot but think that on this matter time is strongly on Whitehead's side. Determinism is a waning idea. People say that the physicist Bohm has proposed a way to reinstate determinism in quantum mechanics. However, if they looked into his book, they would find Bohm declaring that chance is as real as law.[12] His proposal (which has not so far been accepted, I gather) is not motivated by a belief in absolute regularities, which indeed he denies, but (to put it very roughly) in the tactical wisdom of looking for such regularities, in order to make sure that we do not overestimate in a particular case the (admittedly genuine) role of chance.

Naïve Realism.—Contemporary writings on the theory of knowledge seem dominated by one rarely challenged assumption, that the alternative to the "sense-datum" theory (generally viewed as discredited) regarding the *given* in perception can only be something like plain old-fashioned "naïve realism" (so-called, for I agree with Lovejoy that the plain man does not hold this view). Since Whitehead holds neither of these doctrines, nor yet quite Russell's identity theory (that the sensation is the neural process itself), his distinctive and carefully elaborated theory of perception is not readily understood. Whitehead is a direct presentational realist—but not of the naïve variety. He holds that the primary datum in sense perception is some phase of the neural process itself; but this does not mean that our sensory experience simply is the process. Human experiences consist of actual entities coming temporally just after the subhuman actualities constituting the cellular activities which are given in these experiences. There is a "prehensive" relation of experience to its datum, and this relation is not that of identity. A temporal distinction is involved, and the datum, being prior, is quite independent of the particular human experience in question (though not of all earlier human experiences).

Against the contention that the neural process is given, we have the violent negation (again, I speak from experience): "Whatever may be given in normal vision, it is certainly not the optical process itself!" Is this denial an empirical or a linguistic statement? It seems sometimes to be intended as a species of the former, for we are reminded that until physiologists discovered neural processes no one knew there were such things; hence they could not all along have been given. Again we have an appeal to facts which, as interpreted, are known to certain philosophers only, but not to scientists, or to certain other philosophers. Granted, many truths about nerve cells were not known until physiologists discovered them; but just so, many truths about rocks (e.g., their crystalline structure) were not known until physicists and chemists discovered them, although, according to naïve realism, rocks had been directly experienced for ages.

But, it will be urged, at least men did know that there were rocks, and they did not know that there was nervous tissue, except by autopsies; hence in ordinary vision nervous tissue cannot be given. Answer: it cannot be given *as* tissue (or as anything so definitely categorized), for (as many forget) the directly given, merely as such, is not categorized at all, though there is feeling of its quality and spatiotemporal spread. It begs the question at issue to say that men do not directly experience some of the very qualities and shapes really characterizing nervous tissue. For the view which Whitehead holds (something like that of Spinoza, if I understand the latter correctly) is that the sensory quality and shape given in a sensation does qualify, first of all, a physical process going on inside our bodies, and only less directly and precisely the extrabodily physical thing. To object that it is not *as* something inside our bodies that we experience that process is to forget that locating a process in public space involves correlating data from more than one sense, or it involves correlating processes actually given but not "seen" (i.e., not reflecting light to our normally functioning eyes) with objects that are seen. The theory of the inner bodily datum of visual experience does not mean that this datum, rather than the light-reflecting object, is what is seen. For to "see"—Ryle is correct in this, of course—means to gain information about something, or adjust to it, by means of the light which it transmits to our eyes. But the theory in question holds that this information is an evaluation, which has become largely instinctive or automatic, of something still more directly had or possessed. It is a reading of reliable signs, not themselves noted as such (Whitehead's "transmutation"); somewhat as when we read a book we take conscious note, not so much of the words as of the things meant, or as when we watch a cinema we often seem to observe people, not lights and shadows on a screen.

Now one current belief is that all this is obviously not so. We not only see the extrabodily object, but that, and nothing within the body, is what is directly experienced. A possible source of this confident pronouncement seems to be a certain semantic confusion. Thus the yellowish-red patch which I experience when I see an orange in a tree is certainly given as outside the flesh-colored expanse experienced in seeing my hand just before me, or any other part of my visual field similarly representing my physical organism. But on the neural theory, this is but the physiological truism that the part of the bodily process directly had in seeing the orange is spatiotemporally separate from the part had in seeing one's own body. There is no contradiction here of any kind, nor any conflict with known fact. Nor is it known fact that the "orange" quality directly sensed (which does not mean, "a certain wave length") is not any quality of a neural process. Science does not locate qualities, it uses qualities in our experience as signs of quantities [and structures], these being what it locates. As for the shape of the orange, a neural process does have spatiotemporal pattern, and so far as I can find out from physiology, the given patterns *may* all be represented in the inner bodily patterns. There are some apparent exceptions or qualifications, but I believe they are due to ambiguity or vagueness in the meaning of "given," or to careless observation of perception.[13]

It will perhaps be asked: if the inner bodily patterns are given, must it not be *certain* that they have the properties we directly experience? Hence how can the "may" in the above sentence be in order? The answer is this: since the patterns are directly given, they must exist, and *that* at least is not to be put in doubt. But whether they exist inside or outside our bodies is a distinct question, to be answered only after we have considered carefully what we know about both the inner and the outer physical worlds, those inside and outside our skins. The physical and physiological evidence supports the view that there is no universal correlation between given patterns and any patterns existing outside the body; whereas the evidence is at least compatible with there being a universal correlation with the inner bodily process. Since what is given cannot be in contradiction with what it is given as (by the meaning of "given"), we are led to prefer the hypothesis that the spatial location of the given is in, not outside, the body.

Those who reject this reasoning land in the following predicament. They say that the seen oranges, and other external objects, are directly experienced, or at least, nothing else is, in certain cases, and so far as vision is concerned. But when we close our eyes and have an after-image, or when we submit our eyes to intense stimulation and then suddenly put ourselves in total darkness, and yet for sixty or a hundred seconds perhaps experience brilliant light and color qualities, what is it that we directly experience? Clearly nothing outside the body! There are then three possible interpretations: (1) we experience merely a succession of "images," in other words of sense data; (2) we experience merely our own experiences—of what? (3) we experience the highly stimulated neural process. The first two versions are, by all tests I can think of, indistinguishable from each other and equally absurd; the third is Whitehead's version. But, accepting this version, it would be strange to suppose that when we turn the light on again, the neural process suddenly ceases to be given at all. I cannot imagine any scientist finding this an attractive theory. For there is a straightforward account of the change from the one situation to the other which makes readily intelligible (a) how and why it is that in the second case we are, and in the first we are not, gaining reliable information about the extrabodily world, although (b) in both cases the primary, directly experienced object is (in part at least) the same general sort of neural process. Under (a) we merely need the processes of learning plus the Darwinian scheme of natural selection and nonsurvival of organic structures and built-in impulses which fail to give the organism what it needs in order to cope with its environment.

I call attention to the fact that, in spite of all the brave talk about dispensing with mere sense data (and Whitehead could agree they should be dispensed with), not many of our contemporaries have really shown us *how* to dispense with them. Ryle's attempt to talk dreams and images out of existence is hardly a solution. He may have few of these things; some of us, at least, have had many, and quite indubitable, instances of them. And what else can one say of vivid visual images in darkness than that they are either mere sense data, or else neural processes directly experienced? And if this latter sort of thing happens at all, why not experiment with it in a general theory of sense experience? Is this not normal empirical procedure? And we have here little room for alternatives. For the mere sense-datum theory is semantically, not just factually, suspect. It seems to make experience constitute its own datum, and this looks like nonsense. The given is precisely—given; it is not created by, or a molding of some waxlike substance of, the experience for which it is given. To experience is to experience something not just that very experience. At best, the sensum theory is likely to fall before Occam's razor. Thus Whitehead's view is, in one aspect, based upon logical analysis, and in the other aspect (that of locating the datum in space-time) it is a reasonable empirical hypothesis. But few are discussing it as such. Rather, dogmatism is regnant in current epistemology, the dogmatism of a slightly new linguistically furbished sophisticated naïvete: the axiom that the "seen" and the sheerly given must be one.

Inadequacies in Whitehead's Method of Justifying His View.–It often seems as though Whitehead were merely "telling us" things which, in some secret way, he has found out about reality. A well-known logician said to me: "I don't expect anybody to prove things in philosophy; this is impossible. But I do like them to half-prove things. Whitehead doesn't even do that." I can't entirely agree; there are a fair number of half-proofs in Whitehead. But still the complaint has some justification. Whitehead the metaphysician was elderly; he needed his energy to define his rather extensive stock of ideas; and he tended to skimp on the elaboration of reasons. For instance, why introduce God into the system? Whitehead has reasons for this, and not one but a number. However, they are sketched, suggested, hinted at, not set out in neat, scholastic order. This can be done, however. And it needs to be done.

There is need also to meet the analytic-synthetic challenge. Whitehead says his method is "descriptive"; but then he also speaks of "necessity," not indeed for all of his cosmological views, because some of them merely claim to report matters of fact belonging to our "cosmic epoch," but for those claiming "ultimate metaphysical necessity." This is a serious problem and cannot be left just where Whitehead left it. Yet I believe that here too a reasonable view can be worked out in general harmony with his thought.[14]

Whitehead's Platonism, and (insofar) Eclecticism–Pepper's Charge.[15] – Our age is somewhat nominalistic and, as I personally think, in part for good reasons. With a number of others, I have always found "eternal objects" either ambiguous or dubious. But anyone who sets out to refute the entire system, as some have tried to do, by showing the difficulties of "Platonism" in this sense is overestimating the commitment of the system to this doctrine. Only minor changes are needed, I believe, to make the view decidedly more nominalistic. And so far from introducing inconsistencies, this, as I am not alone in believing, renders the system more consistent. The key to his philosophy, Whitehead says very plainly, is creativity, taken as "creative synthesis." This is scarcely Platonism. And it is not merely *a* Whiteheadian principle, but *the* principle–"the category of the ultimate." Everett Hall showed long ago that a philosophy of process of this kind has no obvious need to entertain a set of eternal objects as a multitude of distinct entities.[16] Some eternal ideal or principle of process there is doubtless need for; but this is not necessarily, if even most plausibly, conceived as a set or multitude.

Slips in Exposition.–Whitehead much of the time expresses himself with care and precision. But now and then he makes real "blunders" (his own word, in this connection) in the language he uses. Thus he has sometimes spoken as though each thing in the universe, according to him, depended logically upon every other thing, no matter where or when in all space-time. All close students of Whitehead know that this is by no means what he wishes to say. Yet he did appear to say it occasionally, thereby obscuring the fact that what he himself refers to as "external relations" are as essential to his doctrine as internal relations. Again, there are sentences about the Primordial Nature of God that seem really to refer more correctly to the Consequent Nature. There is the use, in two meanings, of "transmutation" (one with reference to God), without discussion of the great difference between them. And so on.

Whitehead's Apparent Ignorance of Those Who Most Nearly Anticipated Him.—Whitehead knew the main philosophical and theological traditions well enough to know why he could not agree with them, and to avoid egregious "straw-man" fallacies in his criticisms. He also found a good many of the anticipations of his doctrines; e.g., in Plato, Bacon, Descartes, Locke, Spinoza, Leibniz. But on some points he seems not to have known at all that certain Western thinkers before him (Socinus, Fechner, Lequier, to name only three) had held views with striking similarities to his own. He seems also not to have noted the particularly striking analogies between his theory of process, as more concrete than substance or being, and the entire Buddhist tradition. In some ways, indeed, he overstates his divergence from tradition, and in others understates it. As an example of the latter, he imputes a kind of flux to the divine, but in not a few expressions seems to lean back dangerously far toward the timeless deity of the Middle Ages. As an example of the former: a "dipolar" notion, such as his, of deity makes it possible, as I hope to show elsewhere, to employ a revised form of certain traditional proofs for God. All in all, the relations of his doctrines to tradition need more adequate statement than he could give them.

II

I wish to correct an egregious misstatement in Collingwood's posthumous essay on *The Idea of Nature*, to the effect that Whitehead was unaware, until it was pointed out to him, that his view of God was essentially that of Aristotle.[17] As is carefully explained in *Process and Reality*[18] it is not God as conceived by Whitehead who is (nearly) coincident with God as thought by of Aristotle, but—a radically different thing—the Primordial Nature of God. No two entities could be more diverse, the one the purely "abstract" form, radically empty or "deficient in actuality," of deity in its bare eternal identity, and the other the incomparable richness of the concrete divine actuality.

It is not among the best-known names in the history of Western theology and philosophy that Whitehead's nearest analogues are to be found. Yet there are analogues, and we shall never attain proper perspective regarding the importance of Whitehead until we realize that what he did was neither merely to reiterate the "great tradition," with minor deviations or corrections, nor yet to affirm a simply new conception, but rather to give more articulate development, in a great speculative system, to old religious and philosophical insights hitherto neglected by the great system makers of the West, but long present in philosophy and theology, struggling for a more adequate hearing.

Whitehead once remarked to me that he was not unaware of his defects as a philosopher. "I have certain advantages," he said, "but I can readily imagine that one of you may say the things I ought to have said." My judgment now, after nearly thirty-five years, is this: while Whitehead's approach certainly does not exhaust the speculative possibilities open to us—and I hope personally to show before long that significant advances are immediately available—yet he does, with Peirce, and on the whole probably more than Peirce, represent our greatest speculative model since Leibniz. Like that philosopher he knew much of the exact science of his day, and yet was sensitive (indeed even more than Leibniz) to the totality of human interests. Like him he had, as few others in history have had, the "architectonic" capacity to conceive philosophical inquiry as a definite, articulated whole. Like him, and unlike the post-Kantian idealists, he was able to think in terms of unambiguous logical patterns, so that the skeleton of the Whiteheadian view, like the Leibnizian, can be grasped most readily by seeing certain simple assumptions of a sharply logical kind.

Let us consider, as Leibniz's basic technical tenets: (1) sufficient reason, (2) *in-esse*, or the doctrine that no predicates of a concrete unit-reality or monad can be inessential or accidental, (3) logical independence of every monad from every other (lack of "windows"), (4) monadic character of the human or animal soul, (5) universal validity of the psychical analogy between the human monad and any others (doctrine that monads, as such, have some form of perception and appetition), (6) timeless reality of God and hence of all truth. From these tenets there are deduced pre-established harmony and a logical impossibility that a given person or individual should ever, as that individual, have done otherwise than in fact it has done. Optimism too is implied: "whatever is, is right." It is these three consequences which give the system its air of artificiality. And they lead to a grand inconsistency: that the monads are closed to one another and yet open toward God, who also (this would not be admitted, but it follows from the meaning—any possible meaning—of cognitive perfection or omniscience) is open toward the monads. By pre-established harmony, the monads know of and in a sense influence each other; but God knows of and also influences them in some *absolutely* different way. Thus the system rests, as Whitehead saw very clearly, upon a principle which it never articulates and, without a fresh start, cannot articulate. And he also saw that the medieval systems differ from Leibniz in this respect only by being less clear and candid.

Whitehead carefully and brilliantly avoided these difficulties, while retaining, as no one else had been able to do, the basic insights whose one-sided expression had led to the impasse. The result is as follows: (1) Sufficient reason assumes a more moderate form, as we shall see. (2) *De inesse* is retained, because, properly understood, it is analytic, and only loose thinking ever led to its being denied. There cannot, on the most concrete level of "subject," be two ways of having predicates: (a) that of requiring them for its, the subject's, identity, and (b) that of not requiring them. The distinction between "essence" and "accident" must lie on a secondary, somewhat abstract, level. It is the relatively abstract which can have inessential qualifications (the reason being that it does not really "have" them at all, since this is but a way of talking about the characters of the more concrete). (3) Whitehead also retains a certain logical independence of the unit-realities, but yet, without contradiction, upholds their partial logical dependence.

He does this by making several changes in Leibniz. Thus he drops, and in all his later writings (unless perhaps in a few passages about God), never forgets that he has dropped, the idea that the most concrete level of subject or entity is that of individual persons or other enduring individuals; instead he adopts, as apparently Leibniz never once dreamt of doing, but untold multitudes of Buddhists have done, the unit-becoming, or unit-event, as the concrete sample of reality.

Also he limits mutual independence to relations between contemporary events, of which neither is past or future to the other.

Again events are seen as related to their predecessors by "prehensive" relations (corresponding in part, but only in part, to Leibniz's *petites perceptions*—see 5 above) which render the later event logically dependent upon the earlier, no matter to what enduring individuals or "societies" the two belong. Here too, probably unknowingly, Whitehead repeats Buddhistic views. In contrast to Leibniz, Whitehead refuses to countenance the notion that the datum of experience can be simply a property of that experience itself; he refuses to treat a mind as a picture gallery to which something independent *might* correspond. The primary data for an actuality are other and independent actualities.

Finally, Whitehead denies prehensive relations forward in time, so far as concrete entities are concerned. No event prehends or depends upon a later event, as a concrete particular actuality. I think he would not grant that psychic research could upset this prohibition; though there may well be some subtle and difficult questions to consider in that connection, as also perhaps with reference to the "reversal" of time in [some versions of] quantum mechanics.

What is the result of these principles? That the world can be seen as a unified system of causal influences, every item, by its own nature, placing itself in a unique locus in the system ("identity of indiscernibles"), and yet every item being free and contingent. The necessity that a unit be where and when it is is not a necessity that it *be* or occur. The necessity is hypothetical: if that entity, then just there. But the entity was not prehended or logically required by its predecessors. The principle here is the familiar one, $\sim [(p \rightarrow q) \rightarrow (q \rightarrow p)]$, entailment is not necessarily (or normally) reversible.

What about pre-established harmony? It exists, but in the mild and reasonable form of statistical uniformities, relative regularities of behavior inspired by the influence of deity upon all prehending subjects. A certain amount of "disorder is as real as order." There is no implication that whatever is is right. Yet the world has a basic coherence, and every item, by strict though hypothetical necessity, places itself just where and when it is.

Sufficient reason remains in this moderate form: looking backward, from effect to cause, we find a certain definite past to be implicated as furnishing the "real possibility" of the sort of effect which has taken place; looking toward the future, the effect is implicated only as a kind, or class, of really possible effects, some instance or other of which must occur. If the effect is a decision, and concretely and in the singular it always is that, causation is "creative," that is, not the mere unwinding of any necessity or predetermination, or the mere consequence of any law. No matter what antecedently or externally given "motive" may influence a decision, since any motive is more or less abstract and general (otherwise it would be the act itself), the act cannot be implied, but in its further particularity must be created arbitrarily.

If Whitehead had ever considered Leibniz's proposal that God would not have made a world at all were it not that one possible world is best, I imagine that he would have said, with typical good sense: "Since some world is better than no world, the suggested divine behavior would be irrational, and downright peevish, just as the ass who starved because one bundle of hay was no better than the other, would indeed be asinine in its obliviousness to the superiority of eating over starving."

What then about the order of the world, which Whitehead holds expresses the influence of God upon things? This influence, like any influence in this philosophy, can only operate by the influencer getting himself prehended by the things influenced; and therefore, by the asymmetry of prehensive relatedness, there can be no strict entailment of the result. No matter what God decides for the world, the result, the world's prehensive response, involves an element of self-determination or creative freedom. Moreover, although the divine decisions manifest infinite "wisdom," they yet cannot be deduced from any ultimate necessity because (a) they take into account previous cosmic epochs, and previous events in this epoch, all of which are contingent, and (b) there is no one best way for God to react creatively in a given situation (by the very meaning of creative), though there are, as I personally see it, ways of which it can be said that no other could have been better. Whitehead, no more than Leibniz, I think, would admit that God could ever have done better; yet since the world is in part self-created, the result could always have been better.

The timelessness of factual truth and of God (except in his most abstract aspect) goes by the board. The idea that both truth and divine knowledge receive additions is not nearly so new in theology as some think, nor I suspect is it so easily refuted.[19] Creative synthesis (or synthesizing) is here taken as reality itself, after two millennia of trying out the notion that pure being, nonsynthesizing and noncreative in essence, is reality itself, or at least its primary and superior form.

That Whitehead has reinstated the rationalists' vision without its most obvious defects may be seen further by considering an item or two in the Kantian criticism of Leibniz. In *Dreams of a Ghostseer*,[20] Kant rebukes those who had laughed at Leibniz's panpsychist theory of matter; for, said Kant, if we are to look for a positive conception of physical reality as it is in itself, Leibniz showed us the only possible way to form such a conception. But, Kant went on to remark, if we took this path, we should then confront the impenetrable mystery of one monadic subject interacting with others to form a dynamic system, for instance in the human body. But this problem is directly and clearly solved (in principle) in Whitehead's modified Leibnizianism. A unit-reality *consists* of a complex act of prehending various other units; it is an experient occasion whose only possible concrete objects of experiencing are other such occasions. Clearly, to prehend X, to feel its feelings, is, in a certain definite way, to be influenced by X. There is no further problem or mystery of influence passing from one monad to another. Thus Kant was simply mistaken if he supposed . . . that what the Leibnizian form of monadism could not do, no other form could do either.

Again Kant (in the first *Critique*) criticized Leibniz for arguing that the concept of a divine nature consisting of all positive predicates or perfections could not involve any inconsistency, since contradiction requires negative as well as positive properties; on the contrary, said Kant, two positive properties may be "really repugnant," even though both are equally positive—for example, velocities in contrary directions. Now Whitehead agrees with Kant, but draws a more radical conclusion. God cannot, for nothing can, actualize every positive quality, or all possible value, since positive properties and values are typically alternatives to each other: red [here now] instead of blue or green, a sonnet instead of a ballad, or vice versa. But there is another way of defining perfection. We must distinguish between perfect and imperfect *capacities* for positive predicates. No being can have all positive properties, for they involve mutual incompatibilities; but a being can be capable disjunctively of any positive property and any compossible set of such properties. Properties accrue to an actuality through its experiences or prehensions: the divine capacity for prehensions is to be conceived as subject to no limitation whatever, as between various compossible sets of objects or events. God could not have all, but he could have any, among internally compossible sets of positive properties; in other words, no world state or positive actuality could be such that he could not experience it. This is his infinite *potentiality* for properties. His *actuality*, which must, like all actuality, be in some respects finite, is composed of his actual prehensions of the de facto cosmos. I call this the Consequent State (for "Consequent Nature" is ambiguous, alas!). This state sums up without any loss or deficiency the total reality and value of the cosmos prehended, which is a partly new one with each new state of the prehending deity. The cosmos is not only totally embraced, but the act of embracing it has its own supreme value, which is absolute in its adequacy, in the "wisdom" with which the given totality is received into the divine reality.

This is a concept of divine perfection which never clearly dawned upon Kant, or even Hume—who came closer to it—but which has a long line of descent, at least from some religious thinkers of the Reformation, if not from some Patristic and Islamic theologians of centuries earlier. It can be shown, though not in this essay, that the theistic proofs must one and all be transformed if they are to be made relevant to this conception; and when they are thus transformed, it turns out that Hume's and Kant's critiques of the proofs are no longer, as they stand, decisive, or perhaps even pertinent. The whole issue is reopened, if we are intellectually candid and avoid reasoning according to "guilt by association."

Admirers of Kant will perhaps have asked themselves, What about the Antinomies? Has Whitehead properly considered the difficulties which appear when we try to conceive the space-time reality as a whole? I believe that he must have given this matter some thought, and I know that he had long meditated upon Kant's views. But I feel it as a defect that he did not more explicitly discuss the question of the infinity of the past, which he seems to take for granted, and [the finitude or infinity] of space, about which he has little to say, and the regress toward the infinitely small, which he appears to reject. But one thing is clear to me: at least two of Kant's Antinomies depend upon the classical (deterministic) concept of causality which Whitehead rejects. He believes in real possibility in a sense which requires a reformulation of the very meaning of "cause," or of occurrence "according to rules." But the relationships to Kant ought to be worked out by someone. . . . Those who reject metaphysics on the ground that necessary propositions "assert nothing" (Wittgenstein) do not show us that and how they themselves avoid taking the Humean doctrine of universal external relations—or some other view on the basis of which Whitehead is rejected—either as an extralinguistic yet a priori pronouncement, or alternatively as a factual statement, which is nevertheless vouched for by none of the sciences of fact and is widely disputed among philosophers. I submit: the status of Whitehead's metaphysics of process is a postponed, not an adjudicated, matter.

Reprinted from *The Relevance of Whitehead: Philosophical Essays in Commemoration of the Centenary of the Birth of Alfred North Whitehead*, ed. Ivor Leclerc (London: George Allen & Unwin, 1961), pp. 21-43. Minor passages have been omitted, as indicated by ellipses.

CHAPTER ELEVEN

Whitehead's Novel Intuition

It may seem that Whitehead's system is not particularly new. Thus he is a theist, an epistemological realist, a pluralist, an indeterminist, a metaphysical idealist or psychicalist—in the sense of denying any mere matter ("vacuous actuality") irreducible to mind or experience as such—and have there not been many theists, realists, pluralists, indeterminists, psychicalists? Even this combination of doctrines is not altogether new. For instance, Fechner, Varisco, James Ward, and Bergson approximated it. To be sure, Whitehead qualifies his pluralism by the recognition of a profound organic unity of reality, but so did the philosophers just mentioned, and also Royce, Lotze, and still others. Again, the "philosophy of organism" holds that past events are immortal as constituents in subsequent process, but did not Bergson say as much? Finally, Whitehead stands for a seemingly neoplatonic version of eternal forms as integral to the divine reason, an old doctrine indeed! Is, then, his system merely a somewhat new combination of old factors, an eclectic contrivance, as Pepper once suggested?

According to Bergson, a great system is the elucidation of a single novel intuition. Is there such an intuition in Whitehead?

I believe that intellectual affairs are too complex for Bergson's contention to be wholly sound. Probably no philosophy, not even Bergson's, is limited to the elucidation of an organic insight. Eclectic elements, I suspect, always enter in.

However, I also think that Whitehead is a strongly intuitive as well as highly original philosopher. And he wrote one phrase which comes as close as any to capturing the novel insight which his philosophy expresses: "The many become one and are increased by one" (*Process and Reality*, p. 32). Since this assertion is used to elucidate "the category of the ultimate," we have Whitehead's own word for its central position. Let us see how various aspects of his philosophy are implicated in this supreme category.

Pluralism is indicated by "the many." There are numerous realities, not just one, or a mystical reality beyond number. So far the doctrine is simply pluralism. But what pluralist had ever clearly stated that it is the destiny of the many to enter into a novel unity, an additional reality, which, since we are dealing with a principle, not a mere fact, must in its turn be united with the others in a further unity, and so on without end? We have here an admission not merely of emergence, but of emergent or creative *synthesis* as the very principle of process and reality. This is brought out in another phrase, defining the "Principle of Relativity": "To be is to be a potential for every [subsequent] becoming" (cf. *Process and Reality*, p. 33). Each item of reality has the destiny of forming material for endlessly compounded and recompounded acts of synthesis—producing new and more complex realities.

This "pluralism" is original in so many ways at once that I scarcely know in what order to take them. The many *are* not one, they *become* one. This is not the usual "Organicism." First an item is, on its own, through its own unification of its presupposed items; then it is included in, possessed by, subsequent items. In other terms, relationships to prior entities are internal to the given entity, but not conversely. Thus we have both internal and external relations. Bradley and Hume (or Russell) are alike left behind, with all the paradoxes of their two extreme positions.

Again, the "many" are not existing individuals or substances, in the usual sense, but "actual occasions" or unit-events. "Actual" is opposed to "potential," and in any individual thing or person there are always both the actual individual past and the potential individual future. In an occasion, however, there is only actuality, so far as that unit of reality is concerned. It is indeed a "potential" for subsequent becoming; but the actualization of *this* potentiality can never be a possession of the occasion itself, but only of later occasions. The occasion *is*, it does not have, the potentiality, and it is contradictory for a potentiality to be or have its own actualization.

In other language, it is not the items of actuality which change; change is merely their successive becoming. Here Whitehead takes a step beyond Leibniz, who interpreted spatial multiplicity in terms of many reals (not in terms of mere parts of reals), but did not so interpret temporal multiplicity, succession. Whitehead takes this additional step. Succession, he holds, never concerns merely a single unit-reality. Thus process is individualized in time as well as in space. The final "individual" is a spatiotemporal unit, an event, which becomes as a single entity. (Bergson seems to deny any definite units.) Of course there is a radical difference between time and space, for in temporal multiplicity we have the creation of new unities out of the previous ones. Still the units are least terms of actual succession, as well as of coexistence in space. (Vere Chappell's critical remarks,[1] the validity of which I do not wish here to deny or affirm, concerning Whitehead's epochal theory of becoming, seem to be neither intended nor adapted to upset the main point of Whitehead's doctrine of spatiotemporal unit-actualities.)

Whitehead's indeterminism is implicit in what has been said. If the new unity were deducible from the old, it would logically be no addition at all, and the degree of multiplicity would not be "increased." Any causal laws used for the deduction must be viewed as mere abstract aspects of the previous multiplicity; and in any case, how can a law prescribe just how a set of items is to be embraced in a new equally unitary item?

What of the Whiteheadian denial of mere matter (or "vacuous actuality")—that is, the rejection of dualism as well as of materialism? Whitehead's epistemology comes in here: we must always look to experience for our model of reality. An experience is precisely a synthesis emergent upon, and not deducible from, its data. The category of the ultimate tells us that all process, and so, in this philosophy of process, all concrete reality, must at least in this respect be analogous to experience. Moreover, Whitehead sees no way to distinguish between cases of emergent synthesis, or creativity, which are experiences of some sort (however different from the human) and cases which are just not experiences of any kind. For one thing, how would the latter sort be given or known? When given, an entity is taken into the unity of one or more experiences, and this unity is a case of "feeling of feeling," not a case of the subject's feeling the merely insentient as such. How could one feel this? We can sense or feel how various already-actualized occasions sensed or felt; we cannot sense or feel that they simply did not sense or feel at all. A dualism of experiences and nonexperiences would at best be a grave obscurity in the theory of process as creative synthesis.

Two doctrines of Whitehead seem not to be covered by our account, his view of God and eternal objects. I believe that the latter doctrine, so far as I grasp it at all (and I may misconceive it), is to some extent a genuinely eclectic affair, not wholly pertinent to the central insight. I shall not argue this here, but simply say that I think a somewhat more nominalistic version would improve the coherence of the system.

How does God come in? There are many ways (I shall mention but two of them) in which creative synthesis requires a divine level of synthesizing. In the ordinary case most of the items entering into an experience are but ineffectively present in it. They are "negatively prehended," which seems to amount, for most purposes, to not being prehended at all. Only a divine prehension could effectively and positively unify its data. And is not the intelligibility of "negative prehension" dependent upon the reality of some positive prehension of the same items? What makes it *true* that an item is *not* effectively prehended, if this is the whole story? Whitehead himself says that the truth itself is but the way in which "all things are together in the Consequent Nature of God." Only in contrast with his definitive and positive prehension of an item can it make sense to speak of the deficiency of *our* prehension of it.

In another way, God is needed because the order of process is unintelligible without his influence. Each unit of process is a partly free act, somewhat transcending its conditions and any mere causal regularities or laws. But sets of data cannot be synthesized at all unless there is a sufficient degree of order in them. Process would come to an end if limits were not imposed upon the development of incompatible lines of process. The comprehensive order of the world is enjoyed, but not determined or created, by ordinary actual entities. Since the particular order is logically arbitrary, it must be either a blind fact wholly opaque to explanation or the result of a synthesis which deliberately selected it. The only alternative to such selection is the chance agreement of the multitude of acts of synthesis. The theistic explanation meets the difficulty head on. A divine prehension can use its freedom to create, and for a suitable period maintain, a particular world order. This selection then becomes a "lure," an irresistible datum, for all ordinary acts of synthesis.

Is this the traditional theistic view? It seems not. For (1) it conceives even God as endlessly enriched by new data, and (2) it conceives the divine creativity as the supreme, but not the sole, case of creative decision. The old problem of Job cannot then arise in its customary form. If *all-mighty* means "having power unilaterally to decide the details of the world process," then for Whitehead's philosophy the term is meaningless, or contradictory. God's power may in some sense be perfect, but it is not "absolute," for power in its very definition is relative, power to deal with antecedent decisions as data and to influence all subsequent decisions; and thus a monopoly of decision-making exercised in a single act or by a single agent is nonsense. How, nevertheless, power may in God be ideally great or "perfect" is a point which is not explicitly elucidated by Whitehead, but which I believe can quite well be rendered in terms of his basic conceptions.

Thus the category of the ultimate really does express the central intuition of Whitehead's philosophy, with some qualification as to eternal objects.

It is my personal view that a metaphysics can also be integrated by taking as intuitive starting point, not creativity or the category of the ultimate, but deity, defined in Anselm's words as a reality such that none greater (meaning better) can be conceived—provided we understand this to connote, not unsurpassability in every sense, but only unsurpassability *by another*. It can then, I hold, be shown that divine self-surpassing will not only not be ruled out, but will be implied. Also that the self-surpassing, otherwise unsurpassable, deity exists necessarily and eternally, and in addition, that nondivine creativity must also have actual instances. One will in this way have derived the equivalent of "the category of the ultimate" from the religious idea alone. For self-surpassing deity must be creative. In other words, the theistic intuition, properly understood and expressed, without distortions due to neoplatonic prejudices about the absolute superiority of being over becoming, or of the absolute or infinite over the relative or finite, will yield the essence of the Whiteheadian metaphysics. The foregoing is but a hint or two. Certain parts, at least, of the reasoning involved are set forth elsewhere.

William Christian's beautifully argued but to me unconvincing version of Whitehead's account of pastness[2] I take to be destructive of one of the most important elements in the system. This account puts emphasis upon one side of the puzzle of negative prehending and misses the equally essential aspect that even the negatively prehended is present in the "subjective form." Also he has, I think, mistaken the meaning of "past" or "perished." "Past" is a relative term, and cannot describe a quality of the actual entity, taken in itself. "Perished" seems to describe such a quality, implying that the entity is dead, lacking in subjective activity. For this reason I think that the metaphor was an unfortunate one. On the contrary, the principle of process means that the entity *is* its activity, and to say that it lacks this activity is to say that the entity is not what it is. Nor does it help to say that it "no longer is what it was." For this "no longer" takes one outside the entity within which the "was" is meaningless. The conclusion is that the pastness of an entity is the *same* as its being objectified by successors. It is not first past and then objectified; rather it first completes its process of becoming, and then it is objectified. There is nothing between, unless you want to say that its readiness for becoming past, that is, for becoming objectified, is between. The pastness itself is only potential until objectification has taken place. When we are told that the indeterminacy of the actuality's self-creative process has "evaporated" with the achieving of a determinate satisfaction, this only means, I take it, that the particular resolution of the indeterminacy is henceforth definitive; i.e., the "decision" cannot be made over again or otherwise. But the process of deciding is not done away with, since it *is* the actual entity, and this, we are expressly told, can never change. "Perishing," as a sort of drying up of subjective immediacy, would be a change, or nothing that I can imagine. We should remember too that the very "being" of an entity is its availability for objectification (principle of relativity). Hence how can it "be" unavailable? And indeed, if being past is relative, meaning that some new present has the entity as its past, then there can be no legitimate puzzle as to how what is past and gone can be yet now had. For what else is its pastness than this being now had as past? The only "loss" through perishing is due to negative prehensions in an entity's successors, and I cannot concede that these are attributable to God as prehending the creatures (or in any other way). Apparently contrary texts in Whitehead I have dealt with elsewhere.[3] Nor do I concede that nothing is past to the divine prehensions. . . . There is only one form of concrete prehension, "inheritance," and to be inherited and to be past for the prehending experience are one and the same.

Perhaps this view is indeed "too simple." But if so, I do not know what complication would really help. The view is rather less simple than Christian's, so far as God is concerned, for it makes him a society of actual entities, not a single entity. I take Whitehead to have been rather seriously confused in those remarks in which he seems to imply such singularity. If the many in becoming prehended into a novel unity is thereby "increased by one," then in the case of God there is a new entity with each of his unified prehensive acts. To say that there is only one such act is to say either that God never does attain subjective unity or satisfaction at all, or else that his actuality is the *totum simul* of Boethius, surveying all time once for all.

Neither alternative seems to have any place in the Whiteheadian philosophy.

On one point Christian and I agree: Whitehead did not always say unambiguously what he meant, and, therefore, to achieve clarity and consistency we must resolve certain ambiguities at our own risk. But

Christian's risks seem excessive. True, he can take Whitehead's "God is an actual entity" literally, and I cannot. But with some other passages it is my account, not his, which can accept the literal meaning. And Whitehead told me himself that he felt his account of deity to be "very vague," and he went on to suggest that certain other features of his philosophy were more adequately defined in his writings.

It should, I think, be added that there is nonetheless a good deal of admirable clarity in the Whiteheadian discussion of deity. Thus it is perfectly clear that God is viewed as perceiving or prehending the evolving world and thereby endlessly acquiring new content and enhancing the aesthetic richness of his own experience; also that the strictly eternal, infinite, or nonderivative aspect of deity is "abstract" or "deficiently actual," by itself, while only the aspect which is derivative ("consequent"), "in flux," and "in a sense temporal," is concrete or fully actual; further, that this aspect not only perceives, but consciously perceives, the world in all its aspects and thus forms "the unification of all things" whereby they achieve immortality. Thus the divine form of creativity is a perpetual and ideal summing up of *all* anterior products of creativity, and so, in the penetrating though simple colloquial phrase, things always "add up to something," for God never fails to perform the addition.

In essence this doctrine is not new. Intuitively it was, I believe, always present in religious thought. And as early as the Socinian catechism it became, in some respects, lucidly explicit. In vain—for Europe had other things to do, even with respect to Socinianism, than to read this part of the catechism intelligently. Later, Fechner, Lequier, W. P. Montague, and many others gave fairly clear anticipations of the Whiteheadian doctrine. I myself first acquired such a view from my teacher W. E. Hocking. I cannot believe that any theism which fails to include an equivalent of the features mentioned in the preceding paragraph can do justice to the intellectual situation which has resulted from the realization that the medieval or neoplatonic form of theism is not only a doctrine riddled with antinomies but one which never did have a genuine warrant from religious experience, or from the idea of worship, but was rather the result of certain philosophical biases introduced into European thought by Parmenides and Plato. We have, in fact, become aware that to worship Being—or the infinite, immutable, absolute, or independent—may be to worship not God, but an idol. Perhaps deity is eminent becoming as much as eminent being. Is not divinity in the "eminence," rather than in an identity with one category as opposed to the other? In supposing that pure being would be the same as eminence, what did we do if not worship a category instead of God? Eminence may not consist in being on one side of ultimate polarities, such as infinite-finite, nonrelative-relative, eternal-temporal. Eminence may overflow these simple and easy dichotomies, and be in its own unrivaled fashion on both sides of them. Thus the *way* in which God's concreteness is "consequent" upon the world is radically and in principle superior to the way in which we are consequent upon it. And nothing less than deity *could* be consequent upon *all* other things, by means of prehensions positively inclusive of them in all their aspects.

Yet the neoplatonists (including Aquinas under this designation) were still, from the Whiteheadian standpoint, correct in an important point. God, to be sure, is not exclusively eternal, infinite, absolute; but yet he and he alone has even an aspect of his individuality (the Primordial Nature) which is these things. He and he alone is the finite-infinite, the relative-absolute, the consequent-primordial form of creativity; other forms are exclusively finite, relative, consequent. Thus Whiteheadian theism essentially embraces classical theism, but not conversely (though the doctrines of the Trinity and of the Incarnation point, in some respects, toward a Consequent Nature). Here is the crucial problem in religious metaphysics, the decision between God as supreme Being, and God as supreme Becoming or process, inclusive of an abstract element of eternal Being.

It is my conviction that in Whitehead Western metaphysics moved appreciably closer than ever before to a technical language capable of formulating without inconsistency the content of the ancient saying, "God is love." This could not be accomplished so long as the magnificent achievements of the Greeks blinded men to the grave limitations and defects of the platonic (or perhaps pseudoplatonic) exaltation of the fixed and impassible. The "many become one" only because the new unity is one of "feeling of feeling," sympathetically appropriating the feeling-content of the previous entities. Experience is never merely of some insentient "object," but is always experience of others' experience. But what is the root idea of love but this, participation by one subject in the life of others? This is the very process of realization, in Whitehead's system. Obviously no immutable form can engage in such participation. Nor can the Aristotelian "thinking of thinking," unless Aristotle failed badly in explaining his meaning.

Almost the whole of Greek ethics is based upon the notion of substances which never overlap in their being. In one way or another the attempt is made to derive love from self-interest, for instance as a means of remedying deficiency by comparison with the absolute model of beauty.

But if value is essentially found in participating, in living the life of another, then supreme value must be the supreme form of such integration of the many into one, and then there cannot be an absolute case, for the novel unity becomes a potential item for a further act of synthesis, and there can be no final stage. There can only be an inexhaustible progress of the divine life as summing up ever anew the de facto actualities. "Divine love" means "divine relativity" in the concrete or consequent aspect of deity, and absoluteness only in the abstract eternal form of perfection common to all possible stages of the divine creativity. Perhaps Plato had glimpses of such an idea, but certainly Greek thought never clearly elucidated it.

Apart from his eternal objects, Whitehead's mode of thought is, to a remarkable extent, reminiscent of ancient Buddhism, the venerable tradition which most adequately rights the balance against certain exaggerations in the Greek tradition. The Buddhists renounce the effort to explain love by self-interest; indeed, they deny the ultimacy of the idea of self as capable of an [individually unique yet ever] identical interest through the vicissitudes of time. Whitehead once remarked, with a quizzical smile, "I sometimes think that all modern immorality is due to the Aristotelian notion of individual substances." A Buddhist would understand this remark without difficulty. But would those immersed in the platonic tradition understand it?

However, Whitehead is deeply original even when taken as a neo-Buddhist. He sees the synthetic nature of the momentary realities or actual entities (which Buddhism alone of the great traditions realized were the concrete units of reality) and he understands—as the Buddhists seem not to have done—the fashion in which each such entity prehensively sums up its predecessors (but *not* its successors). This *asymmetrical* organicity was made into a formal, clearly stated category for the first time (so far as I know) in *Process and Reality*. Here is the key to a philosophy of process according to which, so far from its being the case that "all things change," no concrete reality changes at all, though every concrete reality becomes by its act of self-creation. (Even God is self-created, with the difference that there can never have been a first and can never be a last divine becoming.) Thus the fear of transition, influential in Buddhism as well as in Greek thought, is overcome without either the futile attempt to explain becoming as a special and inferior case of being or the renunciation of rational explanation altogether. Becoming is no longer the enemy of permanence, but its everlasting foundation. The many are not lost in the new unity, but preserved in it with all their concrete distinctiveness.

Values seemingly lost (through negative prehensions) on lower levels of emergent synthesis abide "evermore," thanks to the operations of the highest level. And thus one of Whitehead's principal aims, to give "importance" to the passing moment, is fulfilled, and fulfilled upon the rational plane. It is an old aim, but when and where was it achieved before with so much clarity and coherence?

Of course there are aspects of Whiteheadian originality not covered in the foregoing account, such as the distinctive theory of relativity in physics, the theory of extensive abstraction, and some aspects of the logic of *Principia Mathematica*. But the central intuitive novelty seems to be in the idea of synthetic psychical creativity, which feeds on its own previous products, and (except, perhaps, for eternal objects) on nothing else whatever.

Reprinted from *Alfred North Whitehead: Essays on His Philosophy*, ed. George L. Kline (Englewood Cliffs, N.J.: Prentice-Hall, 1963), pp. 18-26. ⓒ 1963. Reprinted by permission of Prentice-Hall, Inc.

CHAPTER TWELVE

Whitehead and Ordinary Language

How wide is the gap between Whitehead's metaphysics and "linguistic analysis" taken as the central method in philosophy? To judge from the neglect of this metaphysics in England the gap is wide indeed. There seems indeed to be virtually no discussion of the question among English philosophers. Is this because the lack of linguistic sophistication and clarity in Whitehead is too obvious to need any demonstration? My view is that Whitehead is neither hopelessly defective nor anything like impeccable in his uses of words and that the gap in question can and should be crossed, and in various ways by various persons.

First of all, Whitehead is partly on the side of the current methodology in one significant issue, that of phenomenology. He thinks that we cannot simply confront the given and read off its characters by virtue of an act of "bracketing" whatever is inferred or assumed, rather than directly and unmistakably given. He thinks we must approach the given with definite ideas as to what it *might* be, and that a principal source of such ideas is the "wisdom embodied in language." Otherwise the subtlety and complexity of immediacy will hopelessly confuse or baffle us. He once called metaphysics a "descriptive science"; but he did not suppose that immediacy can furnish us with the tools for describing itself, or that the validity of a description will ever be entirely "clear and distinct," or infallible. He might have had some sympathy with Austin's phrase "phenomenology of language." But he also seems to have thought that we need to know what the great philosophers of the past have made of the data of experience.

In the second place, Whitehead has a deep respect for linguistic traditions. He has formally (in conversation, as told to me by the student addressed) denied inventing any new words as philosophical instruments. Perhaps "superject" is the one exception, and it is by no means indispensable. "Prehension" is Leibnizian: besides, it is simply "apprehension" without the complication implied by the "ap–"; in addition, "prehensile tail," by an obvious metaphor, brings out the point. Whitehead wants a word which expresses the subjective side of the idea of the datum, or the given, i.e., that much of the rest of the world which an experience "grasps." Apprehension, or even "perception," is more than just having data; it includes also some use made of, interpretation put upon, the given. Of course there is always at least a minimal form of this, but "prehension" puts the emphasis upon the aspect of givenness. "Perception" is less clear for an additional reason. It suggests a contrast with memory, whereas, according to Whitehead (who I am sure is here in the right), there are data of memory as truly as of perception. Prehension is the common element of perception and memory, abstracting from aspects of inference, interpretation, and judgment. In all the world before Whitehead, East or West, I find no one nearly so clear as he about the similarities and differences between perception and memory. There is another objection to perception as a synonym for prehension. It might be supposed that in dreams we perceive nothing, but at most think we do. But Whitehead holds that there is always prehension, in any kind of experience or mental event whatever. It is impossible to merely think a larger world of which experience is becoming a part; this world is actually given in every case.

Much has been made recently of the naïveté of assuming a simply given and incorrigibly possessed bit of reality, translatable into sacrosanct protocol statements. But it is not Whitehead who is naïve at this point. The given is indeed possessed, actually there in experience, but that it is translatable into incorrigible bits of knowledge is for Whitehead a very different matter. Like Leibniz and many others he has never for a moment accepted the pseudoaxiom that to experience, and to know that and what one experiences, are the same, or that anyone (unless God) can have infallible introspection. The value of a theory of givenness or prehension is not, for Whitehead, what it once seemed to be for C. I. Lewis, and also for Russell and Carnap, that it enables us to have infallible verbalized premises of knowledge. This is not the point, which—put negatively—is rather that if the rest of the world is simply external to experience there is no reason why inferences concerning the world should have even the slightest probability or tendency to be correct. If and only if we directly grasp reality in intuition, or as Whitehead often says, in "feeling," can our conscious interpretations be at least influenced by that reality. This is a long way from infallibility, but it is also a long way from the sheer disconnectedness of experience and the rest of reality which Hume, Russell, and all too many others seem to affirm.

But Whitehead has another quite different reason for valuing his theory of prehension. He wants to find out not merely how knowledge connects with the rest of the world, but how in general parts of the world connect with other parts. He seeks a real "answer to Hume" on causality. For him experience is not merely a bridge which we may cross to reach reality; it is a paradigm case of reality—for instance, of the cause-effect relation. Epistemology and cosmology, insofar, are the same thing, with but a difference of emphasis. Plato, Leibniz, Peirce, many others, are his predecessors in this. (Kant got somewhat off the track here.)

"Actual entity" employs two generally current words in a special but carefully explicated sense. Why "actual"? Because the contrast intended is with "possible" or "potential." Not all possibilities are actualized; what actualizes some possibilities is the occurrence of corresponding concrete events; these are either groups of events more or less arbitrarily considered as single entities, or they are genuinely singular events each with a unity not dependent upon the point of view from which it is regarded. Whitehead is here, for one thing, rejecting the analysis of becoming into continua with successive parts divisible to infinity. There are least actual units of becoming. Time and space as infinitely divisible are abstractions, the concrete (in any limited space-time) is finite not infinite in number. Just as half a man is not a man nor anything concrete at all, so a man's experience in the first half of (perhaps) a tenth of a second may not be an actual experience at all. Perhaps he could have had a temporally shorter experience, but in fact he did not. The paradigm case of actual entity for us human knowers is a single actual concrete human experience.

"Concrete" and "single" rule out such "experiences" as falling in love. Even if this happened in just one experience rather than a sequence, it would be at most an aspect only, however important, of that experience. Various perceptions would be taking place, various memories, thoughts, emotions, only some of which would be expressed by "falling in love." Concrete experiences cannot be defined but must be "pointed to," e.g., the first experience I had after waking this morning.

If you say that the foregoing idea of a concrete singular needs no label, then you are simply rejecting Whitehead's proposal. Can the ground for doing so be linguistic? I fail to see how. If the idea is to be expressed, what better words could have been used? It is normal to speak of actual, but not of "existing" events. Events do not exist, they really happen, or are actual. Should Whitehead have said "actual *thing*"? Surely that would have been misleading. The word thing is too often used for an entity which develops through changing states, a tree, house, or planet. "Substance" would have had this implication even more strongly. Had Whitehead said "actual events" it would have been all too easy to forget that he was talking about singular and concrete events. One might speak of the "outbreak of World War I" as an actual event, yet it would be a long, long way from being a concrete and singular event, corresponding say to one man's momentary experience (but the whole of that experience). So I maintain that had Whitehead gone still more carefully into how we use the words connected with his problem he might very well have come out exactly as he did.

Another term: "creativity." Here, too, is a word in normal use. Artists, scientists, all sorts of people, are said to be creative if they introduce into the world patterns of feeling, thought, action, neither present in it nor distinctly anticipated before. This meaning Whitehead employs in his metaphysical concept. What makes it metaphysical is just its absolute generality, by which is meant that any actual entity must exhibit it. Since what is not an actual entity is either, according to the system, a group of such entities, or an abstraction from one or more of them, everything whatever will in some fashion embody or manifest creativity. Not that one is to say that a river or tree literally creates, but that when the river or tree is analyzed into the concrete singular components constituting its history, creativity will characterize these components, i.e., the actual entities involved. There will be in each a more or less complex quality new to the universe and only relatively or partially predictable from what went before. This is a doctrine one can reject, but can the ground of rejection be that Whitehead is confused about the uses of words? The metaphysical generality of his assertion is not at all that "everything" creates, for only concrete singulars literally do that. But every such singular does so, though not necessarily in more than some extremely minimal degree. What is new and unpredictable in a man's experience will presumably be more considerable than what is so in a mouse's experience, and what is new and unpredictable in a poet more than in an ordinary "uncreative" sort of person. Whitehead is not rejecting such negations, provided literal exactitude is not claimed for them. Adjectives are normally meant in a comparative sense. A "poor man" is not necessarily a man without a penny, and an "uncreative man" is not necessarily a man absolutely without genuine novelty in his experience. There is no such man.

Whitehead's doctrine that creativity pervades actuality is not even an invention. Bergson and Peirce both had it, and the first of these surely influenced Whitehead. I should be surprised if anyone could give reasonable grounds for holding that they could not have taken this view had they considered more carefully and understood better how words function. Peirce's theory of signs was one of the great achievements in its field. Incidentally, Berdyaev, the Parisian Russian, Varisco in Italy, and, perhaps less clearly, Fechner in Germany held rather similar views about the metaphysical ultimacy of creativity, not all using this word, perhaps. True, the doctrine contradicts what some people still assume is the required causal axiom of "necessary and sufficient conditions" for what happens. But various philosophers anticipated Heisenberg in challenging this axiom. Taking the philosophers' and the physicists' arguments together, I conclude that the axiom should now be qualified to read: happenings have necessary conditions, and they have "sufficient" ones provided only this means: sufficient to make necessary (in principle predictable) the approximate sort of thing that happens, not the very happening itself in all its quality. In other words, causal conditions limit what can happen to a more or less narrow range of possibilities. Thus what happens is always more determinate than the conditions imply. How much this "more" of determinateness amounts to depends upon the level of actualities involved. On the human level it amounts to more than on the mouse level, and on the mouse level more than on that of atoms. There is an intelligible rationale (as Bergson saw) for a hierarchy of degrees of indeterminacy. Some of the chief founders of quantum mechanics (though not Planck, Schrödinger, or Einstein) have suggested some such idea.

Whitehead explicates creativity as the process whereby "the many become one and are increased by one." This may seem obscure, but it follows readily from the conception of actual entities as analogous to human experiences. Each such experience is "one," a new singular actuality not hitherto present in reality. But each experience prehends a multiplicity of data (the "many"). Thus there are memories of preceding experiences of the man himself, there are prehensions of unit-events in parts of the body, etc. Many actual entities furnish data for any one new actual entity. Accordingly, the entity is a "synthesis" of the world out of which it arises. The synthesis cannot be causally predictable, except approximately, because it is a subtle contradiction to suppose that many things could dictate their precise mode of inclusion into a synthesis. This synthesis can only be a creation, for by it the definite complexity of reality is "increased." There is now one more determinate, unique actuality. The more cannot be implied by the less. That there will be more can be, and is, implied; but not the particular quality of the addition. Growth in richness of determination can be inevitable, but not the actual path the growth takes. That is a matter of probability and approximateness. We are not talking about our ignorance of conditions but of the very meaning of "conditioning." Determinists, usually uncritically and without clear awareness of the alternative, assume one meaning; the intelligent indeterminists assume another, knowing well the deterministic alternative. Who could fail to know it, since it has been more or less fashionable for over two thousand years? It is, incidentally, false—though often assumed— that determinism has been rejected only because of its believed incompatibility with moral freedom. Bergson, more obviously Peirce, and others have had additional reasons.

The word "condition" suggests an asymmetry which is nullified by the venerable phrase "necessary and sufficient." If p entails q, then the truth of q is a condition of the truth of p. But normally, in such cases, the truth of p is not, in turn, a condition of that of q. That this man is mortal must be true if all men are mortal (and there is this man). But the mere truth that this man is mortal does not entail that all men are. Yet if p is a sufficient *and necessary* condition of q then it is all the same to say that q is a sufficient and necessary condition of p. "Necessary and sufficient" means reciprocal necessity. Thus the asymmetry which haunts the intuition of causality is contradicted. The previous world is necessary for the present world: and also the present world is a necessary consequence of the previous world; thus necessity holds both ways. To me it is somewhat ludicrous that so few have seen the dubious character of this symmetricalizing of causality in a supposedly harmless definition. (But Meyerson and Peirce saw it.) The reason for this oversight is not far to seek. Our scientific and practical interest in prediction looks for sufficient conditions, given which something about the outcome is guaranteed. Anything not guaranteed is beside the point in many such cases. (It may, in the inorganic parts of nature, be largely confined to the microscopic.) But the interest in prediction is only a penultimate not an ultimate interest, which is rather in deciding which of the antecedently not predictable courses of events we try to make happen. Dewey has always been clearheaded on this. Knowing the future is no absolute aim, for until we decide, there is, insofar, no determinate future to know. *To live or be actual is, in this philosophy, to decide the theoretically undecidable.* This applies to animals as truly, though not so significantly, as to man, and to atoms much less significantly, but still truly.

Whitehead says that the actual entity is "self-creative," *"causa sui."* Is this an absurdity? It is initially paradoxical. But one can trace the paradox to an ambiguity which it seems possible to avoid. The actuality is "internally determined and externally free," which means that the antecedent conditions only limit the possibilities to a more or less narrow range, and that hence if one asks what has given the actuality its precise character the answer must be either the paradoxical, "It gives it to itself," or "Nothing gives the definiteness." It does not "come from" somewhere; rather it is created *de novo* in the becoming of the entity itself. It has no "cause," if that means an antecedent yet fully determining influence. To say "self-caused" can only be a generalization of causation beyond the temporal antecedence normally included in the idea. But one need not use such paradoxical expressions. The definiteness is new, not implied by the antecedent or "external" situation; but there it now is. Since the determinateness has come about, it is in that sense an act. But it is an act of no agent unless one internal to the entity, i.e., the entity itself regarded as acting or free. Peirce had almost this idea in his theory of Firstness.

Whitehead's term "eternal object" is for me more problematic than those discussed so far. He uses this phrase instead of "universal" for several reasons, but one of these reasons seems to me to beg an important philosophical question, the question whether or not the independence of "red," say, from time (red yesterday, today, or tomorrow seems just the same quality) is an absolute independence, so that in no matter what "cosmic epoch" or stage of cosmic development there must be such a universal, or distinct "potential," available for instantiation ("ingression") in concrete actualities. I incline with Peirce, and some kinds of nominalism, to suppose that only extremely general abstractions, such as "quality," are absolutely timeless, nonemergent, or eternal, in their relevance. There is a linguistic component in the question, no doubt. I shall not pursue the matter here.

When Whitehead calls God "an actuality" I do have linguistic trouble. For in his philosophy an actuality is a novel synthesis of many antecedent actualities, themselves syntheses of their predecessors, each new actuality adding itself to the previous "many," thus forming a new plurality to be subsequently synthesized, and so on forever. If then God were a concrete singular, he would be but an episode in cosmic becoming. In addition, religious terms about God take him as analogous to a person or individual, not to a single momentary experience of an individual. For Whitehead a person is a sequence of predecessor-prehending actual entities. This is not a mere class in the logician's sense, and insofar as it is a class it must be construed as having possible as well as actual members (experiences the person might have had, or may yet have). (Current extensionalist logics may not be able to formulate this.) If Whitehead calls such a sequence, so conceived, a "personally-ordered society of entities," this is because (a) a society in the normal sense is identified by potential as well as actual members (thus the American Ornithological Union will presumably come to have members now neither in being nor subject to denotation); also (b) each new member "inherits" qualities characteristic of the society from antecedent members; finally (c) some societies do and some do not form a single linear sequence, A, B, C, . . . The single-sequence societies (broadly analogous to, e.g., the kings of England) are "personally-ordered." This is an extremely abstract analogy, with a human person's sequence of experiences as model. As terminology it is picturesque, but the anthropomorphic suggestions are not misused. The idea is clear enough. What I fail to see, though some close students of Whitehead disagree with me here, is how God can be a single actuality rather than a socially connected sequence of actualities. I even suspect, having in mind the relativity of simultaneity, that the complexity of deity is greater than the analogy with a person suggests, and that, a little as in Trinitarianism, one must posit a multiplicity of personally-ordered societies in the divine life.

However this may be, "actual entity," "prehension," and "creativity" will be involved. These three terms, and not eternal objects or God as an actual entity, are for me the hard core of Whiteheadianism. And the three terms seem linguistically valid and good. I say the same of Whitehead's basic value theory, which views aesthetic good as intensity and harmony of feeling, and ethical good as the generalized will to maximize aesthetic good in future actualities, ultimately, as the inclusive achievement, in divine actualities, by which alone the rest are adequately prehended "forevermore." And I hold that the metaphysics, with the qualifications hinted at above, and some yet to be mentioned, gives the right setting for this sublime theory. This philosophy is akin to Buddhism in the radical way in which it deprives self-interest theories of their specious rationale, but it is more clearly an affirmative (as opposed to "escapist") doctrine than Buddhism, even in the Zen form.

I have not yet discussed the problems connected with what Whitehead terms "genetic analysis." He seems, at least verbally, to affirm two sorts of real succession, succession of actual entities, and succession of "phases" within a single entity. My present judgment, so far as it goes, is that this is a mistake, and that there are no successive genetic phases within an actual entity. The datum is not *first* grasped, *then* thought about (intellectual prehensions), but is grasped thinkingly (so far as there is thought in the experience) from the outset, and if there is a succession of acts, first of grasping, and then of thinking about, the second act is located in a subsequent actual experience. Insofar I am not prepared to defend Whitehead's actual language. That he needed to talk about successive phases in the becoming of an entity I am not convinced. Anything that needs to be said may fall either into talk about sequences of entities, or into talk about possibilities. The entity grasped in a certain intellectual way could have been grasped with less thought. To grasp X thinkingly *logically presupposes* grasping X somehow. In that sense the more physical prehension, having X somehow as datum, is "prior" to any particular complexity in the manner in which X is grasped. William A. Christian thinks Whitehead needs some third sense of succession, distinct from temporal and logical succession.[1] I wonder if this is really so.

I have not mentioned that Whitehead uses "actual occasion" as synonym for actual entity (with the qualification that God is not an occasion). "Occasion" seems reasonable enough as a literary alternative to entity. It is not self-explanatory, but no term can be expected to be wholly so in philosophy. No one, to my knowledge, has ever been misled by the word in this context. The term does suggest a spatiotemporal locus, but that is part of the Whiteheadian concept. Since God for Whitehead is ubiquitous and primordial-everlasting it would be strange to term God an occasion.

"Feeling" has been held to be misused in Whitehead. I hold that his defense against this criticism is valid. He is by no means saying that everything feels, e.g., trees or planets. Many "things" do not feel, and yet feeling is pervasive. For if a thing does not feel, its actual entities can be held to do so. Thus tree cells, in their singular actualities, are credited with some radically subhuman form of sentience. If this doctrine is wrong it cannot, so far as I can see, be on any merely linguistic ground. Nor is the question empirical in the proper sense. As I have often argued, there is no nonquestion-begging criterion of the absence of feeling in concrete singular realities. In other words, the absence of feeling cannot in principle be distinguished from the absence of concrete singularity. This is a logical problem, or linguistic one if you like; but it is not Whitehead, in my opinion, who is misusing words, but his critics. Ordinary language does not limit feeling to human beings, and the question of the limits of the psychical in nature radically transcends the concerns of common sense, or linguistic good sense, in any philosophically relevant sense of these phrases. My arguments on this point, like those of Peirce, Whitehead, and others, have not, so far as I can see, been refuted by the anti-White-headians.

There are many who take Whitehead to be misusing words in contending that the concrete units of reality are not individual persons or things but events or states. We say that John did this or that, not that John's state or actual entity (or entities) at time t did so. Now I think that Whitehead knew this as well as anyone. He never objected to the normal uses of proper nouns and pronouns. But consider the following: "John spoke and John was silent." We all agree that the appearance of contradiction is removed by the qualification, at time t_1 John spoke, at time t_2 he was silent. However, there are two possible theories as to how this removes the contradiction. (1) There is a single subject, John, who has the predicates: speaking-at-time-t_1, silent-at-time-t_2. There is no contradiction, because the predicates are compatible. (2) There are two subjects, John-at-time-t_1, John-at-time-t_2, but only one predicate, speaking, and its contradictory. Since either interpretation removes the contradiction, they are, insofar, equivalent. Yet they are not for all that equivalent in every sense. And the philosophical question that Whitehead sees is, which view is correct for all purposes, i.e., really correct?

An analogy is helpful. John is red and not red: red in his hair, not red in his eyes, etc. A spatial whole can have incompatible properties if they qualify diverse parts, since the real predicates are, p-in-one-part, not-p-in-another-part. If space and time are simply dimensions of a coexisting manifold, then the same analysis can apply to predicates at different times. In one temporal part John is speaking, in another he is silent. But this spatialization of time is, for Whitehead as for Bergson, illegitimate.

The clear-headed proponent of the view Whitehead rejects was Leibniz. The clear-headed proponent of the alternative to Leibniz is Whitehead. I hold his view for reasons that were originally derived from Bergson and James. But it was Whitehead who made me see the implication of the reasons. It is John-now that acts now, not just John. The latter is a mere abstraction standing for nothing concrete. States are not predicates, accidents, in persistently identical substances; rather substances are identical aspects in the concrete realities which are unit-events. Different entities can have identical elements or aspects, but the same entity can have different aspects only if these are coexisting parts of the entity. Space, not time, is the order of coexistence. Time is the order of successive existence, a concept which was never clearly analyzed before Bergson, Peirce, and Whitehead and is still poorly understood by most philosophers.

An old linguistic objection—about as old as Buddhism, I suppose—to an event philosophy is that change requires persistent changing things or substances; and surely a philosophy of process or events must admit change! This is a typical semantic problem which contemporary analysts seem not to be interested in clarifying. My contention is: in just the sense in which Whitehead needs to admit change, in that sense he admits changing persisting things (which he calls societies) and in just the sense in which he denies changing things, he also denies change itself. What he does not deny is becoming. Change is a penultimate, not an ultimate concept, for the philosophy of process. Given a sequence of successive instances of becoming (or creation), one can speak of change, thereby referring to the contrast between earlier and later units in the sequence of successively created actualities. Common speech reflects this meaning when we speak of "changes in public opinion," "changes in the weather," etc. We are referring to differences between earlier and later states of opinion or of the weather. Changes in a man differ from this by virtue of the far greater significance in this case of the relationships between later and earlier states and the greater definiteness or concreteness of the states. These relationships are not merely those of similarity, but of inheritance. Memory is one form of the more or less conscious inheritance of the past in the present. Perception is the other form, inheritance not of my past but of the world's past—"impersonal memory," as I like to call it. Is this a misuse of the words? I venture to think it a paradigm of how philosophy needs to use words. Memory in the normal sense is an intuitive awareness of the personal past; by legitimate generalization perception is memory, intuitive awareness, of the impersonal past. I hear the explosion that has already occurred.

Contemporary critics of event theories of the self[2] repeat or develop further the old Hindu objection to Buddhism that a man remembers *himself* as having experienced this or that. However, *either* the himself remembered is simply or absolutely identical with the remembering self or it is not simply identical. Take the first alternative and you have the paradoxes of the Leibnizian monadology. Take the second and you open the door to Whitehead's view. By "simply identical" I mean that the present self as a whole is identical with the past self as a whole. But this is utterly paradoxical, since the present self has what the past self lacked, namely memory of that past self with its experiences. I sadly remember how conceitedly I spoke yesterday. The sadness belongs to today's self, not to yesterday's. Whatever in the present self was there yesterday does not include the present sadness. Thus identity is a somewhat abstract view of a personal history. This is all that Whitehead is contending. He admits real identity as well as similarity, but it is identity of an element of present reality with the past. The present reality as a whole is numerically new, only the part is the same.

Memory of experience E includes E, but it is more. True, the inclusion is not distinct for introspective consciousness, but Whitehead is one of the philosophers who never forget that to feel or have a datum is one thing, to judge or know that and how one feels is another. We feel the very past itself, but we do not necessarily know what it is that we feel. An infant hardly knows anything, but does this prevent it from feeling a good deal? We are all babies, by some standards. This, too, Whitehead never, or seldom, forgets. "I am a baby in psychology," "I am a baby in Greek Philosophy," he used to say. Whitehead admits all the identity between present and past self that one can admit without severe paradox, as in Leibniz's doctrine that a substance has at all times the same totality of qualities. When one considers the vague but massive "apperceptive mass" of dim memories and sense of the bodily processes which constitutes the real content of selfhood, and thinks how slight an addition any one experience can make to this mass one sees how largely today's self and yesterday's are indeed identical. But if we try to go back to the self of infancy, where the apperceptive mass would be vastly diminished compared to its present richness, we find that the sense of identity begins to fail. Was I really that child? Am I perhaps remembering experiences I had in my imagination as I later heard people talking about what I did as a smaller child?

It would be naïve to suppose that the foregoing will do much to persuade many "analysts" that Whitehead knew what he was doing linguistically. But it may stimulate some to think more fruitfully than I know how to do about the "gap" I spoke of at the beginning of this article between the current metaphysics of process and the current, and more fashionable, "analytic" philosophy.

Reprinted from *The Southern Journal of Philosophy* 8 (Winter 1970): 437-45.

CHAPTER THIRTEEN

Whitehead and Berdyaev: Is There Tragedy in God?

The obvious differences between A. N. Whitehead and Nikolai Berdyaev seem to have obscured their remarkable similarities. Thus, while one was logician and mathematician, the other was theologian and historian of culture. The one aimed at technical precision and appealed mainly to the secular intelligence; the other frankly employed partly mythical language and appealed mainly to the Christian tradition. The Anglican background of Whitehead contrasts with the Greek Orthodox background of Berdyaev. (Curiously enough, both men did much of their work outside their native countries.) Neither writer seems to have had the slightest influence upon the other (Berdyaev was thirteen years younger, having been born in 1874). These may be the reasons why no one appears to have noted the profound coincidence in the religious philosophy of the two seers, one of their common characteristics being that both seem to call for this appellation. The present discussion will focus attention on the similarities between the two thinkers, largely ignoring differences.

First, we may observe that Berdyaev, although he writes as a Christian, is a man saturated with secular philosophy and culture; and Whitehead, although he never professes to be a Christian, has a deep and partly sympathetic awareness of the history of Christian doctrine. Both men accept as well as reject elements of such doctrine. Moreover, their rejections strikingly overlap. Both sharply and bluntly accuse their theological ancestors of having held a "despot" or "tyrant" conception of deity and consequently of having had, in Berdyaev's language, a "slavish religion."[1] Both feel that cruel and brutal aspects have not been lacking.

Thus Berdyaev views the idea of hell as a piece of sadism; Whitehead says that "theories of atonement have been mostly crude" and that the Book of Revelation "illustrates the barbaric elements that have been retained to the undoing of the Christian intuition."[2] Berdyaev, in strong language, expresses his scorn for the "disgusting" notion that the aim of life is to get one's self into heaven while multitudes of one's neighbors are pushed into hell.[3] Whitehead would think similarly, though perhaps he would go even further, since his theory of the individual as a "society" or sequence of experiences in a certain order and with a certain community of quality inherited through the sequence puts him, if possible, in even sharper opposition to a self-interest theory of motivation and since "sympathy" is a metaphysical principle in his system.[4] Berdyaev again speaks for both men when he says that there is a judgment of history upon the church, as well as of the church upon history. Neither thinker regards Christianity as a depository of infallible dictations from the divine to suitable officials, or even as a stream of unfailingly good lives. Both see our pious ancestors as a tragic blend of love and hatred, wisdom and folly, and their theologies as embodiments of this mixture. Berdyaev would hardly have been startled by Whitehead's query: "Must religion always remain as a synonym for hatred?"[5] He himself declared that Christianity had made man worse as well as better and stated that theologians have "always" included immoral elements in their moralizings. In short, both men take our religious tradition seriously, and both take it critically.

Even when one passes to more technical points of philosophical doctrine, the common basis of divergence from any usual "orthodoxy" continues to be impressive. Both view as supreme mistakes the denial of "movement" (Berdyaev),[6] of "flux" (Whitehead),[7] to the divine consciousness; and both oppose the assertion of God's sheer absoluteness, self-sufficiency, or inability to derive increase of value from the creatures.[8] For both of them this is the technical expression of the tyrant idea of deity. The point is not a vague, merely emotional, one; nor is it simply a question of the nature of God's dealings with the world as just and merciful or otherwise. The point is metaphysical: a despot is one who influences, while seeking to evade influence; who wishes, so far as possible, to exert, but never to suffer, power; who will be cause but not effect; who is the totally "independent" manipulator of things. This is the transcendentalized absolute negation of the principle of democratic rule, which is that the ruler should in a sense also be subject and the subject in a sense also ruler. A responsible ruler is sensitive, responsive to the ruled, and this means that he is effect as well as cause. The three previous sentences have, so far as I know, no close equivalents in the writings of the men we are considering, but both say things which imply that divine power escapes being despotic only because it is not sheer power, sheer one-way causation, but is also receptivity and sufferance of causation. Both hold that God's creating of us is to be balanced against the correlative truth that we genuinely create something in God, so that God, in some elements of his life, is creature as well as creator.[9] He is not "pure actuality" but involves inner potentiality.[10] These seem to be ideas reached in complete independence but substantial agreement by the two authors.

Let us now consider the common metaphysical notions forming the framework of this way of viewing deity. For Whitehead, there is an ultimate, though abstract, principle of all reality, a universal of universals, which he calls "creativity."[11] This he says is not identical with God, nor is it an individual, coordinate with or superior to God. It is a mere universal or an ultimate abstraction, *the* ultimate abstraction. Like all universals, it is real only in individuals, including the one essential individual, God. God is not identical with creativity, because you and I are creative too, with our nondivine but real creative action. Whitehead could perhaps here employ scholastic language and say that, just as in Thomism "being" is not simply the same in God and other things, so in his system "becoming" or "creativity," rather than mere being, is the supreme but analogical unity. What does Berdyaev say? When speaking metaphysically, he generally uses the term "freedom" rather than "creativity," but interchangeability of the two for him, and for Whitehead also, is not hard to establish. Freedom is that by which there can be creation of new realities. And Berdyaev tells us that this freedom is a principle uncreated by God and not identical with him and that the process of creation involves God, the uncreated principle of freedom, and the creative and partly self-creative action of the creatures. God's "call to man" is not answered by God himself or by man using solely elements which God has created in him but by man creating new realities, new qualities of experience. This, of course, is thoroughly Whiteheadian. For Whitehead, the unit-actualities are "experient occasions," which are always in some degree "self-creative," and each such occasion contributes to the divine consciousness, which regards it with "tenderness" after it exists and inspires it with his ideal for its coming-to-be as it comes into existence. Thus there quite definitely is a divine call and a creaturely answer.

Largely common to both thinkers is the theory as to how evil arises. The particular evils in the world are not brought into being by divine fiat but spring from [creaturely] freedom.[12] Through freedom or creativity, potential goods are made actual. But potential goods involve exclusive alternatives, mutually incompatible possibilities of value. This is a root of tragedy inherent in freedom and possibility as such and not due to any fiat of God. Actualization is, in principle, exclusion not simply of some evil but also of some good. Berdyaev says that true tragedy is not a clash of good with evil, but of good with good, of two equally noble ideals; Whitehead means the same thing when he says that evil is good out of season or in conflict with some other good. He explains that values are, in principle, determinate and exclusive, always this but not that, in contrast to the realm of mere possibilities in which there is always both this and that. Actual value must always be finite, and "there is no infinitude of all perfections" (save as bare possibilities).[13] But, since freedom is not a single individual power but an analogical universal embodied in many individuals, what is to prevent such individuals from pursuing incompatible values, so that A's success means B's failure and vice versa? The answer, most clearly set forth by Whitehead perhaps, is that nothing can wholly prevent this. No absolute coordinating of the acts of the various individuals can be effected. For they are free, incapable of being completely determined by another, even God. God inspires and influences their acts—otherwise there would be no harmony whatever and no world order—but he cannot precisely and fully decide these acts, for they are in part self-decided and this self-decision cannot be delegated, even to deity.[14] Thus the course of events is decided by no one individual but is a multiple decision, and this not because of any weakness of deity but because of a certain strength or creativeness of the creatures. Their creativeness may be small and often, as Berdyaev says, imperceptible, but it is never zero. In the multiple-freedom or multiple-decision of actualization inheres an element of not wholly eradicable chaos. Chaos is multiple-decision so far as multiple. Only because there is a monistic aspect, the primary inspiration of deity upon all, is there anything but pure chaos. God is the orderer of the world (Whitehead), making the best use possible of the irrepressible part-chaos of free acts.[15] Fate, says Berdyaev, is the "hardened outcome" of freedom, in interplay with Providence.[16] Chance is real and a major cause of our suffering.[17]

A peculiarity of Berdyaev's language is his description of freedom as "not-being," which is yet distinguished from sheer nothing. It seems that only pure possibility, Whitehead's "pure potentials," can be thus intermediate between full actuality and nothing. A difference between the two metaphysicians is perhaps that for Whitehead there is a primordial multitude of such potentials, "eternal objects," whereas Berdyaev would, I suspect, find this too Platonic. He complains that Platonic philosophy misses the truth that creation is the "production of new images," not the mere actualization of eternal patterns.[18] Thus Berdyaev would perhaps say that freedom or creativity is the only eternal object. However, like Whitehead, he ascribes an eternal character, as well as movement and novelty, to God; and it would be a fine point to show how this differs from the "envisagement of all eternal objects," which, for Whitehead, constitutes this eternal or primordial divine character. The question seems to have only secondary interest for most of the issues I wish to discuss in this article.

Both our authors conclude, from their theory of creativity, that tragedy is an ultimate principle, even for God.[19] Alternative possible values and multiple freedom make the total avoidance of conflict unachievable; and even if the suppression of freedom were possible, it would mean the extinction of good as well as of evil, since freedom is the common root of both. The tragic element of life which God cannot eliminate (since its elimination is metaphysical nonsense) is not something simply external and indifferent to God. God is not sheer cause, mere being, independent of all becoming and creating. He is relative to the world,[20] for the merely absolute is "abstract" (the word is used in this connection by both our authors), deficient in inner life.[21] True, both writers agree that God has an abstract aspect which is absolute, strictly eternal; but they insist that in his full concrete actuality he is receptive to the world's life, so that all creative action contributes something to the divine consciousness. We "enrich the divine life itself" (Berdyaev);[22] God has concrete ("physical") perceptions ("prehensions") of events (Whitehead) which form the content of his "Consequent Nature," which is conscious. But in this way our griefs as well as our joys are communicated to God. He intuits and thus shares in our tragedies.[23] The course of history, says the Russian seer, is a divine as well as a human tragedy.[24] Whitehead is somewhat less emphatic about this, but the doctrine is common to the two men. One recalls Whitehead's description of God as "fellow-sufferer"; his declaration that the attribution of "mere happiness" to deity is a "profanation" and that we may employ the human analogies of "tragedy, sympathy, and actualized heroism" as among the least inadequate.[25] Here, then, are two great minds of our time who think that the Christian idea of sacrificial or suffering love has even more direct and ultimate validity in theology than orthodox systems have supposed. Of course, Schelling had said much the same, as well as Fechner and others. Berdyaev knew much of this tradition; I do not know whether or not Whitehead did. In any case, the doctrine has now a new weight and dignity.

An interesting remark of Berdyaev's is that the famous Nygren dichotomy—Eros or Agape?—overlooks pity, which is neither and than which, he thinks, nothing in man is higher. Whitehead actually uses Eros as a symbol for God in a few passages,[26] though it is plain that for him there is an infinite contrast between human "desire" and the divine "appetition" and "tenderness." He frequently uses the word "love" in theological reference. On the whole, no determinate difference between the Russian and the Anglo-American can be established here.

A methodological difference of some importance is that Berdyaev seems to regard the identification of God with the pure "absolute" as philosophically defensible, though theologically vicious. He says that to appreciate the necessity or possibility of movement, potentiality, and relativity in God we must transcend mere rationalism. Whitehead, on the contrary, holds that the attempt to treat deity as wholly without flux is contrary to reason, since it prevents us from conceiving the relations between the world and God without "contradictions at every step."[27] He thinks it is rationalism and not just religious feeling or insight that demands the conception of God as self-related and hence relativized to the world, receptive of its values, its joys, and its sorrows. Berdyaev seems at times to see this superior rationality of the relative concept; but at other times he reverts to his irrationalistic spiritualism which professes to accept the divine relativity and flux *in spite of* reason.[28] Here I think it is Whitehead who is right. Not reason but certain unthinking prejudices resulted in the absolutistic view. A certain etiolatry (worship of cause),[29] or ontolatry (worship of being),[30] or monolatry (worship of unity) in contrast to effect, becoming, and diversity—these and other similar forms of philosophical idolatry, resulting not from calm analysis but from ecstatic enthusiasm for certain one-sided conceptions, constitute the origin of what Berdyaev too flatteringly labels "rationalism."

A similar difference obtains in the treatment of "pantheism."[31] Berdyaev holds that reason gets into difficulties in trying to conceive of the world as contained in God but that it is nevertheless a mystical or religious truth that the world enters into the divine actuality. (Here Berdyaev is following the Russian theologian, Soloviev, as well as German mysticism.) Rationalism is compelled, he suspects, to oscillate between a religiously impossible dualism—of a merely absolute God who does not include the world in his reality—and a no less impossible pantheistic monism. The monism must deny human freedom—and, indeed, all freedom;[32] and the dualism, if it does nominally admit freedom, renders it without ultimate significance, since in the rigidity of the divine absoluteness there can be no open alternatives, and hence it can never make any difference to deity what course the expression of freedom may take. Berdyaev's conclusion is that freedom is something irrational, which can be dealt with only in "mythical" terms of spiritual experience, not in terms of concepts accessible to secular thought.[33] Here again I think Berdyaev is somewhat confused, in comparison with Whitehead. Logical analysis shows, as I have argued elsewhere,[34] that the usual alternative of theism-pantheism is inexhaustive and that the absurdities of both positions can be avoided by rejecting their common premise, which is that the supreme reality is to be conceived by favoring one pole of the ultimate contraries, such as being-becoming, absolute-relative, necessary-contingent, as against the other. Reason itself leads us, I hold, to accept the law of polarity, which finds the ultimate meanings in terms of the contrast between such polarities, not in either pole itself. There can be no mere being, or mere absolute, or mere necessity. Moreover, becoming, relativity, and contingency are irrational only for a spurious "reason." Reason is tracing of relations; for it to deny relativity is fantastic. Open alternatives are inherent in mathematics itself; and the whole apparatus of logic and mathematics has no other "function" (the very word expresses "becoming") than to interpret becoming in some aspect. The best authorities are coming to see that even Newtonian physics cannot be rigorously deterministic, that physics cannot dispense with the notion of potentiality and of ranges of alternative possibilities or "degrees of freedom." Also, it is becoming clear that "things" or "beings" are known as functions of process, not process as function of beings. We are gradually learning that the contrast of being-becoming, absolute-relative, necessary-contingent, is contained as a whole in becoming, relativity, contingency, not in being, absoluteness, necessity. The final words are process, relativity, or freedom just because these can (indeed, logically must) contain in themselves aspects of permanence, absoluteness, or necessity; whereas within the merely permanent nothing can change, and no constituent of an absolute and necessary whole can be relative or accidental. There is nothing illogical or irrational about the idea of open alternatives as containing something common to them all, and thus necessary. A synthesis of the polar contraries by this path is not in defiance of, but in accord with, reason and is demanded by it.

The doctrine which avoids both the difficulties which Berdyaev finds in pantheism and those he finds in the usual or classical theism had better be called "panentheism" than "pantheism," for both etymological and historical reasons. It posits an eternal absolute abstract essence in a God who, in his full concrete actuality or process of experience, includes all contingent things, as inessential but not, for all that, unreal properties—in other words, accidents. I could still be myself, were it not just now true that the chirp of a sparrow comes to me from outside the house. The sensation of this sound is not essential to me, to my being "myself." But there is nothing unreal about the sensation as a constituent of my actual experience. Inessential is one thing; unreal is another. So God has a multitude of inessential real properties or accidents. In these real accidents, contingent things are contained as data of the divine consciousness, in such fashion that God is active as well as passive in regard to them. He suffers our actions, he does not enact them, and that is how they can still be our actions, though they enter into his experience. This is Whitehead's doctrine, and he offers it as the outcome of rationalism, not its defiance.

To call this doctrine "irrational" or "contradictory" (as some would do) because it makes the absolute God relative or the perfect God imperfect is question-begging sophistry. For nothing compels the panentheist to suppose that God, or any existent entity, *is in all aspects* absolute or perfect, in the sense of "at an absolute maximum" or "incapable of increase." There is another sense of perfect which the panentheist regards as the theologically fundamental one, namely, "incapable of being rivaled (equaled or surpassed) by another individual." God is the object of worship: since it is other individuals than God who do the worshiping, if God is exalted above others beyond the possibility of rivalry, then God is indeed God, the appropriate object of universal reverence; and there is no contradiction in supposing that, although in no aspect can God be rivaled by another individual, he can in some aspect surpass himself by growing in content. Fechner (perhaps not read at all by Berdyaev or Whitehead) seems to have been the first, unless it was Schelling, to discern this meaning of "perfect" and its relevance for religion.

Of course, to relate this analysis to Whitehead in detail, it would be necessary to make explicit his theory of the individual as a "personally-ordered society" or linear sequence of experiences. Berdyaev is not concerned with this problem and seems not sharply committed either for or against Whitehead's analysis. In view of his emphasis upon perpetual creation of new realities, however, it seems he ought to accept the Whiteheadian view that the final concrete realities are experient occasions, not enduring individuals. But it is well to admit in passing that Berdyaev falls into some strange phrases about the creation of the soul "in eternity" that appear to contradict all this. Yet, before taking this difficulty too seriously, we need to inquire into the meaning of "eternity" for this author.

Both writers sometimes seem to treat God as simply nontemporal, as though they accepted the venerable notion that the contrast between being and becoming is invidious, though with the superiority all on the side of becoming. But both authors make amends for this in other passages. Berdyaev puts it well with his distinction between integrated and disintegrated time.[35] For us the past tends to be negligible and pale in content, because of our eager concentration upon the present and our anxiety about the future. This, however, is our human deficiency, not an absolute metaphysical principle. The highest mode of experience would retain vivid interest in the past and would create ever new values in the present yet would be free from distracting anxiety concerning the future. The theory is not very fully sketched, but this seems to be the intention.[36] There is a "divine history" as well as a human one; but the divine history is that of growth without loss and without distracting anxiety, although not without suffering, owing to the actual conflicts between creaturely volitions and actions. Thus "eternity," in the previous paragraph, may refer to integrated, rather than disintegrated, time.

Whitehead's view seems similar. He terms "everlastingness" the power of retaining experiences in their full immediacy as elements in subsequent experiences containing also novel elements—in short, the growth of experience without loss, addition without subtraction.[37] The denial of loss is unequivocal so far as concerns God's relation to his own previous experience, but there is some uncertainty or wavering as to how completely the past of the world is preserved in God. There is a saving of "what can be saved." There are reasons against taking this to mean that something is dropped out. It might rather mean that, although the whole of each event is taken into God and preserved there, some of the desires and purposes for the future which the event contained must, because of incompatibility, be frustrated.[38] We do not accomplish all that we sought to accomplish, but our actually achieved feelings and thoughts are imperishable.[39] One reason supporting this interpretation is the saying that the truth itself is only how things are in the Consequent Nature of God,[40] for then it cannot be true that something is left out.

A slight difference, at least of emphasis, between the Whiteheadian metaphysics and that of Berdyaev is this, that, in the former, creativity is sometimes spoken of as though it were a sort of power alongside God, so to speak; whereas Berdyaev says that freedom, though not divinely created, is still *in* the Godhead, a primordial element of his reality as conceived in mystical pantheism.[41] Berdyaev is here influenced by Böhme and Schelling. Whitehead can, without much difficulty, be assimilated to this point of view. For he does say that the Consequent Nature is the unification of all things; so, surely, creativity is included. What Whitehead wants us never to forget is simply that the divine sort of creating, which, like all creating, involved an aspect of self-creation, is not the only sort of creativity. All actualities are "self-created creatures." Creativity is analogical, not just univocal, in that it is both divine and nondivine. But, for all that, all creativity may be *in* God; for, since he is active as well as passive, he can contain creative decisions he does not make. He contains his own divine decisions as making them and nondivine ones as suffering them. Fechner was perhaps the first to expound this idea with some clarity. Putting it another way, a perception or prehension includes its data, and a subject includes its prehensions. The correlation subject-object belongs, with both its terms, to the subject rather than to the object. God as adequate cosmic subject, correlative in a unique way to the total universe of lesser realities, includes all instances and kinds of creativity, either as his own act-forms or as their contents. Thus God is all in all, and this without prejudice to creaturely freedom and individuality.

One might go so far as to say that "creativity" and "freedom" are simply aids to our understanding in trying to conceive the divine life as genuinely related to our lives and to all lives. If we understand well what "God" means, we know all that can be conveyed by "freedom" or by "nondivine creatures." There is nothing but God, as necessarily existing yet contingently experiencing ourselves and other things. No power and no obstacle oppose deity, and nothing conditions him, except as you and I and other more or less free sequences of actualities oppose or condition him. Thus there is no new problem, but the old standard problem of God and the world, approached, however, with new means of analysis. That God cannot extinguish freedom and hence cannot extinguish all evil is no external constraint upon him but just his own essence. It is his eternal essence to be free himself and to deal with free creatures, some creatures or other, but not necessarily just these or those. God has not and cannot have any wish that there be no free creatures; there is no motive or possible desire for an alternative to freedom, which is the root of all good as well as of evil. The only "constraint" here is upon our own confusion, which may lead us verbally to suppose an alternative to freedom. Thus the familiar query "Why did God make free beings, with all the dangers this involved?" is meaningless, since it supposes an alternative where there is none. Possible alternatives are within freedom, not to it. The very idea of divine making or power presupposes a free individual, God, as already actual and hence already in relation to other free beings, furnishing determinate individual objects of awareness. Other "persons" in a Trinitarian Godhead are not enough; for what principle of individuation could really distinguish and give determinate content to three beings, all divine, all with adequate awareness of all truth, and yet in relationship to nothing except each other?

Both our philosophers see deep wisdom, but misinterpreted wisdom, in the orthodox theory of the Trinity. Whitehead says that the principle of mutual immanence between individuals first appeared in this theological guise but needs to be made a general metaphysical principle, replacing the old theory of substances not immanent to each other.[42] Berdyaev says that the theory of divine begetting of Son and Holy Ghost implies an admission of relativity and of becoming in the divine life, which needs to be completed by admitting also a receptivity toward the creaturely becoming whereby the latter can contribute content to the divine becoming.[43]

Our two authors both speak of God as creator, but neither accepts without qualification the doctrine of creation *ex nihilo* as the distinguishing feature of the divine action.[44] Both the statement that man creates only by modifying a given material and the statement that God's creation presupposes nothing but the divine power are alike found unacceptable as they stand. The notion that a new experience or event is merely a new predicate of a material already there is confused, as Whitehead has shown.[45] It conveys no positive insight, since we can perceive or conceive nothing that makes the "matter" the same before and after it has the new quality or shape. That such an account is purely verbal is virtually admitted by Aquinas when he says that we can never know prime matter directly but only by analogy, as with the clay which is in the hands of the potter. But this merely restates the question, which is, What constitutes the identity of the clay in successive events? And, besides, if the same entity really "has" both earlier and later events, then time is frozen and denatured, since it falls within an identity. If we drop these verbalisms, all we have is that human creating makes use of, or profits by, antecedent events. If, and only if, such and such has already happened, can certain human acts now happen. This is what we know positively. The final actualities are events, and the events we know vividly are those constituted by occasions of human experience. If, then, Beethoven had power in part to determine his own musical experiences, insofar he had power to create not mere adjectives of some actuality but actualities themselves.

How far is it different with divine acts?

The most obvious difference is that, although any act of God creative of present actuality in the world presupposes (as we shall see in a moment) earlier events as having already occurred, it does not presuppose occurrences prior to the very existence of God, for deity is primordial and ungenerated; whereas our acts, on the contrary, always depend upon events some of which were antecedent to our personal existence altogether. Divine acts refer only to antecedent events which themselves also embodied divine acts. Anything which God in a given phase requires has also required him in a previous phase of his life. This is not the case with us and our requirements. So creation *ex nihilo* may be taken as an elliptical way of stating that the divine action presupposes nothing anterior to God himself.

That divine creation, at least of present actualities in the world, does presuppose previous events seems evident if we look beyond mere words and try to form even the vaguest conception of what the words mean. Does God make the mature man out of nothing or out of the immature man? Surely the latter. It is a downright contradiction to think of adult memories of childhood made not out of childhood but out of nonentity. To be "remembered," in the proper sense, the earlier events must have occurred. (For Whitehead, the mother is unconsciously remembered by the infant, and no absolute beginning is reached.) Earlier events are data required to give content for the present event—if you will, its presupposed materials. The later events are not, for all that, just these same materials acquiring new qualities. They are new actualities, having some qualities of the earlier ones and also novel qualities. It seems self-evident that a single new quality means a new total reality. The whole Ab is not identical with the whole A, no matter now insignificant the b may be.

But did not God create the first events, the first state of the world, out of nothing? It seems the answer must be yes, provided that there was a first state. But why assume this? A first moment could have no memories, and an experience without memory is not an experience in any recognizable Whiteheadian sense. (Berdyaev seems not to have talked to this point; but I am at least not sure he would have held a radically different view.) Indeed, a first state of the world would be utterly unlike anything we can conceive. It would point to no prior events. If Adam had a navel, this pointed to his having had a mother; if not, was he a man? The father of Edmund Gosse worried about this for years, until he arrived at the "solution" that God had no choice but to create a first state of the world looking in all respects as though it had not been the first state. He was compelled to practice a gigantic deception upon human scientists. But perhaps that is a *reductio ad absurdum* of the notion of a first state. Present-day physicists have some ingenious suggestions here, but we cannot pursue the matter further.

Apart from a hypothetical, if at all conceivable, first event, God, as well as man, creates with reference to events already in being, thus not out of nothing, although in the divine case the reference is never to events that precede his own existence. Of both the divine and the ordinary creative action the result is a new actuality, not merely a new adjective of an old actuality. In spite of these analogous factors, there is an infinite, not a merely finite, superiority in the divine action, since the latter operates cosmically and not locally, always and not sometimes, with invincible power to achieve its basic objective—the perpetuation of the cosmic process for the benefit of the creatures and the enrichment of its own life—and since the divine action at each moment involves a new phase of the divine experience, which alone is an adequate perception of all space and all past events. It is too often forgotten that there is no logical need to choose between an absolute and a merely finite difference, since there is the intermediate case of an infinite (yet not absolute) difference. One may contrast infinity and zero, or a large finite and a small finite, or, finally, infinity and the finite. The old view was that God had infinite power, we no power, to turn nothing into something; the difference was absolute. But suppose we have a finite power to turn nothing (that is, potentiality, which is at least no determinate-being) into something; it does not follow that God differs from us "merely in degree" of power, if that means merely finitely. Between an infinite degree and any finite degree there is an infinite difference. That God always has a definite potentiality—that is, past events as data—to work with does not make his power merely finite. Power consists in ability to use data to make new actualities; infinite power to do this means ability to do it primordially and everlastingly and to achieve always and infallibly a personal synthesis of the data which could not be rivaled by any other person and which then enters subconsciously into all lesser creative action and thus guides the world in the light of its history. Something like this is what Whitehead and Berdyaev substitute for the too simple doctrine of creation *ex nihilo*.

Let us now consider the attitude of our authors toward ethical questions. Berdyaev wants us to be creative and to cherish creativity in others, to love each other as beings creative on the ultimate metaphysical level of adding to the divine life itself. He rejects the aspects of intolerance, envy, egotism, legalism, moralism, which have so often disfigured Christian ethics and made it seem almost irrelevant to man's spiritual adventure in art, science, statesmanship, and other fruitful endeavors. Such endeavors are not to be viewed as mere obedience to God (why should he care about such mere obedience?) but as means of enriching his life by virtue of his loving participation in ours. Whitehead's view seems about the same. He says that we need patterns of social order, which must change from time to time to maintain their freshness of interest, but that the criterion of the value of an order is its contribution to individual lives as appreciated through love and as finally appropriated forever by the divine love.[46] There seems to be a difference between the two men insofar as Berdyaev exhibits a note of asceticism in regard to sex (seemingly contradicted in some places) which I do not find in Whitehead. The latter's warning against contentment with "obvious enjoyments" does not seem equivalent to Berdyaev's statement that in sex pleasure there is always poison.[47] On the whole, however, the general harmony between the two thinkers applies also to their ethical views.

Of course, one could systematically emphasize the differences, particularly of terminology, between Russian and Englishman, just as I have emphasized the similarities. Granting this possibility, I do wish to maintain the significance of the convergence which I hope I have demonstrated. We have illustrated here a new philosophical and religious climate of opinion, in which the long-reigning bias toward cause-worship and being-worship or, in plainer English, worship of sheer power no longer plays a role. A great change has taken place. It is now possible to be conscious of the difference between the worship of peace, eternity, being, security, independence, oneness, absoluteness, activity, cause, and the worship of God, who to men like Berdyaev, Whitehead, Schelling, and many others is something very different—yes, infinitely different—from these one-sided qualities. It is now open to us to use concepts of process, becoming, self-creation, receptivity, complexity, relativity, passivity, sensitivity, effect, and tragedy (without, however, any invidious exclusion of their contraries) as aids to expression of our sense of the individual whose majesty is exalted beyond possible rivalry, the all-worshipful God. We do not have to worship power or "completeness" or inability to grow in content or an exhaustive (and therefore self-contradictory) actualization of value. Rather we worship love, including sensitivity, responsiveness, an infinitely delicate way of appropriating and preserving created values, of synthesizing ever new phases of itself as sole adequate effect of all antecedent causes (and, therefore, supreme cause of all subsequent effects), uniquely complex, uniquely integrated, matchlessly subtle in passivity to its data. All this stands in no conflict with the idea that God is in every way unrivaled by others, actual or possible. He is unrivaled temporally; for no other is primordial and everlasting, no other has an individual character with essential traits that *cannot* alter—for example, the trait of immunity to rivalry itself. (The supposition that the world has no beginning or ending in time does not mean that there is an individual other than God with equally universal temporal scope, for "the world" is not an individual but simply "all individuals other than God.")

It is a vital discovery, I suggest, that the thesis of etiolatry, the denial of relativity and process to God, cannot be deduced from the religious idea that God is the all-worshipful, that is, the one to whom there cannot be a rival. This discovery sets us free from the supposed necessity to worship mere power or self-sufficiency. The causative power of God is really due, we may believe, to his unique facility in responding as effect to all things as causes, that is, to his loving appropriation of all lives. God has power over us because we cannot but love him, at least unconsciously. "The power of God is the worship he inspires" (Whitehead), and we love him not because he is in some other sense powerful or because he is unaffected by, and thus neutral with respect to worldly alternatives but rather because he is the fullness of loving sympathy and sensitivity, so that alternatives in the world make more difference to him than to anyone else; for only he can adequately appreciate the scope of these alternatives.[48] Thus he is the least neutral or "independent" of any individual in his actual concrete experience, and, for that very reason, in his essential abstract individuality (common to all experiences possible for him) he is the most neutral or strictly independent. Whatever happens, God, with his previously acquired values, will persist because he cannot lose his unlimited passive power of receiving any cosmic datum whatever into his consciousness. He can, it is true, receive it only for what it is worth, and we serve him by making it worth all that we can; but it will in any case be an enrichment without prejudice to the values already enjoyed. Our own passive power is infinitely inferior. We must often lose consciousness and always must forget nearly all the past, when confronted with new data. The question never is, Will the divine experience be divine, or will it receive all the particularity of the world? It is rather, How much enrichment over previous divine experience will result, and how much will there be divine joy rather than divine sorrow? Indifference to suffering rather than suffering as a result of loving sympathy with the sufferers should be rejected as unworthy to be predicated of God.

An objection sometimes made to the notion of divine suffering is that one can help sufferers better if one does not feel their pangs. This is a good test case for the question as to where the real danger of anthropomorphism in theology lies. Let us first note that we men have very limited passive powers. If we take in strong feeling from one other person, we can take in very little else; and we have little energy left over to react creatively, to explore possibilities, to think clearly. This limitation as to scope of passivity and as to total energy is our real weakness, not the passivity itself. If it were the passivity, then an insect would be vastly stronger than we; for surely we have a much greater scope of passive sensitivity than an insect! We are more variously passive and more variously active than an ant. There is no contradiction in this. God, having unlimited scope of passive reception, can always assimilate any presented datum, including any strong emotion of another, and yet retain full freedom of attention for all other data and all relevant possibilities of creative reaction thereto. "God," says Whitehead, "is the evaluation of the world,"[49] limited only in his presented content, not in his power to do it justice. To "adapt" with matchless efficiency to every state of affairs is not to be concretely uninfluenced by such states, is not to be in every sense independent of them, but it is to be totally secure of personal survival and integrity and in that sense totally independent of all occurrences. All this is only what "omniscience" means when interpreted without etiolatrous precommitment.

Let us sum up. For Whitehead and Berdyaev, God is not cause rather than effect, being rather than becoming; neither is he effect rather than cause, becoming rather than being. He is supreme in all these respects. Since all the basic conceptions are used, none is viewed idolatrously as synonymous with God. All must be supplemented by their contraries; for deity transcends these contrasts because his unrivaled majesty is found at both poles of the categorial contraries. (Ethical evil is not categorial, but a special case of the truly categorial principles, and in this it is unlike suffering, which is universal in scope. I omit discussion of this point, which is similar to Berdyaev's "tragedy lies beyond good and evil.")[50]

If we follow these two guides, we shall worship the unrivaledness, the supreme excellence, of the divine cause-effect, activity-passivity, which alone makes God worthy of universal reverence. We shall present our lives to him as all that we have with which to serve him in the only way in which an individual whose essence is love can be served, namely, by the production of happiness in individuals other than himself, and we shall try to avoid causing him to suffer in the only way in which he can be caused to suffer, through the unhappiness or nonfulfillment of these other individuals. We worship in deity an unqualified independence of essence and existence, his Primordial Nature, which is absolute, necessarily existent, but abstract; and we worship an equally matchless receptivity, passive power or derivativeness of experience, his Consequent Nature, which is relative, contingent, concrete, and actual (not merely "existent," since this means only that the essence is embodied in some suitable actual experience or other). Finally, in the words of Berdyaev, "we can only reconcile ourselves to the tragedy of the world because God suffers in it too. God shares his creatures' destiny."[51] Or, in the words of Whitehead, "God is the fellow-sufferer who understands."[52]

Notes

Chapter 2

1. See Alfred North Whitehead, *Process and Reality* (New York: Macmillan, 1929), p. 76 (hereafter cited as *P & R*).

2. Alfred North Whitehead, *Science and the Modern World* (New York: Macmillan, 1925), pp. 174-75, 223; *Adventures of Ideas* (New York: Macmillan, 1933), pp. 247-56; *P & R*, p. 470. It is true that Whitehead mainly emphasizes internal rather than external relations, partly because he is primarily combatting not Absolute Idealism (which has been somewhat out of fashion) but rather, atomistic and other more or less extreme pluralisms. Also, I suspect, he inclines (as a rule, not always) to avoid the phrase "external relations" because, to say "relation to B is external to A" is really to say, "A has no relation to B." (See chap. 2 of my *The Divine Relativity* [New Haven: Yale University Press, 1948].) An entity's relations are all internal to the entity, but it does not follow that X's relations to Y must all be internal to Y. A relation may involve terms not all of which involve the relation. And Whitehead in effect holds that no actuality ever has relation to a particular actuality subsequent to it in time.

3. See *P & R*, p. 246.

4. W. E. Agar, *A Contribution to the Theory of the Living Organism* (Melbourne: Melbourne University Press, 1943).

Chapter 3

1. L. Susan Stebbing, review of *Process and Reality*, *Mind*, n.s. 39 (1930): 466-75.

2. Ibid., p. 467.

3. See, e.g., ibid., p. 474.

4. A term due to A. E. Murphy. See his article, "Objective Relativism in Dewey and Whitehead," *Philosophical Review* 36 (March 1927): 121-44. See also Charles W. Morris, *Six Theories of Mind* (Chicago: University of Chicago Press, 1932), for an excellent defense of this doctrine. Murphy's articles on Whitehead are reprinted in *Reason and the Common Good*, ed. W. H. Hay, M. G. Singer, and A. E. Murphy (Englewood Cliffs, N. J.: Prentice-Hall, 1963).

5. See C. I. Lewis, *Mind and the World Order* (New York: Charles Scribner's Sons, 1929), pp. 81, 82.

6. See A. E. Murphy, "The Development of Whitehead's Philosophy," *New World*

Monthly 1, no. 2 (February 1930): 81, 100. See pp. 92 f.

7. Thus one critic declares, speaking of Whitehead's ascription of "social instincts" to molecules: "The points of identity covered by these vague terms are so tenuous as to be relatively insignificant, and it is only by reference to the respects in which molecules and minds are not alike that we can attach much significance to the assertions just given. And with regard to such features the assertions are more than misleading, they are simply wrong" (A. E. Murphy, review of *Symbolism* by Whitehead, *Journal of Philosophy* 26 [1929] : 492). For a more mature and less dogmatic judgment see Murphy's *Reason and the Common Good*, pp. 67-78, 163-72, 234-40.

8. See, e.g., H. Harlow and R. Stagner, "The Psychology of Feelings and Emotions," *Psychological Review* 39 (1932): 570-89. [On the subject of this paragraph see my *Philosophy and Psychology of Sensation* (Chicago: University of Chicago Press, 1934); reissued in 1968 by Kennikat Press, Inc., Port Washington, N.Y.]

9. See A. E. Murphy, "The Development of Whitehead's Philosophy," p. 93.

10. See Alfred North Whitehead, *Adventures of Ideas* (New York: Macmillan, 1933), p. 255, and *Process and Reality* (New York: Macmillan, 1929), p. 188 (hereafter cited as *P & R*).

11. Murphy's comment, "Thus is change caught, killed, and stuffed, and the realization, in a subjective and 'pre-established harmony' of feeling, of an ideal of satisfaction or attainment, again unconscious as a rule, is made the cosmological expression of the occurrent novelty of the universe," implies that this prevision of future satisfaction which acts as divine final cause is absolutely definite. This can scarcely be Whitehead's meaning, yet insofar as there is ambiguity in the doctrine of eternal objects, insofar genuine novelty, or creativity as something more than the mere copying in time of the eternal objects, is imperiled. We need a clear statement of the degree of definiteness, or the opposite, attaching to an eternal object as such. Such a statement, so far from destroying other features in the system, would, I believe, strengthen them. (See A. E. Murphy, "The Development of Whitehead's Philosophy," pp. 97-98.)

12. The evolution of all essences, aside from the categories, is the theme of a posthumous essay by Charles Peirce on "The Logic of Continuity," which will appear in vol. VI of his *Collected Papers*. [All eight volumes of *Collected Papers of Charles Sanders Peirce*, ed. Charles Hartshorne and Paul Weiss (Cambridge: Harvard University Press, 1935-60) are now in print. Vols. VII and VIII were edited by Arthur W. Burks.]

13. See, e.g., Dorothy M. Emmet, *Whitehead's Philosophy of Organism* (London: Macmillan, 1932), chap. 5, "Are the Eternal Objects Platonic Forms?". Also Everett W. Hall, "Of What Use Are Whitehead's Eternal Objects?," *Journal of Philosophy* 27 (Jan. 16, 1930): 29-44. Reprinted in *Alfred North Whitehead: Essays on His Philosophy*, ed. George L. Kline (Englewood Cliffs, N. J.: Prentice-Hall, 1963), pp. 102-16.

14. A. O. Lovejoy, *The Revolt Against Dualism* (New York: W. W. Norton, 1930), pp. 155-75.

15. Between this absolutely unique quality and the most comprehensive universal there are all degrees, so that the distinction between universal and particular becomes "blurred," as Whitehead says, i.e., becomes a matter of degree. This remark Stebbing regards as "a great muddle." Perhaps the reason is her own adherence to the doctrine that "the absolutely specific shade of white is abstract," that is, "it can be within more than one particular occasion" (L. Susan Stebbing, *A Modern Introduction to Logic* [New York: Thomas Y. Crowell, 1930], p. 444). The assumption is that we can observe two different objects to be "exactly similar" in quality. Lovejoy, in the

passage referred to, makes the same assumption. Since, as we shall presently see, the assumption is open to serious question, we have here a fine example of how easily metaphysical assumptions creeep in unnoticed when topics are treated apart from a systematic metaphysical inquiry. *Absolute* similarity (except of mathematical concepts) is as transcendent as omniscience.

16. It is, however, erroneous to say, as Stebbing does, that the "immortality" of past events renders "eternal objects" as such superfluous. Can she have forgotten that, while immortality can be deduced from eternity, the converse is not true? Immortal essences need not be primordial. Yet primordial aspects the universe must have; for instance, time itself, as such, must be such an aspect.

17. See G. F. Stout, *Studies in Philosophy and Psychology* (New York: Macmillan, 1930), chap. 17.

18. "If we allow for degrees of relevance, and for negligible relevance, we must say that every actual entity is present in every other actual entity" (*P & R*, p. 79).

19. I feel bound to point out that in the late G. H. Mead's remarkable book, *The Philosophy of the Present* (La Salle: Open Court, 1932), p. 1, occurs a highly questionable interpretation of Whitehead's doctrine of time. If Whitehead anywhere in his discussions of the divine consciousness commits himself to the notion of the timeless absolute ascribed to him by Mead, then insofar he destroys whatever distinctive features his theory of real process, with its professed provision for genuine novelty and indetermination, involves. I suggest that no such commitment will be found.

20. The best presentation of the contrary view known to me is found in Mead's *Philosophy of the Present*.

21. Since writing this article, I have come to feel that the most important criticisms of Whitehead are those which would be made by the "logical positivists" (the Vienna Circle). The great task seems to me this: to purify and strengthen Whitehead's synoptic insights by the methodological instruments explicit or implicit in the really "positive" aspects of positivism.

Chapter 4

1. See my *Philosophy and Psychology of Sensation* (Chicago: University of Chicago Press, 1934), p. 208.

2. Ibid., sec. 4.

3. See W. R. Dennes's paper, "Preface to an Empiricist Philosophy of Religion," in *College of the Pacific Publications in Philosophy*, vol. 3, ed. Paul Arthur Schilpp (Stockton: College of the Pacific, 1934), p. 114.

Chapter 5

1. Cf. Alfred North Whitehead, *Process and Reality* (New York: Macmillan, 1929), pp. 519 f., 526 (hereafter cited as *P & R*); *Modes of Thought* (New York: Macmillan, 1938), pp. 92-95, 111 f., 164 (hereafter cited as *M of T*).

2. Cf. *P & R*, p. 225; *Adventures of Ideas* (New York: Macmillan, 1933), p. 356 (hereafter cited as *A of I*); *M of T*, pp. 72-75.

3. *M of T*, p. 136.

4. Whitehead says that every actual entity transcends its actual world, even including God. But this means it adds itself as a new value to existence, and since God and God alone *fully possesses* or prehends every such addition, God "transcends" or excels others in a special or pre-eminent sense, and that is the sense in which I am using the term.

5. Cf. *A of I*, p. 330; *P & R*, p. 69.

6. *P & R*, p. 521.

7. Ibid., p. 529.
8. Ibid., p. 532.
9. Alfred North Whitehead, *Science and the Modern World* (New York: Macmillan, 1925), p. 258 (hereafter cited as *SMW*); *Religion in the Making* (New York: Macmillan, 1926), pp. 153, 155 (hereafter cited as *RM*).
10. *P & R*, p. 528.
11. *SMW*, p. 258.
12. *A of I*, pp. 330, 333, 356.
13. Cf. *P & R*, pp. 523-27.
14. Cf. *A of I*, pp. 215, 217; also *P & R*, p. 529.
15. Cf. *P & R*, pp. 521, 523 f.
16. Cf. *M of T*, p. 128.
17. Cf. *P & R*, pp. 524 f., 530.
18. Ibid.
19. Ibid.
20. Cf. *A of I*, p. 357.
21. *SMW*, p. 258.
22. *P & R*, p. 529.
23. Cf. *RM*, pp. 94 f.; *P & R*, pp. 343 f., 525 f.
24. Cf. *P & R*, p. 68.
25. Cf. *A of I*, p. 216.
26. *P & R*, p. 532.
27. Cf. *A of I*, pp. 342, 344.
28. *P & R*, pp. 525, 532.
29. This is sometimes admitted by Neo-Scholastics. See for instance E. I. Watkin, *A Philosophy of Form* (London: Sheed and Ward, 1938), p. 47. This writer tries to mitigate his admission by reasoning which I am prepared to show is fallacious.
30. *P & R*, p. 73.
31. Cf. *M of T*, pp. 139 ff.
32. Ibid., pp. 140 ff.
33. Ibid., pp. 151, 159, 162-65.
34. *A of I*, chap. 7. See also Alfred North Whitehead, *Symbolism, Its Meaning and Effect* (New York: Macmillan, 1958), chap. 2, for Whitehead's "answer to Hume," an answer which, however, cannot be understood apart from the doctrine of God. See also *M of T*, pp. 162 f., and *RM*, pp. 104 f.
35. Cf. *RM*, p. 160; *The Function of Reason* (Princeton: Princeton University Press, 1929), pp. 21-23, 72.
36. Cf. *P & R*, p. 161; *RM*, p. 158. For an analysis and defense of the doctrine, ancient in religion, but almost unexplored in philosophy, that God is love (in a non-Pickwickian sense) see my book, *Man's Vision of God and the Logic of Theism* (Chicago: Willett, Clark & Co., 1941. Hamden, Conn.: Archon Books, 1964). In that book many of the problems dealt with in this essay are given a more detailed treatment.
37. *P & R*, p. 134.
38. *A of I*, p. 267.
39. Cf. ibid., pp. 247, 251; *P & R*, p. 363.
40. Cf. *M of T*, pp. 132, 133 f.
41. Cf. *RM*, pp. 103 ff., 119, 156; *P & R*, p. 142; *A of I*, pp. 362 f.
42. Cf. *RM*, pp. 107 f.
43. On this question, see also below, p. 97.
44. Cf. *M of T*, pp. 30, 32 f., 157; *P & R*, pp. 182 f.
45. Cf. *RM*, p. 153.
46. Ibid., p. 152.

47. Cf. *SMW*, p. 230.
48. Cf. *A of I*, pp. 249, 250 f.
49. Ibid., p. 328.
50. *SMW*, p. 257.
51. Cf. *P & R*, p. 140.
52. Cf. *M of T*, p. 196.
53. Cf. *P & R*, pp. 343, 532.
54. Ibid.; *RM*, p. 159.
55. Cf. *P & R*, pp. 373 f., 520; *RM*, pp. 104 f.
56. *P & R*, p. 532.
57. *The Philosophy of George Santayana*, Library of Living Philosophers, vol. 2, ed. Paul A. Schilpp (Evanston and Chicago: Northwestern University Press, 1940), p. 594.
58. Cf. *RM*, p. 155.
59. Cf. *P & R*, pp. 346, 444; *SMW*, chap. 10.
60. See my essay, "Santayana's Doctrine of Essence," in Schilpp, ed., *The Philosophy of George Santayana*.
61. Ibid., p. 535.
62. Ibid., p. 592.
63. This restriction was first suggested by Dorothy M. Emmet. See her book, *Whitehead's Philosophy of Organism* (London: Macmillan, 1932), chap. 5.
64. Cf. *M of T*, pp. 126-27.
65. The difficult chapter on "Abstractions" in *SMW* (chap. 10) is the basic text for the doctrine of eternal objects. It seems clearly to affirm the eternity of specific as well as generic properties (see *SMW*, p. 232).

Chapter 6

1. For further discussion of this and related problems see my *Man's Vision of God and the Logic of Theism* (Chicago: Willett, Clark & Co., 1941. Hamden, Conn.: Archon Books, 1964).
2. Alfred North Whitehead, *Religion in the Making* (New York: Macmillan, 1936), p. 158.
3. Alfred North Whitehead, *Process and Reality* (New York: Macmillan, 1929), p. 161.
4. Ibid. Also p. 525.
5. Ibid., p. 531.
6. Ibid., p. 533.
7. Ibid., pp. 530-31. (Italics mine.)
8. *The Philosophy of Alfred North Whitehead*, Library of Living Philosophers, vol. 3, ed. Paul A. Schilpp (Evanston and Chicago: Northwestern University Press, 1941). This volume contains an essay by me on "Whitehead's Idea of God" [reprinted here as chapter 5, above].
9. Ibid., p. 698.

Chapter 7

1. *Alfred North Whitehead: An Anthology*, selected by F. S. C. Northrop and Mason W. Gross (New York: Macmillan, 1953).

Chapter 8

1. Alfred North Whitehead, *Essays in Science and Philosophy* (New York: Philosophical Library, 1948), p. 89.

Chapter 10

1. Nathaniel Lawrence, *Whitehead's Philosophical Development: A Critical History of the Background of Process and Reality* (Berkeley: University of California Press, 1956); Ivor Leclerc, *Whitehead's Metaphysics: An Introductory Exposition* (London: Allen & Unwin; New York: Macmillan, 1958); William A. Christian, *An Interpretation of Whitehead's Metaphysics* (New Haven: Yale University Press, 1959); W. Mays, *The Philosophy of Whitehead* (London: Allen & Unwin; New York: Macmillan, 1959). A fifth book, by Robert Palter, undoubtedly excellent, is about to appear. [Robert M. Palter, ed., *Whitehead's Philosophy of Science* (Chicago: University of Chicago Press, 1960).] And I have seen a fine manuscript [by Sherburne] on the application of Whitehead's philosophy to aesthetics. For constructive and searching criticism of the second and third of the above works see V. C. Chappell, "Whitehead's Metaphysics," *Review of Metaphysics* 13 (1959): 278-304. Personally, I think his criticisms of Leclerc are too drastic and those of Christian not drastic enough; but the article deserves attention.

2. Ivor Leclerc, "Whitehead's Philosophy," *Review of Metaphysics* 2 (1957): 68-93.

3. Mays, *The Philosophy of Whitehead*, p. 61.

4. Ibid., p. 65.

5. Ibid., pp. 64-65.

6. Alfred North Whitehead, *Process and Reality* (New York: Macmillan, 1929), pp. 46, 50, 52l (hereafter cited as *P & R*).

7. *The Philosophy of Alfred North Whitehead*, Library of Living Philosophers, vol. 3, ed. Paul A. Schilpp (Evanston and Chicago: Northwestern University Press, 1941), pp. 114 f.

8. Mays, *The Philosophy of Whitehead*, pp. 64-65, 71.

9. Ibid., p. 60.

10. Ibid., pp. 225-28.

11. A. J. Ayer, *The Problem of Knowledge* (London: Macmillan; Baltimore: Penguin Books, 1956), p. 27.

12. David Bohm, *Causality and Chance in Modern Physics* (London: Routledge and Kegan Paul, 1957), pp. 132, 136, 153, 169.

13. See my "Professor Hall on Perception," *Journal of Philosophy and Phenomenological Research* 21 (1960-61).

14. See my "Some Empty though Important Truths," *Review of Metaphysics* 8 (1955): 553-68; "Metaphysical Statements as Nonrestrictive and Existential," ibid. 12 (1958): 35-47.

15. See S. C. Pepper, *World Hypotheses* (Berkeley: University of California Press, 1942), p. 106.

16. See Everett W. Hall, "Of What Use Are Whitehead's Eternal Objects?," *Journal of Philosophy* 27 (1930): 29-44.

17. R. G. Collingwood, *The Idea of Nature* (Oxford: Oxford University Press, 1945), pp. 169 ff.

18. *P & R*. See fn. 6.

19. There is indeed a problem of relating this to the "semantic concept" of truth accepted by formal logicians. But at least F. Waismann's attempt in ordinary language to refute the notion of new truths seems to me a failure. His supposedly unanswerable questions can be answered. See his essay, "How I See Philosophy," in *Contemporary British Philosophy*, 3rd ser., ed. H. D. Lewis (London: Allen & Unwin; New York: Macmillan, 1956), pp. 449-58.

20. See the final paragraph of the first division of Part I, including fn. [I fear I have simplified and perhaps somewhat distorted what Kant says in this paragraph.

But my main point holds: Kant was in no position to judge the possibility of a psychicalistic explanation of matter. He was too close to Leibniz to see the revisions required to salvage the positive insights in Leibnizianism.]

Chapter 11

1. Vere C. Chappell, "Whitehead's Theory of Becoming," in *Alfred North Whitehead: Essays on His Philosophy*, ed. George L. Kline (Englewood Cliffs, N. J.: Prentice-Hall, 1963), pp. 70-80.

2. William A. Christian, *An Interpretation of Whitehead's Metaphysics* (New Haven: Yale University Press, 1959), chaps. 6-8. In his essay in Kline, ed., *Alfred North Whitehead*, pp. 93-101, Professor Christian indicates that on this issue his mind is less closed than it once was.

3. Charles Hartshorne, "The Immortality of the Past," *Review of Metaphysics* 7 (1953): 98-112.

Chapter 12

1. William A. Christian, *An Interpretation of Whitehead's Metaphysics* (New Haven: Yale University Press, 1959), pp. 80 f.

2. E.g., Sydney Shoemaker, *Self-Knowledge and Self-Identity* (Ithaca: Cornell University Press, 1963).

Chapter 13

1. Alfred North Whitehead, *Adventures of Ideas* (New York: Macmillan, 1933, 1948), pp. 216 ff. (hereafter cited as *A of I*); also *Process and Reality* (New York: Macmillan, 1929; Social Science Bookstore, 1949), p. 520 (hereafter cited as *P & R*). Nikolai Berdyaev, *The Destiny of Man* (New York: Charles Scribner's Sons, 1939), pp. 35 f. (hereafter cited as *Destiny*); also *Spirit and Reality* (New York: Charles Scribner's Sons, 1939), p. 193 (hereafter cited as *Spirit*); *Slavery and Freedom* (New York: Charles Scribner's Sons, 1944), pp. 92-93 (hereafter cited as *S & F*).

2. *A of I*, p. 218; cf. Berdyaev, *Freedom and the Spirit* (New York: Charles Scribner's Sons, 1935), pp. 174 f. (hereafter cited as *Freedom*); *Destiny*, pp. 156, 358-59.

3. *Destiny*, p. 146.

4. *A of I*, p. 236.

5. Ibid., p. 221.

6. *Freedom*, pp. 190 ff.; *The Meaning of History* (New York: Charles Scribner's Sons, 1936), pp. 34-51 (hereafter cited as *History*); *Destiny*, pp. 38 f.

7. *P & R*, pp. 526 f.; *Modes of Thought* (New York: Macmillan, 1938), pp. 111 f. (hereafter cited as *M of T*); *A of I*, p. 357.

8. *S & F*, p. 51; *Destiny*, p. 37; *Freedom*, pp. 138 f., 191 ff.

9. *P & R*, pp. 343 f., 528; *Spirit*, pp. 155, 174.

10. *Freedom*, pp. 332 f.

11. *P & R*, pp. 10 f., 31 f.

12. *Spirit*, pp. 113 ff., 126; *Destiny*, pp. 39-42.

13. *A of I*, pp. 330, 333 f., 356 f.; *Essays in Science and Philosophy* (New York: Philosophical Library, 1948), p. 80 (hereafter cited as *Essays*); *M of T*, pp. 73-75 (the same passage also in *The Philosophy of Alfred North Whitehead*, Library of Living Philosophers, vol. 3, ed. Paul A. Schilpp [Evanston and Chicago: Northwestern University Press, 1941], p. 685).

14. *Spirit*, pp. 36, 147 ff., 154 f., 174; *Destiny*, p. 57; *S & F*, p. 90.

15. Alfred North Whitehead, *Religion in the Making* (New York: Macmillan, 1926), pp. 94, 99, 104 (hereafter cited as *RM*); *M of T*, pp. 70 f.

16. *Destiny*, p. 42.
17. *Spirit*, p. 103.
18. *Destiny*, p. 97.
19. Ibid., pp. 40, 41; *Spirit*, p. 114 f.
20. *S & F*, p. 85.
21. *Destiny*, pp. 37 f.; *Freedom*, p. 190; *S & F*, pp. 51, 84; *P & R*, pp. 50, 522.
22. Nikolai Berdyaev, *The Russian Idea* (New York: Macmillan, 1947), p. 243.
23. *S & F*, p. 51.
24. *History*, pp. 45 f.; *Freedom*, p. 192.
25. *Essays*, p. 72 (The identical essay is also found in Schilpp, ed., *The Philosophy of Alfred North Whitehead*. See pp. 697 f.)
26. *A of I*, pp. 323, 356, 357.
27. *P & R*, p. 526.
28. *Destiny*, pp. 37 f.; *Freedom*, pp. 190 ff.; *History*, pp. 50-55; *S & F*, pp. 82 f.
29. Berdyaev goes so far as to say flatly that God is not a cause (see *S & F*, pp. 26, 82 f.; *Spirit*, p. 114).
30. Cf. *S & F*, pp. 73-82.
31. E.g., *Destiny*, p. 39.
32. *S & F*, p. 90.
33. *Freedom*, chap. 2.
34. Charles Hartshorne, *Man's Vision of God and the Logic of Theism* (Chicago: Willett, Clark & Co., 1941. Hamden, Conn.: Archon Books, 1964).
35. *History*, chap. 4.
36. Nikolai Berdyaev, *Solitude and Society* (New York: Charles Scribner's Sons, 1938), pp. 129-47; *S & F*, pp. 255 ff.
37. *P & R*, pp. 517 f., 524 f., 527, 530 f., 532 f.
38. Ibid., p. 525.
39. *RM*, p. 155.
40. *P & R*, p. 18.
41. *Destiny*, p. 39; *Spirit*, pp. 114 f.
42. *A of I*, p. 216.
43. *Destiny*, pp. 34, 74.
44. Ibid., pp. 33, 34, 36, 85 f.; *S & F*, p. 90.
45. *A of I*, pp. 354 ff.; *P & R*, pp. 76, 86 f., 119-22, 208 f., 239.
46. *A of I*, pp. 99, 331, 376.
47. See *Freedom*, pp. 202-5. Whitehead would approve, I think, of Berdyaev's condemnation of the view that conjugal love has its essential end in propagation (see *S & F*, pp. 229-37).
48. *RM*, p. 155.
49. Ibid., p. 159.
50. *Destiny*, p. 42.
51. Ibid., p. 40.
52. *P & R*, p. 532.

Index of Persons

Agar, W. E., 17
Anselm, Saint, 165
Aquinas, Thomas, 18, 19, 45, 69, 144, 168, 185, 193
Aristotle, 12, 15, 18, 44 f., 46, 48, 51, 54, 63, 72, 76, 119, 120, 121, 127, 134, 154, 168, 169
Augustine, 92
Austin, J. L., 7, 171
Ayer, A. J., 146

Bacon, Francis, 154
Beethoven, Ludwig van, 193
Berdyaev, Nikolai, 132, 134, 175, 183-99
Bergson, Henri, 5, 11, 15, 63, 78, 83, 84, 85, 86, 132, 161, 163, 175, 176, 180
Berkeley, George, 4, 5, 23, 36, 45, 47, 52
Boethius, 166
Bohm, David, 149
Böhme, Jakob, 192
Bosanquet, Bernard, 6, 35, 38
Boutroux, E., 15
Bradley, F. H., 6, 31, 43, 162
Bridgman, P. W., 143

Carnap, Rudolf, 58, 172
Carneades, 63
Chappell, Vere C., 163
Christian, William A., 142, 143, 165 ff., 179

Clifford, William K., 148
Cohen, Morris R., 17
Collingwood, R. G., 154
Comte, Auguste, 38
Croce, Benedetto, 11

Dante, Alighieri, 36
Darwin, Charles, 152
Descartes, René, 4, 10, 25, 38, 132, 154
Dewey, John, 63, 129, 130, 134, 176

Edwards, Jonathan, 86, 130
Einstein, Albert, 22, 175
Ely, Stephen Lee, 99-110
Emerson, Ralph Waldo, 130

Fechner, G. T., 13, 14, 63, 72, 132, 154, 161, 167, 175, 187, 190, 192
Feyerabend, P. K., 6

Gerard, Ralph W., 147
Goldstein, K., 57
Gosse, Edmund, 194
Green, T. H., 6

Hall, Everett W., 153
Hartshorne, Charles, 19, 148
Hegel, G. W. F., 4, 7, 38, 52
Heidegger, Martin, 7
Heisenberg, Werner, 143, 175
Hocking, William Ernest, 167

Howison, George Holmes, 6, 130
Hume, David, 4, 5, 10, 11, 14, 16, 51, 63, 81, 126, 127, 137, 146, 149, 160, 162, 173
Husserl, Edmund, 141
Huxley, Julian, 147

James, William, 4, 6, 10, 11, 15, 34, 38, 61, 64, 75, 107, 129, 130, 134, 180
Joachim, H. H., 6
Johnson, A. H., 19
Johnson, Samuel, 130

Kant, Immanuel, 4, 7, 11, 45, 46, 63, 87, 92, 158, 159, 160, 173
Kline, George L., 170

Lawrence, Nathaniel, 142
Leclerc, Ivor, 142, 144, 160
Lee, Otis H., 61
Leibniz, Georg W. von, 2, 4, 10, 12, 25, 31, 36, 48, 49 f., 51 ff., 63, 91, 120, 121 f., 125, 130, 142, 148, 154, 155, 156, 157, 158, 159, 162, 172, 173, 180, 181, 182
Lequier, J., 132, 154, 167
Lewis, C. I., 11, 172
Locke, John, 4, 10, 23, 154
Lotze, Rudolf Hermann, 161
Lovejoy, A. O., 33, 149
Lowe, Victor, 19, 144

Malebranche, Nicolas de, 92
Marx, Karl, 39
Matthew of Aquasparta, 92
Mays, Wolfe, 143, 144 ff.
Mead, G. H., 85
Merleau-Ponty, M., 5
Meyerson, Emile, 176
Mill, John Stuart, 10
Montague, William Pepperell, 130, 167
Moore, G. E., 6, 7, 15
Murphy, Arthur E., 27

Newton, Isaac, 22, 29, 39, 58
Nicholas of Cusa, 69
Nygren, Anders, 188

Oakes, Urian, 130
Occam, William of, 152

Parker, Dewitt H., 86, 87
Parmenides, 42, 50, 167
Paul, Saint, 2
Pavlov, Ivan Petrovich, 112
Peirce, Charles Sanders, 1, 2, 4, 5, 6, 10, 14, 15, 39, 48, 53, 54, 129, 130, 132, 134, 141, 142, 148, 155, 173, 175, 176, 177, 179
Pepper, Stephen C., 153, 161
Perry, Ralph Barton, 6, 11
Pfleiderer, Otto, 63
Philo, 63
Planck, Max, 175
Plato, 6, 53, 54, 63, 73, 76, 97, 112, 154, 167, 169, 173, 187
Popper, Karl, 142

Renouvier, Charles B., 87
Royce, Josiah, 2, 6, 130, 134, 161
Russell, Bertrand, 6, 7, 63, 88, 111, 112, 146, 149, 162, 172, 173
Ryle, Gilbert, 6, 7, 150, 152

Santayana, George, 33, 63, 80, 85, 93, 95, 96, 129, 130, 134
Schelling, F. W. J., 13, 14, 187, 190, 192, 196
Schilpp, Paul Arthur, 97
Schleiermacher, Friedrich, 63
Schrödinger, E., 143, 175
Socinus, Fausto, 13, 154, 167
Soloviev, Vladimir, 188
Spaulding, E. G., 6
Spinoza, Baruch, 29, 35, 37, 38, 43, 50, 63, 73, 86, 91, 92, 101, 125, 150, 154
Stebbing, L. Susan, 21
Stout, G. F., 33

Teilhard de Chardin, Pierre, 147
Tertullian, 13
Tillich, Paul, 138

Varisco, B., 72, 161, 175

Ward, James, 63, 72, 161
Weiss, Paul, 1
Wisdom, John, 7
Wittgenstein, Ludwig, 6, 7, 160
Woods, James Haughton, 129
Wright, Sewall, 147

Zeno, 38

Index of Subjects

AA, 71, 78
Absolute, 14, 167
Absolute, the, 36, 116, 188
Absoluteness of God, 2, 14, 66 f., 71, 75, 78, 184
Absolute of absolutes, 116
Abstract, the infinitely, 14
Abstract entities, 147
Accidents, 68, 155
Action, 39
Actual entity, 119 ff., 125, 178
Actuality, 12
Actus purus, 73. *See also* Pure actuality
Aesthetic: drives, 14; experience, 26; good, 178; harmony, 81; perfection, 75; principles, 11, 16, 58; richness, 167; teleology, 82; value, 74
Aestheticism, 107
Aesthetics, 26
After-images, 151
Agape, 188
All in all, God as, 192
Alternatives, ground of, 80
Altruism, 2, 17, 89, 103, 105 f., 119, 123
American philosophy, 129
Amoebae, 118
Analogical concepts, 18, 70
Analogy, argument by, 28 f.
Analytic: propositions, 147, 153; philosophy, 182
Animism, 44

Anticipation, 51
Antinomies, 160
A-perfection, 73, 78
AR, 66
AR-CW, 70
Arithmetic, 97
Artist, cosmic, 82
Atheism, 38, 78 f.
Atomicity, temporal, 16, 38. *See also* Time, epochal theory of
Atomism, 41, 43
Atoms, 29, 41, 48, 57 f., 147; freedom of, 131; as organisms, 58
Atonement, 184

Becoming, 10, 113, 169; eminent, 167; higher mode of, 84; theory of, 127. *See also* Process
Behaviorism, 6. *See also* Materialism
Being and becoming, 113, 115, 154
Being Itself, 138
Beings in happenings, 121
Benevolence of God, 99, 102 f.
Best possible world, 91
Bifurcation of nature, 22 ff.
Biology, 16, 41, 118
Body, the, 5, 10, 16, 28 f., 45 ff., 55, 81, 89, 150. *See also* Cells
British philosophy, 4 f.

Buddhism, 5, 130, 135, 156 f., 169, 178

Categorial contrast, 64
Categories, 32, 69, 96; God as exemplification of, 68 f.; argument from, 28 f.
Category of the ultimate, 162
Causal: connectedness, 14, 126; conditions, 175; efficacy, 126
Causality, 3; asymmetry of, 176; as physical memory, 137
Causa sui, 177. *See also* Self-creation
Causation as creative, 157
Cause of all, 64
Causes, final, 44
CC, 65, 71
Cells, 41, 55, 73, 104, 134, 149; feeling in, 28; form in, 45; in biology, 16 f.; of nerveless metazoa, 30; theory of, 38, 54
Change, 127, 162; substantial, 135 f.; and substance, 181
Chaos, 77; borders of, 82
Character, personal, 13
Clarity, Whitehead's, 112
CN, 73 ff. *See also* Consequent Nature
Color, 24, 26, 47, 96, 151. *See also* Vision
Common sense, 46, 55
Commonsensism, 44
Complete being, 37, 64, 67, 71
Compound individual, 38, 41 ff.
Concreteness, theory of, 27; misplaced, 64
Conformation, 81, 126
Consciousness in God, 143
Consequent factor (in God), 65
Consequent Nature, 31, 102, 199; as all-inclusive, 116; as conscious, 143; as in flux, 133; as prehending us, 100; and truth, 191
Consequent state, 76, 119, 138
Contemporaries, 3, 30, 52, 86 f., 125 f., 156
Continental tradition, 4
Contingency, 31, 37, 80, 96; asymmetrical, 86; basis of, 81

Continuity, law of, 52, 57 f.; of quality, 95 f.; of essences, 59
Contradiction and time, 180
Contrast, importance of, 16, 56, 66, 74, 92, 94
Cosmic epoch, 15, 82
Cosmology, 9
Creation, 32, 92, 99; *ex nihilo*, 193 ff.
Creative synthesis, 139
Creativity, 1, 11, 18, 83, 100, 132, 170, 174. *See also* Synthesis
Creativity Itself, 138
Creature: as means, 105; God as, 185
Critical Realism, 48
Cruelty in God, 104
CW, 67 f., 70 ff.

Dance of Shiva, 91
Darwinian, 152
Data, 10, 28, 149. *See also* Given, the
Death, 110, 122 f., 137
Decision, 131, 166; creaturely, 72, 93, 100; objectification of, 73
Decision-making, monopoly of, 164
Defining characteristic, 13, 121
Definiteness and reality, 34
Democracy, economic, 39
Determinables, 32, 95 f.
Determinism, 29, 50, 127, 130, 176; asymmetrical, 86; classical, 149, 189
Difference of degree, 195
Dipolar, 68
Divine: joy and suffering, 197; process, 18; relativity, 169
Dreams, 172
Dualism, 44, 48 f., 57 f., 113 ff., 130

Eclecticism, 153, 161, 163
Ego, 122
Egocentric predicament, 11, 52
Egoism in God, 104, 107
Emergence: of essences, 32 f., 59, 162; of mind, 147
Eminence, 167 f.
Empiricism, 10, 17

End, a public and everlasting, 110
Energy, degradation of, 56
Epistemology, 173
Equality, economic, 39
Eros, 188
Eternal: objects, 2, 31, 77, 116, 163, 177, 202 n.; ideal, 153
Eternity, 32, 191
Ethical: God as, 107; good, 178
Etiolatry, 188, 197 f.
Event, 120, 174
Everlasting, 85
Everlastingness, 191
Evil, 18, 68, 72, 90, 94; aesthetic, 69; ethical, 198; problem of, 72, 90-94, 105, 108, 185, 192
Evolution, 15, 152
Existence: as social, 73; as ground of possibility, 80; as public, 81
Existents, contingent, 68
Experience, 5, 125, 173; human, 7, 131; practical, 27; as inclusive, 114; as spatiotemporal, 18; unity of, 48
Explanation: in a circle, 25; of lower by higher, 131
Expression, aesthetic, 26
Extended, mind as, 10
Extensive abstraction, 59, 94

Feeling: absence of, 148, 179; animal, 132; social, 93, 142, 163, 168; multidimensionality of, 26, 28; participatory, 52; singular subjects of, 148; surd to, 148
Feeling of feeling, 17, 24 f., 28, 67
Feelings, ocean of, 148
Finite-infinite, 168
Form and matter, 49
Forms of definiteness, 95
Freedom: and chaos, creaturely, 72, 90, 104, 106; of God, 13, 133; human, 57, 61, 99; of indeterminacy, 126; no alternative to, 192 f.; as notbeing, 186
"Fringe," 107

Future, the, 51, 121
Future events, 31

Genesis, book of, 101
Genetic analysis, 178
Genius and rules, 92
Gestalt, 49
Given, the, 46 f., 48, 150 ff.; world as, 172. *See also* Data
Givenness, 172
God, 36, 56, 89 ff.; as abstract, 64; as active and passive, 68 f.; as actual and potential, 13 f., 177; as beyond rivalry, 197; as compound individual, 60; as derivative, 77; as efficient and final cause, 92; as public and everlasting end, 110; as experiencing, 14; as fellow sufferer, 68, 93, 187, 199; as growing, 37, 66, 75; as immutable, 4, 36, 38, 167; as inclusive, 61; as independent, 65, 184, 197; as individual, 13; as in flux, 133; as inheriting the world, 133; as limited, 70; as living, 35, 37; as loving, 73; as nontemporal, 83; as personal, 14, 89; as prehending and prehended by all, 31 f.; as a principle, 61, 90 f.; as righteous, 93; as a society. *See also* Divine
God-now, 117
God's: concepts, 77; happiness, 103, 108, 187; power, 101, 165, 197; righteousness, 93. *See also* Categories; Consequent Nature; Love; Omnipotence; Omniscience; Past; Power; Present; Primordial Nature; Religion; Truth; Wisdom
Greek tradition, 169

Happiness, 103
Heaven, 122, 184
Hell, 122, 184

Idealism, 11, 38, 155; absolute, 15, 127, 201 n.; true, 52
Ideals of perfection, 108
Identity of indiscernibles, 157
"Identity theory," 149

Immanence, 56
Immediacy: altruism of, 52; preserved in God, 107
Immortality: conventional, 134; of facts, 51; objective, 12, 142; of the past, 51, 84, 108 f.; personal, 2, 105 f., 108, 123, 142. *See also* Everlastingness
Immutable deity, 4, 167
Importance, 105, 170
Impure potentials, 74, 95 f.
Inanimate nature, 29, 118
Incarnation, the, 168
Incompatibility, 37, 71, 186; of positive qualities, 159
Indefinables, 25
Indeterminism, 52, 126, 163, 175 f.
India, 43
Indistinctness. *See* Perception
Individual, 13, 42 ff., 71; final, 163
Individual, the, with universal functions, 139
Individuals, 44; as preserved in God, 184, 197
Inesse, 155
Infinity, 36; of the past, 101
Inheritance, 166; social, 16
Insignificance, whiff of, 134
Intellectualism, 38
Internal. *See* Relations
Intuition, 78

John-now, 180

Knowledge, 11, 64, 67, 74, 172; integration of, 30; perfect, 104

Language, ordinary, 179; rules of, 146 f.
Laws of nature, 56 f.; as imposed, 82; as statistical, 150, 157
Life in nature, 29, 133
Linguistic analysis, 171
Logic, extensionalist, 178; formal, 6; relational, 14; subject-predicate, 43, 49
Love, 2, 195 f.; conjugal, 208 n.; sacrificial, 187. *See also* God

Many become one. *See* Ultimate, category of the
Materialism, 6 f., 17, 26, 36, 43, 58, 114, 130, 147
Mathematics, 25, 95, 97
Matter, 17, 58, 113; dead, 5, 37, 52, 82, 90; and form, 44; mere, 17
Maximalistic attitudes, 111
Maximum, absolute, 67
Memory, 3, 6, 11, 14, 51, 118, 194; cosmic, 35, 60; God's, 138; impersonal, 3, 130; of infancy, 182; molecular, 118; physical, 3, 137, 144; personal, 3, 130; and substance, 181
Metaphysical: compliments to God, 70; ground, 72
Metaphysics, 9, 17, 27, 36, 38, 91, 125
Microscopic realm, 47
Mind and matter, 113 ff.
Minimalistic attitudes, 111
Misplaced concreteness, 25
Molecules, 29, 57, 146
Monads, 31, 49, 155 f., 181
Monism, 42 f., 188
Monolatry, 188
Monotony, 77, 94
Most real being, 64, 159
Muddleheaded, Whitehead as, 111

Naturalism, 147
Necessary: being, 80, 88; propositions, 160
Necessity, metaphysical, 153; of God, 18
Negative prehensions, 164 f.
Neoplatonic, 165, 167
Nervous system, 29, 56
Neural: conditions, 137; process, 149
New Realism, American, 48
Nominalism, 48

Objectification, 166
Objective relativism, 23
Occasions, 119; experient, 119
Omnipotence, 77, 99 f.
Omniscience, 64, 73 f., 103, 105, 198
Ontolatry, 188
Order: aesthetic, 14, 82; cos-

mic, 82; problem of, 133; and disorder, 157
Orderer, God as, 88, 186
Organisms, 41; in organisms, 54

Pain, 6
Panentheism, 54, 189 f.
Panpsychism, 23, 28 ff., 52 f., 58, 158
Pantheism, 54, 72, 188
Participation, 168, 196
Particulars, 13
Parts, internal, 55; external, 55; imperfect, 77
Past, causal, 30
Past, the, 34, 51, 127, 165; as finite or infinite, 87; as given, 85; God's relation to, 83 f.
Patience, 72, 81
Perception, 6, 118 f., 125, 136, 150, 181; and being, 126; indistinctness of, 34, 48. *See also* Prehension
Perfection of God, 64, 70, 73, 190. *See also* AR, R
Perishing, 2, 84, 123, 127, 165
Person, 177
Personal: identity and memory, 181; order, 3, 13, 71, 83, 90, 95, 178
Personality, 135
Persuasion, 92
Phenomenology, 171
Philosophy, future of, 129
Physical: objects, 29; reality, 18
Physics, 27, 30, 117, 147. *See also* Quantum; Relativity
Piecemeal: philosophizing, 22; supernaturalism, 75
Plants, 57
Platonism, 153, 187
Pluralism, 146, 201 n.; macroscopic, 44, 48; microscopic, 48
PN, 73
Poet of the world, 2
Polarities, 69
Positivism, 60, 146
Possibility: as indefinite, 32; as inexhaustible, 71, 82; requires a ground, 79. *See also* Incompatibility

Posterity, 105; the ultimate, 133
Potency, 64
Potentiality, 12, 71, 159, 162
Power: division of, 72, 100, 164; worship of, 196. *See also* Etiolatry
Prediction, 15, 176
Pre-established harmony, 156 f.
Prehension, 11, 14, 72, 92, 109, 118, 125; God's, 103, 144; negative, 2
Prehensive relation, 149, 156 f.
Present, divine specious, 87
Primary achievement, Whitehead's, 55
Primary properties, 6, 22 ff.
Primordial Nature: in relation to medieval theology, 36; in relation to Plato's demiurge, 54; complete yet deficient, 71; symbolized by PN, 73; as A-perfect, 75; as necessarily existent, 88; independent of particulars, 102; the Absolute of absolutes, 116; as God in eternity, 133; not an actuality, 145; possibly confused with Consequent Nature, 154; abstract, 199
Principium individuationis, 31
Principle of limitation, 90
Privacy, 6 f.
Problem of evil, 90, 93 f., 108. *See also* Evil
Process, 74, 76, 117; philosophies of, 130; principle of, 83, 153, 165; theory of, 92
Process Itself, 138
Proofs for God, 79, 109, 154, 160
Properties, nonrelative, 10. *See also* Relations, internal
Protocol statements, 172
Providence, 75
Psychologists, 26
Psychology, 119; comparative, 30
Pure actuality, 64, 73
Purpose, 79

Qualities, secondary, 22, 26, 47

Quantum: mechanics, 16, 57, 83, 175; uncertainty, 56
Quantum of process, 119, 173

Rationalism, 10, 158
Realism, 5, 11, 149
Reason, 92, 189; presupposes creation, 91
Receptivity, 73
Relations, 6, 14 f.; internal, 6, 109, 126, 154, 162; external, 6, 15, 48, 154, 160, 162; of God to world, 144. *See also* Prehension
Relative-absolute, 115 f., 168
Relative of relatives, 116
Relative perfection, 71. *See also* R-perfect
Relativity, 10, 113; ordinary, 77; physics of, 31, 86; principle of, 162
Relevance, negative, 31; negligible, 31
Religion, 79, 99, 184; God of, 13, 35, 63
Religious experiences, 144
Rhythms in nature, 58
Right and wrong, 110
R-perfect, 71, 75, 78
rr, 78
RR, 66

Satisfaction, 166
"See," 152
Self, 121 ff.
Self-creation, 1, 15, 18, 91, 169, 177, 192
Self-determining, 100, 158
Self-identity, 16, 108, 123
Self-interest, 2, 11, 17, 103, 105 f., 123, 178, 184
Selfishness, 123
Self-moved, mind as, 54
Self-surpassing, 71
Self-transcendence, 80
Self-transcending transcender of others, 89
Sensation, 24, 26. *See also* Vision
Sense-data, 26, 152
Sense qualities, 26. *See also* Qualities
Sensitivity, 198
Sentient and insentient, 30, 115, 132, 147

Sex, 196, 208 n.
Simplicism, 42 f., 45, 56
Simultaneity, 31, 86, 178
Singulars, concrete, 5, 173 f., 177, 179
Social: feeling, 25 f.; interdependence, 93; nature of reality, 73, 107 f.; nature of motivation, 105; all realization is, 70; relations, 55
Societal philosophy, 131
Societies; nonliving, 59; of occasions, 3, 13, 54; of societies, 55, 90
Society, cosmic, 83
Socinian, 167
Solipsism, 5; epistemological, 52
Soul, Buddhist denial of, 130
Space, 25
Space-time, 56
Spatiotemporal: patterns, bare, 22, 119; structures, 127
Specificity, 96
Speculative philosophy, 112 f.
Spontaneity, 1, 131
State, divine, 75
Stimuli, 24, 118
Straw-man fallacy, 3
Structural properties, 27. *See also* Spatiotemporal
Subjective and objective forms, 139, 165
Subjectivism: Berkeleyan, 45; reformed, 14, 57
Subjectivity, 11
Subject-object, 11, 46, 125, 192
Subjects of predication, 10
Subject-superject, 91
Substance, 3, 89, 154; Buddhist denial of, 130; and accidents, 88; as mutually immanent, 89; theories of, 42
Substantial composition, 42
Substantialism, 88
Succession: in God, 84; three kinds of, 179
Suffering in God, 106, 198
Sufficient: condition, 175; reason, 155 f.
Superject, 89, 172; God as, 109

Supreme: Becoming, 168; Being, 69 f.; love, 83; Unity, 108
Supremely social, 73, 168
Sympathy, 11, 16, 28, 67, 123, 168, 184
Synthesis, 175; creative, 153, 158, 162; free, 72
Synthetic propositions, 146, 153
System, philosophical, 22

Tenderness, 81
Theism, 38, 110, 189; classical, 63 f., 167
Theologians, 63, 72
Theologies, 184
Thing in itself, 4
Things, 135, 189
Thomism, 19, 185
Time: asymmetry of, 50, 86, 157; as cumulative, 85; epochal theory of, 88, 173; integrated, 191; as key to the categories, 86; spatialization of, 180
Token-reflexive terms, 117, 121
Totum simul, 166
Tragedy, 93, 108, 186, 198 f.; in God, 106
Transcendent, 14
Transcendentals, 69
Transmutation, 47, 150
Trees, 30

Trinity, the, 168, 178, 193
Truth: and Consequent Nature of God, 191; and time, 85; as union of opposites, 5; value of, 74
Types, theory of, 78
Tyrant conception of God, 183

Ultimate, category of the, 126, 175
Ultimate irrationality, 91
Unconscious, the, 81
Unit-becoming, 119, 145, 147, 163, 173
Universals, 12, 15, 33. *See also* Eternal objects
Universe, 117; as an individual, 43, 50, 60

Vacuous actuality, 17 f., 90, 163
Vagueness, 33, 35
Value: and fact, 113, 115; always finite, 186; as particular, 102; as temporal, 64
Variety, no maximal, 74
Vision, 117 f., 150 ff. *See also* Color
Void, 44

Wisdom of God, 158
World, this actual, 68
World-solidarity, 33
World soul, 54
WW, 65